EASTON AREA PUBLIC LIB.
1901 9100 058 765 5

THE OLD MASTERS

OF

BELGIUM AND HOLLAND

[Les Maîtres d'Autrefois]

By EUGÈNE FROMENTIN

TRANSLATED BY

MRS. MARY C. ROBBINS

BOSTON AND NEW YORK
HOUGHTON, MIFFLIN AND COMPANY
The Riverside Press, Cambridge
1900

The Riverside Press, Cambridge, Mass., U. S. A.
Printed by H. O. Houghton & Company.

PREFACE.

I HAVE just been viewing Rubens and Rembrandt in their own homes, and at the same time the Dutch school in its unchanging frame of agricultural and maritime life, of downs, pastures, huge clouds, and low horizons.

Here are two arts, distinct, perfectly complete, entirely independent of each other, and very brilliant, which require to be studied at once by an historian, a thinker, and a painter. That the work should be properly done requires the union of these three men in one; and I have nothing in common with the two first, while as to the painter, however a man may have a feeling for distances, he ceases to be one in approaching the least known of the masters of these privileged countries. I shall traverse the museums, but I shall not review them. I shall stop before certain men: I shall not relate their lives, nor catalogue their works, even those preserved by their compatriots. I shall define simply as I understand them, as fully as I can seize them, certain characteristic sides of their genius or talent. I shall not grapple with too great questions; I shall avoid profundities and dark places. The art of painting is only the art of expressing the invisible by the visible. Whether its roads be great or small, they are sown with problems which it is permitted to sound for one's self as truths, but which it is well to leave in their darkness as mysteries. I shall only speak concerning certain pictures, of the surprise, the pleasure, the astonishment, and with no less precision of the vexation, which they have caused me. In all this I shall only translate with sincerity the inconsequent sensations of the mere amateur.

I warn you that there will be no method, no course pursued in these studies. You will find here many gaps, preferences, and omissions, without this want of balance detracting at all from the importance or the value of the works of which I may not have spoken. I shall often recall the Louvre, and shall not fear to conduct you thither, that examples may be nearer, and verifications easier. It is possible that some of my opinions may conflict with those generally received. I shall not seek, but I shall not avoid, any revision of ideas which may arise from these disagreements. I entreat you not to see in this any indication of a guerilla spirit, which seeks to distinguish itself by boldness, and which, while travelling the beaten path, would fear to be accused of observing nothing, if it did not judge everything differently from others.

To tell the truth, these studies will be only notes, and these notes the disconnected and disproportionate elements of a book to be made in a more special manner than those which have been made up to this time, — a book in which philosophy, æsthetics, nomenclature, and anecdotes will hold less place and the questions of the craft much greater place.

It should be like a sort of talk about painting, where the painters would recognize their habits, where men of the world would learn to better know painters and painting. For the moment my method will be to forget everything which has been said on this subject; my aim, to raise questions, to produce a wish to think about them, and to inspire in those who would be capable of rendering us such a service the curiosity to solve them. I call these pages, The Old Masters, as I should speak of the severe or familiar masters of our French tongue, if I were speaking of Pascal, of Bossuet, of La Bruyère, of Voltaire, or of Diderot, — with this difference, that in France there are schools where respect for and study of these masters of style are still maintained, while I scarcely know where in these days the advice is given to respectfully study the ever exemplary masters of Flanders and Holland.

I shall, moreover, suppose that the reader whom I address is enough like me to follow me without too much fatigue, and yet different enough to give me the pleasure of contradicting him, so that I can put some ardor into my attempts to convince him.

BRUSSELS, July 6, 1875.

CONTENTS.

PART I. — BELGIUM.

PART II. — HOLLAND.

PART III. — BELGIUM.

LIST OF ILLUSTRATIONS.

RUBENS.

PAUL POTTER.

REMBRANDT.

PART I.

BELGIUM.

THE

OLD MASTERS OF BELGIUM AND HOLLAND.

BELGIUM.

I.

THE MUSEUM AT BRUSSELS.

THE Brussels Museum has always had much greater value than renown. What injures it in the eyes of people whose minds instinctively take long flights, is its being but two steps from our own frontier, and consequently the first stage in a pilgrimage which conducts to sacred shrines. Van Eyck is at Ghent, Memling at Bruges, Rubens at Antwerp. Brussels possesses as its own none of these great men. She did not witness their birth; she scarcely saw them paint; she has neither their ashes nor their masterpieces. A pretence is made of visiting them at home; but it is elsewhere that they await us. All this gives to this pretty capital the appearance of an empty house, and exposes it to being quite unjustly neglected. It is not known, or it is forgotten, that nowhere in Flanders do the three princes of Flemish painting march with such an escort of painters and able men, who surround them, follow them, precede them, and open for them the gates of history, — disappearing when they enter, but still causing them to enter. Belgium is a magnificent book of art, whose chapters, fortunately for provincial glory, are to be found everywhere, but whose preface is at Brussels, and only at Brussels; and I would say to any one who should be tempted to skip the preface to reach the book, that he makes a mistake, that he opens the book too soon, and that he will read it unprofitably.

This preface is very fine in itself; it is, moreover, a document whose place nothing supplies. It informs one what is to be seen, prepares for, suggests, explains everything; setting in order the confusion of proper names, and works which are entangled in the multitude of chapels, where the chance of time has disseminated them, and classing them here without mistake, thanks to the perfect tact which has united and classified them. It is a kind of list of what artists Belgium has produced up to the time of the modern school, and really a record of what it possesses in its divers places of deposit, museums, churches, convents, hospitals, town halls, and private collections. Possibly she herself scarcely comprehended with exactness the extent of this vast national treasure, the most opulent in the world, except that of Holland, and second only to that of Italy, before she came into possession of these two equally well kept registers, the museums of Antwerp and Brussels. In a word, the history of art in Flanders is capricious, even romantic. At each moment the thread is broken and found again; one imagines painting lost, gone astray upon the great highways of the world; it is a little like the Prodigal Son returning when he is no longer expected. If you would have an idea of its adventures, and learn what happened to it during its absence, examine the museum of Brussels; it will tell you all, with that facility of information which an abridgment can offer, — an abridgment, complete, truthful, and perfectly clear, of a history that has endured for two centuries. I am not speaking merely of the management of the place, which is perfect. Fine rooms, good light, works choice from their beauty, their rarity, or merely for their historical value; the most ingenious exactitude in determining the value of works coming from abroad,— in fine, a taste, a care, a knowledge, a respect for the things of art, which make to-day of this rich collection a model museum. Understand, it is especially a Flemish museum, which gives it a family interest for Flanders, and for Europe an inestimable value.

In it the Dutch school is scarcely seen; you scarcely look for it. It would find here habits and beliefs foreign to its own, — mystical, catholic, and pagan, with none of which it would feel at home. Here it would encounter the legends, the ancient history, and the direct or indirect memorials of the dukes of Burgundy, the arch-dukes of Austria, the Italian dukes, the Pope, Charles V., Philip II., that is to say, all the things and all the people that it did not recognize or which it denied, against which it combated for a hundred years, and from which its genius, its instincts, its needs, and consequently its destiny, sharply and violently separated it. Between Moerdyk and Dordrecht there is only the Meuse to pass, but a whole world separates the two frontiers. Antwerp is the antipodes of Amsterdam, and by his good-natured eclecticism and the gay and sociable side of his genius, Rubens is more ready to fraternize with Veronese, Tintoretto, Titian, Correggio, or even with Raphael, than with Rembrandt, his contemporary, but his intractable contradictor.

As to Italian art, it is here only as a reminder. It is an art that is falsified by acclimation, and which alters its very nature in entering Flanders. In perceiving, in the least Flemish part of the gallery, two portraits by Tintoretto, not excellent, much retouched, but typical, one fails to understand them beside the works of Memling, of Martin de Vos, of Van Orley, of Rubens, of Vandyck, even of Antonio Moro. It is the same with Veronese; he is out of place, his color is faded and bears traces of distemper, his style seems a little cold, his pomp studied and almost affected. The work is, however, a superb one in his finest manner; it is a fragment of triumphal mythology detached from one of the ceilings of the ducal palace, one of the best; but Rubens is beside it, and that very thing suffices to give to the Venetian Rubens a foreign accent. Which of the two is right? In listening only to the tongue so excellently spoken by these two men, which is the better, — the correct and learned rhetoric they employ in Venice, or the emphatic, grandiose, and warm incorrectness of the Antwerp speech? In Venice one inclines to Veronese, but in Flanders Rubens is better understood.

Italian art has that quality common to all strongly constituted arts, that it is at once very cosmopolitan because it has been everywhere, and very haughty because it has been sufficient to itself. It is at home in all Europe except in two countries,

— Belgium, whose spirit it has visibly impregnated without ever mastering it, and Holland, which at first seemed to consult it, and finally did without it; so that, while it lives on friendly terms with Spain, and reigns in France, where, at least in historical painting, our best painters have been Romans, it encounters in Flanders two or three very great men of lofty and indigenous race, who hold sway, and mean to divide their empire with none.

The history of the relations of these two countries, Italy and Flanders, is curious; it is long, it is diffuse. Elsewhere it is confusing; but here, as I have told you, it can be read easily. It begins at Van Eyck, and ends on the day that Rubens left Genoa and returned, bringing with his luggage the cream of Italian lessons, that is, all of it that the art of his country could reasonably support. This history of the fifteenth and sixteenth centuries in Flanders forms the medium part and the truly original foundation of this museum.

We enter by the fourteenth century; we end with the first half of the seventeenth. At the two extremities of this brilliant course we are struck by the same phenomenon, — rare enough in such a little country, — we see an art which was born of itself, on the spot; and an art which was born again when it was thought to be dead. Van Eyck is recognized in a very fine Adoration of the Magi; Memling is suggested by certain fine portraits; and there, at the very end, a hundred and fifty years later, Rubens is perceived; — each time a sun rises, and then sets with the splendor and the brevity of a beautiful day without a morrow.

While Van Eyck is above the horizon, he casts gleams which reach to the very confines of the modern world; and it seems as if it were these gleams, that it recognized and which illumined it, that awakened the modern world. Italy is warned of it and comes to Bruges. Thus it was, that from a visit of workmen curious to know what they must do in order to paint well, with brilliancy, with consistency, with ease, with permanence, there began between these two peoples those comings and goings which, however they changed in character and direction, never ceased. Van Eyck is not alone; around him swarm works, — works rather than names. They cannot be well distinguished either among themselves or from the German school: it is a jewel case, a reliquary, a sparkling of precious gems. Imagine a collection of painted jewel work — in which is recognized the hand of the enameller, of the glass-worker, of the engraver, and of the illuminator of psalters; whose sentiment is grave, whose inspiration is monastic, whose destination is princely; which show already experienced handling and dazzling effect — in the midst of which Memling remains ever distinct, unique, candid, and delicious, like a flower whose root is unattainable, and which has sent forth no shoots.

After the extinction of this fair dawn, the fading of this lovely twilight, night descended upon the North, and Italy was seen to shine. Quite naturally the North rushed thither. Flanders was at that time at that critical moment in the life of individuals and of peoples when, if they are no longer young, they must ripen; for when one almost ceases to believe, one must know. Flanders did to Italy what Italy had been doing to antiquity; she turned towards Rome, Florence, Milan, Parma, and Venice, even as Rome and Milan, Florence and Parma, had turned towards Latin Rome and Greece.

The first to go was Mabuse, who went to Italy about 1508; then Van Orley, at the latest in 1527; then Floris, then Coxcie, and others followed. For a century there existed on classic ground a Flemish academy, which formed excellent pupils and some good painters; which came near stifling the Antwerp school by force of culture without greatness of soul, by lessons well or ill learned, and which finally served to sow the unknown. Do we here find the precursors? At least these are the original stock, the intermediaries, the men who study with a will, who desire renown, who are charmed by novelty, tormented by ideal excellence. I cannot say that in this hybrid art everything was of a kind to console for what no longer existed, or to excite hopes of what was coming.

But in any case they all captivate, interest, instruct us, even if we only learn from them to understand one thing, which seems common because so definitely proved,—the renewal of the modern by the ancient world, and the extraordinary gravitation which drew Europe towards the Italian Renascence. The Renascence was produced in the North exactly as it was in the South, with this difference, that at the time we have reached, Italy precedes, Flanders follows; and while Italy possesses schools of rare culture and noble understanding, Flemish scholars hasten thither.

These scholars, to call them by a name which does honor to their masters, — these disciples, better so named from their enthusiasm and according to their merits, are diverse, and diversely impressed by the spirit which speaks to all of them from afar, and charms them when near, according to their natures. Some of them Italy attracts but does not convert, like Mabuse, who remained Gothic in mind and in execution, and brought back from his excursion only the taste for fine architecture, already preferring palaces to chapels. There are some whom Italy retained and kept, others whom she sent back, freer, more supple, more nervous, even too much inclined towards moving attitudes, like Van Orley; others she despatched to England, Germany, or France; and still others returned unrecognizable, notably Floris, whose turbulent and cold manner, irregular style, and thin execution were hailed as an event in the school, and gave him the dangerous honor of forming, it is said, one hundred and fifty pupils.

It is easy to recognize, amidst these deserters, certain rarely obstinate souls who, ingenuous and powerful, remain extraordinarily attached to their native soil, and, ploughing it, discover on the spot something new, — witness Quentin Matsys, the Antwerp blacksmith, who began with the wrought-iron well, still to be seen before the portal of Notre Dame, and later, with the same honest hand, precise and powerful, and the same metal-worker's tool, painted the Banker and his Wife in the Louvre, and the admirable Burial of Christ in the Antwerp Museum.

Without leaving this historical hall of the Brussels Museum, one might make extensive studies and discover many curiosities. The period comprised between the end of the fifteenth century and the last third of the sixteenth, that which begins after Memling, with Gérard David and the Stuerbouts, and which finishes with the last pupils of Floris, — for instance, Martin de Vos, — is really one of the periods in the school of the North that we can poorly understand from our French museums. Here are found names wholly unknown among us, like Coxcie and Connixloo. We can learn to understand the merit and the transitory value of Floris, and at a glance can define his historical interest; as to his glory, it will forever astonish, but can be better explained. Bernard van Orley, in spite of all the corruptions of his manner, his mad gesticulations when he grows animated, his theatrical rigidity when he is self-conscious, his faults in drawing, his errors in taste, is revealed to us as an exceptional painter, first, by his Trials of Job, and finally, and even more surely, by his portraits. You find in him something Gothic and something Florentine, Mabuse mingled with an imitation Michael Angelo, the anecdotic style in his triptych of Job, his historical style in the triptych of the Virgin weeping over Christ, — in one, the heavy and pasty style, the sombre color, the tiresomeness of a pale rendering of foreign methods; in the other, the violence and the happy hits of the palette, glittering surfaces, and the glassy brilliancy appropriate to a practitioner from the workshops of Bruges. And yet such is the vigor, the inventive force, and the power of this eccentric and changeful painter, that in spite of his extravagances, he is recognized by an indescribably imposing originality. At Brussels he has some surprising works. Observe that I do not speak to you of Franken, — Ambroise Franken, a pure Fleming of the same epoch, who has nothing in the Brussels Museum, but who figures at Antwerp in an altogether wonderful way, and who, if he is wanting to the series, is at least represented by analogous painters. Observe, too, that I omit those pictures poorly defined and catalogued as *unknown masters,* — triptychs, portraits of various dates, beginning with the two life-sized figures of Philip the Fair and the Mad Joanna, two works rare from the value attached to them by iconography, charming in their execution, most instructive by their appropriateness. The museum possesses about fifty of these anonymous numbers. No one expressly claims them. They recall certain pictures of better determined origin, sometimes connect and confirm them, make their relationship clearer, and better fill out their genealogical tree.

Consider, moreover, that the primitive Dutch school, that of Haarlem, which is confounded with the Flemish school till the day when Holland ceased to be confounded entirely with Flanders, this first effort of the Netherlands to produce indigenous fruits of painting, is to be seen here, and I pass it by. I will only mention Stuerbout, with his two imposing panels of the Justice of Otho, and Heemeskerke and Mostaërt, — Mostaërt, a refractory spirit, an aborigine, a gentleman of the household of Margaret of Austria, who painted all the important personages of his time, a genre painter remarkably tinged with history and legend, who in two episodes of the life of St. Benedict represents the interior of a kitchen, and paints for us, as they did a hundred years later, the familiar domestic life of his time, — Heemeskerke, a pure apostle of linear forms, dry, angular, glaring, blackish, who cuts out of hard steel his figures vaguely imitated from Michael Angelo.

It is easy to mistake a Dutchman for a Fleming. At that date it made very little difference on which side of the Meuse a man was born; what mattered, was to know if such a painter had or had not tasted the troubled waters of the Arno or the Tiber. Had he or had he not visited Italy? Everything is in that, and nothing can be stranger than this mingling, in large or small doses, of Italian culture and persistent Germanisms, of a foreign tongue and the indelible local accent which characterizes this school of Italo-Flemish mongrels. Journeys are in vain; something is changed, but the substratum exists. The style is new, movement is to be found in the grouping, a hint of chiaroscuro begins to dawn upon palettes, nudities appear in an art hitherto wholly clothed and costumed according to local fashions, the height of personages increases, the groups are more numerous, the pictures more crowded, fancy mingles with the myths, an unbridled picturesqueness is combined with history; it is the moment of Last Judgments, satanic and apocalyptic conceptions, and grimacing deviltries. The imagination of the North yields with joyful heart, and gives itself over, in the whimsical or in the terrible, to extravagances which Italian art never suspected.

In the first place, nothing deranges the methodical and tenacious foundation of Flemish genius. Execution remains precise, sharp, minute, and crystalline: the hand remembers having not long since manipulated polished and dense substances; recalls the chiselling of copper, the enamelling of gold, the melting and coloring of glass. Then gradually the trade changes, the coloring is broken, the tone is divided into lights and shades; it becomes iridescent, preserves its substance in the folds of stuffs, evaporates and whitens at each salient point. Painting becomes less solid, and color of less consistency, in proportion as it loses the conditions of force and brilliancy which came from its unity; it is the Florentine method which begins to disorganize the rich and homogeneous Flemish palette. This first ravage well established, the evil makes rapid progress. In spite of the docility with which it follows the Italian teaching, the Flemish spirit is not supple enough to bend entirely to such lessons. It takes what it can, not always the best, and something ever escapes it, — either the method when it tries to seize the style, or the style when it succeeds in approaching the method. After Florence, Rome dominates it, and at the same time Venice. At Venice the influences which it undergoes are singular.

One can hardly perceive that the Flemish painters have studied the Bellini, Giorgione, or Titian. Tintoretto, on the contrary, has visibly impressed them. They find in him something grandiose, a movement, and a muscularity, which tempt them, and a certain transitional coloring, from which that of Veronese will separate itself, and which seems to them more useful to consult for the purpose of discovering the elements of their own. They borrow from him two or three tones, his yellow especially, with the manner of accompanying them. It is to be remarked that in these disconnected imitations there are not only many incoherences, but striking anachronisms.

They adopt more and more the Italian fashion, and yet they wear it ill. An inconsequence, a badly assorted detail, an odd combination of two manners which do not go well together, continue to manifest the rebellious side of the natures of these incorrigible scholars. In the full tide of the Italian decadence, on the eve of the seventeenth century, there are found still among these Italo-Flemings men of the past who seem never to have remarked that the Renascence was over and done. They inhabit Italy, and only follow its evolutions from afar. Whether from inability to understand things, or from native stiffness and obstinacy, there seems to be one side of their minds which resists, and will not be cultivated. An Italo-Fleming is invariably far behind the Italian time of day, which explains why during the life of Rubens his master hardly walked in the steps of Raphael.

While in historical painting some are belated, elsewhere there are some who divine the future, and are in advance. I speak not only of the elder Breughel, the inventor of *genre* painting, a terrible genius, an original master if ever there was one, father of a school to come, who died without having seen his sons, yet whose sons are his very own. The museum of Brussels makes us recognize an unknown painter of uncertain name, recognized by sobriquets: in Flanders he is called Henri *met de Bles*, or de Blesse, the man with the tuft; in Italy, Civetta, because his pictures, now very rare, have an owl in place of a signature. A picture by this Henri de Bles, a Temptation of St. Anthony, is a most unexpected work, with its bottle-green and black-green landscape, its bituminous ground, its sky of light Prussian blue, its audacious and ingenious masses of color, the terrible black, which serves for background to the two nude figures, and its chiaroscuro so boldly obtained with a clear sky. This enigmatic painting, which savors of Italy, and announces what Breughel and Rubens will be later, in their landscapes, reveals a skilful painter, and a man impatient to anticipate the hour.

Of all these painters more or less disacclimated, of all these *Romanists,* as they were called on their return into Antwerp society, Italy not only made skilful, copious artists, of great experience, of true knowledge, especially of great aptitude for diffusion and for vulgarizing (I ask their pardon for the word, it being used in its double signification), but she also gave them the taste for multifarious methods. According to the example of their own masters, they became architects and engineers and poets. To-day this fine fire causes a slight smile at the thought of the sincere masters who preceded them, and the inspired master who was to follow them.

They were brave men, who worked for the culture of their time, and unconsciously for the progress of their school. They went away, enriched themselves, and returned home like emigrants whose savings are made with a view to the fatherland. Some of them were very secondary, and local history itself might forget them if they did not all follow each other from father to son, and if genealogy were not in such cases the only means of estimating the utility of those who seek, and of understanding the sudden grandeur of those who find.

To sum up, a school had disappeared, that of Bruges. Aided by politics, war, journeys, and all the active elements which compose the physical and moral character of a people, another school was formed at Antwerp; ultramontane beliefs inspired it, ultramontane art advised it, princes encouraged it, all national needs called for it. It was at once very active and very undecided, very brilliant, astonishingly fruitful, and almost obscure; it was metamorphosed from top to bottom, so as to be no longer recognizable, until it arrived at its decisive and final incarnation in a man born to bend to all the needs of his age and of his country, nourished by all schools, and who was the most original expression of his own, that is to say, the most Flemish of all Flemings.

Otho Vœnius is placed in the museum of Brussels immediately beside his great pupil. It is towards those two inseparable names that we must tend if we would draw any conclusion from what precedes. They are seen from the whole horizon, the former concealed in the glory of the other; and if I have not named them twenty times already, you should be grateful for the effort I have made to induce you to expect them.

II.

THE MASTERS OF RUBENS.

It is known that Rubens had three teachers, — that he began his studies with a well-known landscape-painter, Tobias Verhaëgt; that he continued them with Adam Van Noort, and ended them with Otho Vœnius. Of these three professors, there are but two with whom history concerns itself, and it still accords to Vœnius almost all the honor of this great education, one of the finest from which a master has ever gained fame, because in fact Vœnius directed his pupil until he attained his majority, and was not separated from him till the age when Rubens was already a man, and, at least in talent, already a great man. As to Van Noort, we learn that he was a painter of real but fantastic originality, who was very harsh with his pupils. In his studio Rubens spent four years; but he disliked him, and found in Vœnius a master of more compatible temper. This is about all that is said of this intermediary director, who held this child in his hands precisely at the age when youth is most susceptible to impressions; but according to my idea this hardly accounts for the influence he must have had upon this young mind.

If from Verhaëgt Rubens learned the elements, if Vœnius instructed him in the humanities, Van Noort did something more; he showed him in his own person a character wholly individual, an unconquerable organization, in short, the sole contemporary painter who remained a Fleming when every one in Flanders had ceased to be one.

Nothing is so singular as the contrast afforded by these two men, so different in character and consequently so opposite in their influence, and nothing is more curious than the destiny which led them in succession to concur in that delicate task, the education of a child of genius. Remark that by their disparities they corresponded precisely to the contrasts of which was formed this multifarious nature, as circumspect as it was bold. Isolated, they represent its contrary elements, that is, its incongruities; together, they reconstitute, minus the genius, the whole man with all his forces, his harmony, his equilibrium, and his unity.

Now, when we understand the genius of Rubens in its plenitude, and the contradictory talents of his two instructors, it is easy to perceive, I do not say the one who has given the wisest counsels, but which of the two has most vividly moved him, — the man who appealed to his reason, or the one who addressed his temperament; the irreproachable painter who exalted Italy to him, or the man of the soil who perhaps showed him what he might one day be, by remaining the greatest of his own nation. In any case there is one whose action is explained but scarcely seen, and another whose influence is manifest without being explained; and if a man be absolutely determined to recognize some family feature in this face so markedly individual, I can see but one which has the character and persistency of an hereditary trait, and this characteristic comes from Van Noort. And now I will say what I have to express concerning Vœnius, claiming for a man too much forgotten the right to figure at Rubens's side.

This Vœnius was no ordinary man. Without Rubens he would find it difficult to sustain the renown he has in history; but at least the lustre from his disciple illumines a noble figure, a personage of distinguished mien, of lofty birth, of high culture, a learned, sometimes even an original painter from the variety of his knowledge, and from a talent almost natural, his excellent education forming a part of his nature, the result being a man and an artist each as admirably trained as the other. He had visited Florence, Rome, Venice, and Parma, and certainly it was in Rome and Venice and Parma that he spent the longest time. A Roman in his scrupulousness, a Venetian in his taste, a Parmesan above all, from affinities which are more rarely revealed, but which are most intimate and true, at Rome and in Venice he had found two schools constituted like no other; at Parma he met one isolated creator, without relations, without doctrines, who did not even pride himself on being a master. Had he, on account of his differences, more respect for Raphael, more sensuous ardor for Veronese and Titian, more tenderness at bottom for Correggio? This I believe. His successful compositions are a little trivial, rather empty, rarely imaginative; and the elegance he derives from nature and his association with the best masters as with the best company, the uncertainty of his convictions and preferences, the impersonal force of his coloring, his draperies destitute of truth and of grandeur of style, his untypical heads, his winy tones lacking in great warmth, — all these suggestions, full of good breeding, would give of him the impression of a mind accomplished, but mediocre. He might be called an excellent court master, who teaches admirably lessons too admirable and powerful for himself. He is, however, something much better than that, and as proof of it, I only need his Mystical Marriage of St. Catherine, which is found in the Brussels Museum on the right, above the Magi of Rubens.

This picture struck me forcibly. It was painted in 1589, and is penetrated with that Italian substance on which the painter had been profoundly nurtured. At this time Vœnius was thirty-three years old. On his return to his own country he took the first rank as architect and painter to Prince Alexander of Parma. From his family picture, which is in the Louvre and which dates from 1584, to this, — that is, in five years, — the stride is enormous. It seems as if his Italian memories had slumbered during his sojourn at Liége with the Prince Bishop, and were revived at the Court of Farnese. This picture, the best and most surprising produced from all the lessons he had learned, has this in particular: it reveals a man behind many influences, it indicates at least in what direction his native inclinations lead, and we learn from it what he desired to do, while seeing most distinctly what inspired him. I will not describe it, but, the subject seeming to me to deserve that one should pause before it, I took some running notes which I here transcribe.

"More opulent, more supple, less Roman, although at the first glance the tone remains Roman. From a certain tenderness of type, an arbitrary crumpling of stuffs, a little mannerism in the hands, we feel Correggio introduced into Raphael. There are angels in the sky who make a pleasing spot; a dark yellow drapery in half-tint is thrown, like a tent with folds turned back, across the branches of the trees. The Christ is charming; the young and slender St. Elizabeth is adorable. She has the cast-down eyes, the chaste and infantile profile, the pretty well-turned neck, the candid air of Raphael's virgins, humanized by an inspiration from Correggio, and by a marked personal sentiment. The blond hair which melts into the blond flesh, the grayish white linens which lead into each other, the colors shadowy or marked, which melt or are distinguished very capriciously according to new laws, and according to the author's proper fancy, all these are pure Italian blood transfused into veins capable of turning them into new blood. All this prepares for Rubens, whom it announces, and towards whom it leads.

"Certainly there is in the Marriage of St. Catherine enough to enlighten and urge forward a mind of such delicacy, a temperament of such ardor. From his Italian souvenirs Vœnius derived these elements, this arrangement, the spots of color; this bending, waving chiaroscuro; this yellow, no longer Tintoretto's, though derived from it; the pearly flesh, no longer the pulp of Correggio, although it has its savor; this thinner skin, this colder flesh, a more feminine grace or a more local femininity; an entirely Italian background, from which, however, the warmth has departed, and in which the red principle gives way to the green principle, with an infinitely greater caprice in the disposition of shadows, and a light more diffused, and less rigorously submitted to the arabesques of form. It is but a slight effort at acclimation, but the effort exists. Rubens, for whom nothing was lost, must have found, when he went to Vœnius seven years later, in 1596, the example of a style of painting already very eclectic and passably emancipated. It is more than one would expect from Vœnius, and enough that Rubens should be indebted to him for a moral influence, if not a decided impression."

As can be seen, Vœnius had more exterior than depth, more order than native richness, and an excellent education; but he lacked ardor, and had not a shadow of genius. He gave good examples, being himself a good example of what may be produced in all things by good birth, a well-trained mind, a supple comprehension, an active and mobile will, and a peculiar aptitude for submission.

Van Noort was the counterpart of Vœnius. He was wanting in almost all that Vœnius had acquired; he naturally possessed what Vœnius lacked. He had neither culture, nor politeness, nor elegance, nor style, nor submissiveness, nor balance; but, on the other hand, real gifts and vivid gifts. Savage, hasty, violent, unpolished, just as nature had made him, he never ceased to be either in his conduct or his works.

He was a man all of a piece, of pure impulse; perhaps an ignorant man, but a somebody, — the opposite of Vœnius, the opposite of an Italian, — a Fleming in race and temperament, who remained a Fleming. With Vœnius he represented marvellously the two elements, native and foreign, which for a hundred years had divided the mind of Flanders, one almost wholly stifling the other. In manner, and allowing for the difference of epoch, he was the last offshoot of the strong national stem of which the Van Eycks, Memling, Quentin Matsys, the elder Breughel, and all the portrait painters had been, according to the spirit of each age, the natural and vigorous product.

Changed as was the old German blood in the veins of the erudite Vœnius, it flowed rich, pure, and abundant in this strong, uncultivated organization. In his tastes, his instincts, his habits, Van Noort belonged to the people. He had their brutality, even, it is said, their love of wine, their loud voice, their coarse but frank language, their ill-taught and rough sincerity, — everything, in a word, except their good-humor. A stranger to society as well as to academies, no more polished in one sense than in another, but absolutely a painter by his imaginative faculties, by the eye and by the hand; rapid, alert, of undisturbed self-possession, he had two motives for daring all, — he knew that he was capable of doing everything without any one's help, and he had no scruples about his own ignorance.

To judge by his works, now become very rare, and by the little that remains to us of a laborious career of eighty-four years, he loved what in his country was scarcely esteemed longer, — an action, even heroic, expressed in its crude reality apart from any ideal, whether mystical or pagan. He loved sanguine and ill-combed men, gray-beards tanned and aged, hardened by rude labor, with shining thick hair, unkempt beards, veined necks, and broad shoulders. In handling he delighted in strong accents, showy colors, great clearness in powerful and inharmonious tones, the whole but little blended, painted broadly, glowing, shining, and rippling. His touch was impatient, sure, and true. He had a way of striking the canvas and imprinting upon it a tone rather than a form, which made it resound under the brush. He massed many stout figures in a little space, disposed them in abundant groups, and drew from numbers a general relief which added to the individual relief of things. Everything that could shine, shone, — brow, temples, mustaches, the white of the eye, the edge of the eyelid; and by this fashion of rendering the action of vivid light upon the blood, the moisture and gleam contracted by the skin from the heat of day which burns it, by much red, intensified by much silver, he gave to all his personages a certain most pronounced activity, and, so to speak, the appearance of being in a sweat.

If these traits are exact, — and I believe them to be so, from having observed them in a very characteristic work, — it is impossible to misunderstand what an influence such a man must have had upon Rubens. The pupil certainly had a good deal of the master in his blood. He had indeed almost everything which makes the originality of his master, but also many other gifts in addition, whence result the extraordinary plenitude, and the not less extraordinary temper of his fine mind. Rubens, it has been written, was *tranquil and lucid*, which means that his lucidity arose from an imperturbable good sense, and his tranquillity from the most admirable equilibrium which has perhaps ever reigned in a brain.

But it is none the less true that there exist between him and Van Noort evident family relations. If that were doubted, one need only look at Jordaens, his co-disciple and his substitute. With age, with education, the traits of which I speak were all to disappear in Rubens, but in Jordaens they have existed underneath his extreme resemblance to Rubens, so that to-day it is by the relationship of the two pupils that one can recognize the original marks which unite both to their common master. Jordaens would certainly have been quite other had he not had Van Noort for an instructor and Rubens for a constant model. Without that instructor would Rubens have been all that he is? and would not one accent have been wanting to him, — that plebeian accent which attaches him to the very heart of his people, thanks to which he has been understood as well by them as by delicate minds and princes? However that may be, Nature seems to have been groping when from 1557 to 1581 she sought the mould in which to melt the elements of modern art in Flanders. It may be said that she tried Van Noort, that she hesitated before Jordaens, and that she only found what she wanted in Rubens.

We have now reached 1600. Henceforth Rubens had enough force to be independent of a master, but not of masters. He departed for Italy, and what he did there is known. He sojourned there eight years, from the age of twenty-three to thirty-one years. He stopped at Mantua, preluded his embassy by a journey to the Court of Spain, returned to Mantua, went to Rome, then to Florence, then to Venice, then from Rome he went to settle at Genoa. There he beheld princes, became celebrated, — there took possession of his talent, his glory, and his fortune. After the death of his mother he returned to Antwerp in 1609, and made himself recognized without difficulty as the first master of his age.

III.

RUBENS IN THE BRUSSELS MUSEUM.

If I were writing the history of Rubens, it would not be here that I should compose the first chapter. I should look for Rubens in his very beginnings, in his pictures anterior to 1609, or else I should choose some marked period, and from Antwerp follow this career, which is so direct that the undulations of the widely developing nature can scarcely be perceived, as it increases its extent without the uncertainties and contradictions of a mind which seeks its way. But remember that I am only turning the leaves of an imperceptible fragment of this immense work. Detached pages of his life are offered by chance, and I accept them thus. Everywhere, moreover, that Rubens is represented by a good picture, he is present, I will not say in all parts of his talent, but certainly in at least one of the finest.

The museum at Brussels has seven of his important pictures, a sketch, and four portraits. If this is not enough to measure Rubens, it suffices to give a grand, varied, and just idea of his value. With his master, his contemporaries, his co-disciples, or his friends, he fills the last division of the gallery, and there sheds abroad that restrained brilliancy, and that soft and powerful radiance which are the grace of his genius. There is no pedantry, no affectation of vain grandeur or of offensive pride, but he is naturally imposing. Give him for neighbors the most overpowering and contrary works, and the effect is the same. He extinguishes those which resemble him, silences those which attempt to contradict him ; from afar he makes his presence consciously felt, he isolates himself, and wherever he may be he is at home.

These pictures, though undated, are evidently of very diverse periods. Many years separate the Assumption of the Virgin from the two dramatic canvases, St. Lieven, and Christ ascending Calvary. Not that in Rubens are seen those striking changes which mark, in the greater part of painters, the passage from one age to another, commonly called their manners. Rubens ripened too early and died too suddenly to have his paintings preserve visible traces of his first ingenuousness, or feel the least effect of his decline. From his youth up he was himself. He had found his style, his form, almost his types, and once for all the elementary principles of his craft. Later, with experience, he acquired still more liberty ; his palette, while it grew richer, became more temperate ; he obtained greater results with less effort, and his extreme boldness, when examined, reveals at bottom perfect moderation, the knowledge, the wisdom, and the pertinence of a consummate master, who is as contained as he is free. He began by working rather thinly and smoothly and vividly. His color, pearly in surface, was more glittering and less resonant, the under tints were less well chosen, the substance less delicate or less deep. He feared a negative tone, not suspecting the learned use of it that he should one day make.

Even at the end of his life, in full maturity, that is, in the full effervescence of brain and method, he returned to this studied manner, which is relatively timid. Therefore in his little anecdotic *genre* pictures made with his friend Breughel to amuse his later years, there is no longer to be recognized the powerful hand, unbridled or refined, which painted at the same epoch the Martyrdom of St. Lieven, the Magi of the Antwerp Museum, or the St. George of the Church of St. Jacques. The spirit in truth never changed; and if one would follow the progress of age, it is the man who must be considered rather than the attractions of his thought; his palette must be analyzed, his method studied, and above all only his great works must be consulted.

The Assumption corresponds to this first period, since it would be inexact to say his first manner. This picture has been much retouched, and though we are assured that on this account it loses a large part of its merit, I cannot see that it has lost that which I am seeking. It is a page at once brilliant and cold, inspired in rendering, methodical and prudent in execution. It is like the pictures of that date, polished, clean in surface, a trifle glassy. The commonplace types lack naturalness; the palette of Rubens resounds already with certain dominant notes, red, yellow, black, and gray, brilliant but crude. These are its insufficiencies. As to merits entirely acquired, they are here applied in a masterly way. Great figures leaning over the empty tomb, all the colors vibrating over a black opening, the light spreading from a central point of brilliancy, broad, powerful, sonorous, wavy, dying in softest half-tints; on the right and left nothing but weak points except two accidental spots, two horizontal strong points which attach the scene to the frame half-way up the picture. Below, some gray steps; above, a sky of Venetian blue with gray clouds and flying vapors, and in this shaded azure, her feet buried in bluish fleecy clouds, her head in a glory, floats the Virgin, clothed in pale blue, with a dark blue mantle, three winged groups of angels accompanying her, all radiating with pearl and rose and silver. At the upper angle, just touching the zenith, a little agile cherub, beating his wings, shining like a butterfly in the light, mounts directly and flies through the open heaven like a swifter messenger than the others. Here are suppleness, breadth, depth of grouping, and a marvellous union of the picturesque with the grand. In spite of certain imperfections all Rubens is here, more than in embryo. Nothing can be more tender, more frank, or more striking. As an improvisation of happy spots of color, as life, as a harmony for the eye, it is perfect, — a summer festival.

Christ in the Lap of the Virgin is a much later work, grave, gray, and black. The Virgin is in sad blue; the Magdalen in a purple-black garment. The canvas has suffered much from transportation, either in 1794, when it was sent to Paris, or in 1815, when it returned. It passed for one of the finest works of Rubens, which it no longer can be called. I confine myself to transcribing my notes, which say enough.

The Magi are neither the first nor the last expression of a subject that Rubens has treated many times. In any case, in whatever rank they are classed in these versions developed from one theme, they follow that of Paris, and very certainly they precede that of Mechlin, of which I will speak further on. The idea is ripe, the arrangement more complete. The necessary elements, of which is to be composed later this work so rich in transformations, types, and personages, with their costumes and their habitual colors, are all found here, playing the rôle designed for them, occupying in the scene their destined place. It is a vast page, conceived, contained, concentrated, summed up, like an easel picture, and for that reason less decorative than many others. It has a great clearness, no tiresome neatness, not one of the chilling drynesses of the Assumption, a great carefulness, with the maturity of most perfect knowledge. The whole school of Rubens might have been instructed from this one example.

With the Ascent of Calvary, it is quite another thing. At this date Rubens had made the greater part of his great works. He was no longer young; he knew everything; he could only have lost, if death, which protected him, had not removed him before he began to fail. Here we have movement, tumult, agitation, in form, in gesture, in countenances, in the disposition of groups, in the oblique light, diagonal and symmetrical, going from the base to the top and from right to left. Christ falling under his cross, the escort of horsemen, the two thieves held and driven by their executioners, are all marching in the same line, and seem to climb the narrow ascent which leads to the place of torture. The Christ is dying with fatigue; St. Veronica is wiping his brow; the Virgin in

tears rushes towards him, extending her arms to him; Simon of Cyrene bears the cross; — and in spite of this tree of infamy, these women in tears and mourning, this struggling victim on his knees, whose panting mouth, moist temples, and haggard eyes excite pity, — in spite of the terror, the shouts, the near approach of death, it is clear to him who can see, that this equestrian pomp, these floating banners, this harnessed centurion turning upon his horse with a noble gesture, in whom are recognized the features of Rubens, — all these cause the execution to be forgotten, and give more manifestly the impression of a triumph.

And this is the individual logic of this brilliant mind. It might be said that the scene is comprehended falsely, — that it is melodramatic, without gravity, without majesty, without beauty, without august character, in fine, almost theatrical. The picturesque, which might well ruin it, is what saves it. Fancy takes possession of it, and elevates it. A gleam of true sentiment pierces and ennobles it. Something like a trait of eloquence enhances the style. Finally, there is an inexpressible fire, an admirably inspired enthusiasm, which make of this picture exactly what it ought to be, — a picture of trivial death, and an apotheosis. I find, on examination, that this picture dates from 1634. I was not mistaken in attributing it to the last and finest years of Rubens.

Is the Martyrdom of St. Lieven of the same epoch? At least it is in the same style, but in spite of something terrible in the rendering, it has more liveliness in its attraction, its method, and its color. Rubens thought less of it than the Calvary. His palette was gayer at that time, the workman more rapid, and his brain less nobly disposed. Forget that this is an ignoble and savage murder of a holy bishop whose tongue has just been torn out, who is vomiting blood, and writhing in agonizing convulsions; forget the three executioners who are torturing him, one with his bloody knife between his teeth, the other with his heavy pincers holding the frightful morsel of flesh to the dogs; look only at the white horse curveting under a white sky, the golden cope of the bishop, his white stole, the dogs spotted with black and white, four or five of them black, the two red caps, the flushed faces with ruddy skins, and all around in the vast field of canvas the delicious concert of gray and azure and pale or dark silver, — and you will receive only the sentiment of a radiant harmony, the most admirable perhaps, and the most unexpected that Rubens ever used to express, or, if you prefer, to excuse, a scene of horror.

Did Rubens seek contrast? Did he need for the altar which it was to occupy in the church of the Jesuits at Ghent, that this picture should be at once raging and celestial, terrible and smiling, a shuddering horror and a consolation? I think that the poetical side of Rubens adopted quite voluntarily such antitheses. Even if he did not think of it, involuntarily his nature would have inspired them. It is well from the beginning to accustom ourselves to these contradictions which produce an equilibrium, and constitute an exceptional genius. Here are much blood and physical vigor, but a winged spirit, a man who fears not the horrible but has a tender and truly serene soul; here are hideousnesses and brutalities, a total absence of taste in form, combined with an ardor which transforms ugliness into force, bloody brutality into terror. This desire for apotheosis of which I spoke in the Calvary, he carries into all he does. If well understood, there is a glory, a trumpet call, in his grossest works. He is very earthy, more earthy than any of the masters whose equal he is, but the painter comes to the aid of the draughtsman and thinker, and sets them free. Therefore there are many who cannot follow him in his flights. There is a suspicion of an imagination which elevates him, but what is seen is only what attaches him below, to the common, the too real, — the thick muscles, the redundant or careless design, the heavy types, the flesh, and the blood just under the skin. And yet there is a failure to perceive that he has formulas, a style, an ideal, and that these superior formulas, this style, this ideal, are in his palette.

Add to this his special gift of eloquence. His language, to define it accurately, is what in literature is called oratorical. When he improvises, he is not at his best; when he restrains his speech, it is magnificent. It is prompt, sudden, abundant, and warm; in all circumstances it is eminently persuasive. He strikes, astonishes, repels you; he irritates, but almost always convinces; and if there is a chance for it, more than any one else he can touch you. Certain pictures of Rubens are revolting, but there are some that bring tears to the eyes, and such an influence is rare in all schools. He has the weaknesses, the digressions, and also the magnetic fire of the great orators. He sometimes perorates and declaims, he beats the air with his huge arms, but there are words he can speak as no other man can. In general, his ideas are such as can only be expressed by eloquence, by pathetic gesture and sonorous utterance.

Remark also that he paints for walls, for altars to be seen from the nave; that he speaks for a vast audience; that consequently he must be heard from afar, must strike a long way off, seize and charm from a distance, whence results the necessity of insisting, of enlarging methods, of increasing the volume of sound. There are laws of perspective, and so to speak of acoustics, which preside over this solemn art, of such immense range.

It is to this kind of declamatory and incorrect, but very moving eloquence, that belongs his Christ coming to judge the World. The earth is a prey to vices and crimes, to conflagrations, assassinations, and violence; the idea of these human perversities being rendered by a bit of animated landscape such as Rubens alone can paint.

Christ appears armed with thunderbolts, half flying, half marching; and while he prepares to punish this abominable world, a poor monk in his woollen robe implores mercy, and covers with his two arms an azure globe, around which is twined a serpent. Does the prayer of the saint suffice? No. Then the Virgin, a tall woman in widow's weeds, throws herself before Christ and arrests him. She neither implores, nor prays, nor commands; she is before her God, but she addresses her Son. Opening her black robe, she uncovers her large immaculate bosom, which she touches with her hand, displaying it to him whom it has nourished. The apostrophe is irresistible. Everything may be criticised in this purely passionate picture, painted without retouching: the Christ, who is only ridiculous; the St. Francis, who is but a terrified monk; the Virgin, who resembles a Hecuba with the features of Helen Fourment, — even her gesture is not without boldness, if one remembers the taste of Raphael, or even the taste of Racine. But I believe it is none the less true that neither at the theatre nor on the tribune, — and this picture recalls both, — nor in painting, which is its true domain, have been found so many pathetic effects from such vigor and such novelty.

I neglect — and Rubens will lose nothing thereby — the Assumption of the Virgin, a picture without a soul; and Venus in the Forge of Vulcan, a canvas too closely related to Jordaens. I pass over likewise the portraits, to which I shall return. Five of the seven pictures, as you see, give a first idea of Rubens not destitute of interest. Supposing that he were unknown, or known only by the Medici Gallery at the Louvre, — and that is an ill-chosen example, — one would begin to suspect what he is in his mind, his method, his imperfections, and his power. From this, one would conclude that he must never be compared to the Italians, under penalty of misunderstanding, and judging him falsely. If we mean by style the ideal of the pure and beautiful transcribed in formulas, he has no style. If we mean by grandeur loftiness, penetration, the meditative and intuitive force of a great thinker, he has neither grandeur nor thought. If taste be requisite, he has no taste. If one delights in a restrained, concentrated, condensed art, like that of Leonardo da Vinci for example, this can only irritate and displease by its habitual exaggerations. If all human types must bear some relation to those of the Dresden Madonna, or to La Joconde, to those of Bellini, Perugino, and Luini, those delicate definers of grace and beauty in woman, no indulgence can be felt for the abundant beauty and plump charms of Helen Fourment. Finally, if, approaching more and more to the sculptural manner, there should be demanded from the works of Rubens the conciseness, the rigid bearing, the peaceable gravity, that painting wore when he began, very little would be left to Rubens, except a gesticulator, a man full of force, a sort of imposing athlete, with little cultivation, — in short, a bad example. In this case, as has been said, " We salute when we pass, but do not look."

It is necessary then to find, apart from all comparison, a special position for this glory which is so legitimate a glory. It must be found in the world of the true through which Rubens travels as a master; and also in the world of the ideal, that region of clear ideas, of sentiments, and emotions, whither his heart as well as his mind bear him incessantly. Those wing strokes by which he there maintains himself must be understood. It must be comprehended that his element is light, that his means of exaltation is his palette, his aim the clearness and evidence of objects. The works of Rubens cannot only be viewed in an amateur fashion as shocking the mind and charming the eye. There is something more to be considered and to say. The Brussels Museum is the beginning of the matter, but we must remember that Mechlin and Antwerp remain.

IV.

RUBENS AT MECHLIN.

Mechlin is a great dreary city, empty, dead, and buried in the shadow of its basilicas and convents, in a silence from which nothing is able to rouse it, neither its industries, its politics, nor the controversialists who sometimes meet there. At the present moment they are having processions with cavalcades, congregations, and banners, on the occasion of the Centennial Jubilee. All this commotion animates it for a day, but on the morrow the province goes to sleep again. There is very little movement in the streets, a great desert in the squares, many mausoleums of black marble, and statues of bishops in its churches; and around the churches that fine short grass which grows in solitude among the pavements. In short, in this metropolitan, or rather I should say necropolitan city, there are but two things which survive its past splendor, — its sanctuaries of exceeding richness, and the pictures of Rubens. These pictures are the celebrated triptych of the Magi at St. John, and the not less celebrated triptych of the Miraculous Draught of Fishes, which belongs to the church of Notre Dame.

The Adoration of the Magi is, as I have previously informed you, a third version of the Magi of the Louvre and of Brussels. The elements are the same, the principal personages textually the same, with an insignificant change of age in the heads, and some transpositions of equally little importance. Rubens has made no great effort to remodel his first idea. According to the example of the greatest masters, he had the good sense to live largely upon himself, and when one rendering appeared to him fertile in variations, he simply made some slight alteration in the repetitions. This theme of the Wise Men coming from the four corners of the earth to adore a homeless infant, born one winter night in the manger of a poor and hidden stable, was one of those which pleased Rubens by its pomp and its contrasts. It is interesting to follow the development of the first idea, as he essays it, enriches, completes, and finally establishes it. After the picture at Brussels, which might have satisfied him, he was able, it seems, to treat the subject better still, with greater richness, more freedom, giving to it that flower of certainty and perfection which belongs only to works absolutely mature. This he has done at Mechlin, after which he returned to it, abandoned himself more entirely, added to it new fancies, astonished still more by the fertility of his resources, but did no better. The Magi at Mechlin may be considered as the final expression of the subject, and as one of the finest pictures of Rubens in this style of grand spectacular canvases.

The composition of the central group is reversed from right to left, — with the exception of this change, it can be almost wholly recognized. Here are the three Wise Men, — the European, as at

Brussels, with his white hair minus the baldness; the Asiatic, in red; the Ethiopian, faithful to his type, here smiles, as he smiles elsewhere, with that ingenuous negro laugh, tender and wondering, so delicately observed in this affectionate race ever ready to show its teeth, only he has changed his rôle and his place. He has been relegated to the second rank, between the princes of the earth and the supernumeraries; the white turban which he wore at Brussels here adorns a fine ruddy head of Oriental type, whose bust is clothed in green. Also the man in armor is here, half-way up the staircase, bareheaded, rosy, fair, and charming. Instead of keeping back the crowd by facing them, he makes a happy counter-movement, bends to admire the child, and by a gesture repels the eager multitude thronging up the steps. Remove this elegant knight of the time of Louis XIII., and it is the East. How could Rubens know that in every Mussulman country people are so intrusive that they crush each other in order to see better? As at Brussels, the accessory heads are the most characteristic and the finest.

The arrangement of color and the distribution of the lights is unchanged. The Virgin is pale, the infant Christ radiating with whiteness under his aureola. Immediately around all is white, — the sage with his ermine collar and hoary locks, the silver head of the Asiatic, finally the turban of the Ethiopian, — a circle of silver, shaded with rose and pale gold. All the rest is black, tawny, or cold. The heads, ruddy or of a burning brick-red, contrast with bluish countenances of a most unexpected coldness. The dark roof melts away in air. A figure in blood-red in the half-tint relieves, finishes, and sustains the whole composition, attaching it to the vault by a knot of color, soft, but very precise. It is a composition that cannot be described, for it expresses nothing formal, nothing pathetic or moving, especially nothing literary. It charms the mind because it enchants the eye ; to a painter, the painting is priceless. To the delicate it must cause great joy, and it must confound the wise. It is wonderful to see how it all lives, moves, breathes, looks, acts, is full of color or fades away, forms a part of the frame or detaches itself from it, melts into it by its lights, reinstates itself and maintains itself there by its force. And as to the crossing of shades, the extreme richness obtained by simple means, by the violence of certain tones, the softness of certain others ; the abundance of red, and yet the coolness of the whole picture, — as to the laws which preside over such effects, they are things absolutely disconcerting.

Analysis reveals only a few very simple formulas, two or three master colors whose purpose is explained, whose action is foreseen, and whose influence every man who knows how to paint to-day understands. The colors are always the same in the works of Rubens ; there are no secrets, to speak truly. The accessory combinations can be noted, his method can be expressed ; it is so constant, and so plain in its application, that a pupil, it would seem, would only have to follow it. Never was handiwork easier to seize, with fewer tricks and reticences, because there never was a painter so little mysterious, either when thinking, composing, coloring, or executing. The sole secret which belongs to him, and which he never yielded even to the most intelligent or the best informed, — even to Gaspard de Crayer, even to Jordaens, even to Vandyck, — is that imponderable, unseizable point, that irreducible atom, that nothing, which in all the things of this world is called the inspiration, the *grace*, or the *gift*, — which is everything.

This is what must be understood in the first place when Rubens is spoken of. Every man of the craft, or a stranger to the craft, who does not understand the value of the *gift* in a work of art, in all its degrees of illumination, inspiration, or fancy, is hardly fit to taste the subtle essence of things, and I would advise him never to touch Rubens nor even many others.

I will spare you the doors of the triptych, which, however, are superb, not only being of his best period, but in his best manner, brown and silvery, which is the last expression of his richness. There is a St. John there of a very rare quality, and an Herodias in dark gray with red sleeves, who is his eternal woman.

The Miraculous Draught is also a fine picture, but not the finest, as they say at Mechlin, in the Notre Dame quarter. The curé of St. Jean would share my opinion, and in good conscience he would be right. This picture has just been restored, and at present it is placed upon the ground, in a schoolroom, leaning against a white wall, under a glass roof which inundates it with light, without a frame, in the crudity, in the violence, in the cleanliness of its very first day. Examined by itself, with the eye close to it, and entirely to its disadvantage, it is a picture which I will not call gross, because the handiwork elevates the style a little; but material, if the word expresses, as I understand it, ingenious but narrow construction of a vulgar character. It is wanting in that something, I know not what, in which Rubens infallibly succeeds when he touches the common, — a note, a grace, a tenderness, something like a kind smile which makes an excuse for heavy features. Christ, relegated to the right, in the wing, as an accessory in this fishing picture, is as insignificant in gesture as he is in physiognomy; and his red mantle, which is not a fine red, is sharply relieved against a blue sky, which I suspect is very much altered. St. Peter, a little neglected, but of a fine winy value, would be, if the Gospel were thought of before this canvas painted for fishermen and entirely executed from fishermen, the sole evangelical person in the scene. At least he says exactly what an old man of his class and rusticity would say to Christ in similarly strange circumstances. He holds pressed against his ruddy and rugged breast his sailor's cap, a blue cap, and it is not Rubens who would be deceived in the truth of such a gesture. As to the two naked figures, one bending towards the spectator, the other turned towards the background, and both seen by the shoulders, they are celebrated among the best academy pieces that Rubens ever painted, from the free and sure manner with which the painter has brushed them in, doubtless in a few hours, at the first painting, with the wet paint clear, even abundant, not too fluid, not thick, neither too modelled nor too rough. It is Jordaens without reproach, without excessive redness, without glitter; or rather it is, in its way of seeing the flesh, and not the *meat*, the best lesson that his great friend could give him. The fisherman with his

Scandinavian head, his flowing beard, his golden hair, his bright eyes in his flushed countenance, his great sea-boots and red garment, is overwhelming. And, as usual in all Rubens's pictures where excessive red is employed as a quietus, it is this flaming personage who tempers the rest, acts upon the retina, and disposes it to see green in all the neighboring colors. Note also among the accessory figures a great boy, — a cabin boy standing on the second boat, leaning on an oar, dressed no matter how, with gray trousers, a purplish waistcoat, too short, unbuttoned, and open over his naked stomach.

These men are fat, red, sunburned, tanned and swollen by the fierce breezes, from their finger ends to their shoulders, from the brow to the nape of the neck. All the irritating salts of the sea have exasperated whatever the air touches, have brightened the blood, flushed the skin, swollen the veins, roughened the white flesh, and in a word stained them with vermilion. It is brutal, exact, taken on the spot : all has been witnessed on the quays of the Scheldt by a man who sees largely, sees truly, both color and form ; who respects the truth when it is expressive, nor fears to express crude things crudely, for he knows his trade like an angel and fears nothing.

What is truly extraordinary in this picture, thanks to the circumstances which permit me to see it so near, and examine the workmanship as closely as if Rubens executed it before me, is that it seems to reveal all his secrets, and that after all it astonishes just as much as if it revealed nothing. I had already said this of Rubens, before this new proof of it was given me.

The embarrassment is not to know how he did it, but how he could do so well by working thus. The means are simple, the method elementary. It is a fine panel, smooth, clean, and white, on which works a hand magnificently agile, adroit, sensitive, and composed. The impetuosity supposed to be his is a way of feeling, rather than a disorderly way of painting. The brush is as calm as the soul is hot and ready to rush forward. In such an organization there is such an exact relation and such a rapid connection between the vision, the sensitiveness, and the hand, such perfect obedience of the one to the others, that the habitual explosions of the brain which directs make one believe in the summersaults of the instrument. Nothing is more deceptive than this apparent fever, restrained by profound calculation, and served by a mechanism practised in every exercise. It is the same with the sensations of the eye, and consequently of the choice he makes of colors. His colors are also very simple, and only appear so complicated on account of the results achieved by the painter, and the part he makes them play. Nothing can be more limited than the number of primary tints, nor more foreseen than the manner in which they are opposed; nothing also is more simple than the habit by virtue of which he shades them, and nothing more unexpected than the result which is produced.

Not one of Rubens's tones is very rare in itself. If you take his red, it is easy to dictate the formula; it is vermilion and ochre very little broken, in its state of first mixture. If you examine his blacks, they are taken out of a pot of ivory black, and serve, with white, for all the imaginable combinations of his dull or tender grays. His blues are accidents; his yellows, one of the colors which he feels and manages least well in point of tint, except the golds, which he excels in rendering in their warm deep richness, have, like his reds, a double part to play,—first, to make the light fall somewhere beside upon the whites; secondly, to exercise in the neighborhood the indirect action of a color which changes other colors,—for instance, to turn into violet, and give a certain bloom to a dull and very insignificant gray, quite neutral when viewed upon the palette. All this one may say is not very extraordinary.

Brown undertones, with two or three active colors, to make one believe in the wealth of a vast canvas; broken grays obtained by dull mixtures; all the intermediary grays between deep black and pure white,—consequently very little coloring matter and the greatest brilliancy of color, great luxury obtained with small expense, light without excessive brightness, an extreme sonorousness from a small number of instruments, a key-board in which nearly three fourths of the keys are neglected, but which he runs over, skipping many notes and touching it when necessary at the two ends;—such is, in the mixed language of music and painting, the habit of this great practitioner. He who sees one of his pictures knows them all, and he who has seen him paint one day has seen him paint at almost every moment of his life. There is ever the same method, the same coolness, the same calculation. A calm and intelligent premeditation presides over his always sudden effects. Whence comes his audacity, at what moment he is carried away and abandons himself, can never be known. Is it when he executes some violent work, some extravagant gesture, a moving object, an eye that gleams, a mouth that shouts, tangled hair, a bristling beard, a hand that grasps, foam that lashes the beach, disorder in array, a breeze in light objects, or the uncertainty of muddy water dripping through the meshes of a net? Is it when he imbues many yards of canvas with a glowing tint, when he makes his red ripple in waves, so that everything around this red is spattered with its reflections? Is it, on the contrary, when he passes from one strong color to another, circulating through neutral tones as if this rebellious and sticky material were the most manageable of the elements? Is it when he gives a loud cry, or when he utters a sound so feeble that one can hardly catch it? Did this painting, which puts the beholder into a fever, burn in this manner the hands whence it issued, fluid, easy, natural, healthy, and ever virgin, no matter at what moment you surprise it? Where, in a word, is the effort in this art, which might be called forced, while it is the intimate expression of a mind which never was forced?

Did you ever close your eyes during the execution of a brilliant piece of music? The sound gushes everywhere. It seems to leap from one instrument to the other; and as it is very tumultuous, in spite of the perfect harmony of the whole, it might well be believed that everything was agitated, that the hands trembled, and that the same musical frenzy had seized the instruments and those who held them; and because the performers move the audience so violently, it seems impossible that they should remain calm before their music rests; so that one is quite surprised to see them peaceable, self-contained, solely attentive to watching the movement of the ebony wand which leads them, sustains them, dictates to each what he should do, and which is itself only the agent of a mind fully awake and of great knowledge. Thus Rubens wields, during the execution of his works, the ebony baton which commands, conducts, and overlooks; his is the imperturbable will, the master faculty, which also directs very attentive instruments, I mean the auxiliary faculties.

Shall we return for a moment more to this picture? It is under my hand, it is an occasion not often to be had, and which I shall never have again. I will seize it.

The painting is done at once, completely, or with very little retouching. This can be seen by the lightness of certain lays of color, in the St. Peter in particular, in the transparency of the great flat and sombre tints, such as the boats, the sea, and all that participates in the same brown, bituminous, or greenish element; it is equally seen in the not less rapid, though heavier execution of the parts which require a thick paint and a more sustained labor. The brilliancy of the tone, its freshness and its radiance, are due to this. The white ground of the panel and its smooth surface give to the color, frankly applied, that vibration proper to all tinting laid upon a clear, resisting, and polished surface. If it were thicker, the material would be muddy; if it were more rugose, it would absorb as many luminous rays as it would reflect, and the effort would have to be doubled to produce the same result of light; were it thinner, more timid, or less generously smooth in its contours, it would have that enamelled character, which, however admirable in certain cases, would suit neither the style of Rubens, nor his spirit, nor the romantic purpose of his fine works. Here, as elsewhere, his moderation is perfect. The two torsi, finished as thoroughly as a bit of nude of this extent can be within the conditions of a mural picture, have not undergone much retouching with the brush. It might well be that in his days so regularly divided by labor and repose, that each figure was the result of an afternoon of joyous work, after which the painter, content with himself with good reason, laid aside his palette, had his horse saddled, and thought no more about it.

With still better reason, in all the secondary and supporting parts, the sacrificed portions, the large spaces where the air circulates, the accessories, boats, waves, nets, and fishes, the hand runs along and does not emphasize. A vast wash of the same brown, which is brownish above and green below, grows warm when there is a reflection, is gilded in the hollows of the sea, and descends from the edge of the vessels to the frame. Through this abundant and liquid material the painter has given the appropriate life to each object, or, according to the language of the studio, "he has *found* the *life*." A few gleams, a few reflections laid on with a fine brush, and you have the sea. It is the same with the nets and their meshes, their planks and corks; the same with the fish struggling in the muddy water, so wet that they drip with the very colors of the sea; the same with the feet of Christ and the boots of the glowing sailor. To call this the last word of the art of painting, when it is severe, or when it seeks, with the grand style in mind, eye and hand to express ideals or epics; to maintain that this is the true method under all circumstances, — would be like applying the picturesque, rapid language, full of imagery, of our modern writers to the ideas of Pascal. In any case it is Rubens's own language, his style, and consequently is appropriate to his own ideas.

The real astonishment, when one thinks about it, comes from the fact that the painter has meditated so little; that, having thought of any subject, no matter what, he is not turned aside, but can make a picture of it; that with so little study he is never trivial, and that with such simple means he can produce such an effect. If the science of his palette is extraordinary, the sensitiveness of his agents is none the less so; and a merit of which one would hardly suspect him comes to the aid of all the others, — moderation, and even I might say sobriety, in the purely exterior manner of handling the brush.

There are many things that people forget in our time, that they appear to misunderstand, and that they vainly strive to abolish. I cannot tell where our modern school found its taste for thickness of material, and that love of heavy masses of paint, which constitutes in the eyes of some people the principal merit of certain works. I have seen no authoritative examples for it anywhere, except in the painters of the visible decadence and in Rembrandt, who apparently could not always do without it, but who knew how to do without it sometimes. Fortunately in Flanders it is an unknown method; and as to Rubens, — the accredited master of transport and fury, — the most violent of his pictures are often the least loaded. I do not say that he systematically thins his lights, as they did up to the middle of the sixteenth century, or that, on the other hand, he thickens all the strong tints. This method, exquisite in its first destination, has undergone all the changes since introduced by the necessities of ideas, and the more multiplied needs of modern painting. However, if he is far from the purely archaic method, he is still farther from the practices in favor since Géricault, — to take a recent example from the illustrious dead. His brush glides and does not plunge. It never drags after it that sticky mortar that accumulates on the salient points of objects, and produces the effect of high relief, because the canvas itself thus becomes more salient. He does not load, he paints ; he does not build, he writes ; he caresses, lightly touches, or bears heavily. He passes from an immense impasto to the most delicate, the most fluid touch, always with that degree of consistency or lightness, that breadth or that minuteness, which suits the subject that he treats, so that the prodigality or the economy of his paint is a matter of local suitability, and the weight or the marvellous lightness of his brush is a means of expressing what demands or does not demand emphasis.

To-day, when divers schools divide our French school, and to tell the truth, we have only certain more or less adventurous talents without fixed doctrines, the value of a picture well or badly executed is of very little consequence. A crowd of subtle questions induce forgetfulness of the most necessary elements of expression. In carefully examining certain contemporary pictures, whose merit, at least as attempts, is often more real than is believed, we find that the hand is no longer reckoned among the agents which serve the mind. According to recent methods, to execute is to fill a form with a tone, whatever may be the tool that performs the labor. The mechanism of the operation seems unimportant, provided the operation succeeds ; and it is wrongly supposed that thought can be as well served by one instrument as another. It is precisely the opposite of this that all the skilful painters, that is to say, the sensitive ones, of these countries of Flanders and Holland, have affirmed in advance by their method, which is the most expressive of all. And it is against the same error that Rubens protests, with an authority which will perhaps have a little better chance of being heeded.

Take from the pictures of Rubens — from this one which I am studying — the spirit, the variety, the propriety of each touch, and you take from it a word which tells, a necessary accent, a trait of physiognomy. You take away from it perhaps the sole element which spiritualizes so much materiality, and transfigures its frequent hideousness, because you suppress all sensitiveness ; and, tracing effects to their primary cause, you kill the life and make a picture without a soul. I might almost say that one touch the less would cause the disappearance of some artistic feature.

The rigor of this principle is such, that in a certain order of productions there is no thoroughly felt work which is not naturally well painted, and that any work where the hand shows itself with success or brilliancy is from that very fact a work which comes from the brain and manifests that fact. Rubens had on this subject opinions which I recommend to you, if you should ever be tempted to scorn a brush stroke made in an appropriate manner.

There is not in this great picture, apparently so brutal and so free in handling, a single detail, small or great, which is not inspired by sentiment, and instantaneously rendered by a happy touch. If the hand did not move so rapidly, it would be behind the thought ; if the improvisation were less sudden, the life communicated would be less ; if the work were more hesitating or less comprehensible, the picture would become impersonal in proportion to its acquired heaviness and its loss of spirit. Consider, moreover, that this unequalled dexterity, this careless skill in playing with ungrateful materials and rebellious instruments, this noble movement of a well-handled tool, this elegant fashion of moving it over free surfaces, the impulse which escapes from it, the sparks that seem to fly from it, — all this magic of the great performers, which in others becomes mannerism, or affectation, or purely a spirit of common alloy, — in him (I repeat it to satiety) is only the exquisite sensibility of an eye admirably healthy, a hand marvellously submissive, and finally and especially, of a soul truly open to all things, happy, confident, and great. I defy you to find in the great repertory of his works one perfect work ; but I also defy you not to feel even in the manias, the faults, I was going to say the trivialities, of this noble mind, the marks of incontestable grandeur ; and this exterior mark, the last seal placed upon his thought, is the imprint of the hand itself.

What I say to you in many phrases far too long, and too often in the special jargon which it is hard to avoid, would doubtless have found a more suitable place elsewhere. Do not imagine that the picture I dwell upon is a finished specimen of the finest merits of the painter. In no degree is it that. Rubens has frequently conceived better, seen better, and painted far better; but the execution of Rubens, so unequal in results, scarcely varies in principle, and the observations made with regard to a picture of medium merit, are equally applicable, and with much better reason, to whatever he has produced that is excellent.

V.

THE ELEVATION OF THE CROSS AND THE CRUCIFIXION.

MANY people say Antwerp, but many too say the Home of Rubens; and this way of speaking expresses still more exactly all the things which make the magic of the place, — a great city, a great personal destiny, a famous school, and pictures ultra-celebrated. All this is imposing, and the imagination becomes more than usually active, when in the midst of the Place Verte is seen the statue of Rubens, and beyond, the old Basilica, where are preserved the triptychs which, humanly speaking, have consecrated it. The statue is not a masterpiece, but it is he in his own home. Under the figure of a man who was merely a painter, with the attributes only of a painter, in very truth is personified the sole Flemish royalty which has been neither contested nor menaced, and which certainly never will be so.

At the end of the square Notre Dame is seen, in profile, drawn at full length from one of its lateral fronts, — the darkest, because it is the weather side. Its surrounding of light low houses increases its size and makes it darker. With its wrought architecture, its rusty color, its blue and shining roof, its colossal tower, where shines in the stone, smoky with the Scheldt fogs and the winters, the golden disk and golden hands of the clock, it gains immeasurable proportions. When, as to-day, the sky is lowering, the clouds add to the grandeur of its lines all the freaks of their caprice. Imagine then the invention of a Gothic Piranesi, exaggerated by the fancy of the North, wildly lighted by a stormy day, and traced in irregular spots upon the great background of a tempest-swept sky, all black or all white. No preliminary scenic effect could be combined more original and striking.

In spite of coming from Mechlin and Brussels, in spite of having seen the Magi and the Calvary, and of having formed of Rubens an exact and measured idea, in spite of having familiarly examined him until you feel quite at your ease, you will not enter Notre Dame as you would a museum.

It is the hour of three, — the clock in the air has just struck; hardly a sacristan makes a sound in the quiet naves, clean and bright as Peter Neefs has reproduced them, with an inimitable sentiment of their solitude and their grandeur. It rains, and the light is changing; gleams and shadows succeed each other upon the two triptychs, attached unostentatiously, in their narrow frames of brown wood, to the cold smooth walls of the transepts; yet these superb paintings only appear more distinct amid the glaring lights and the obscurities which struggle with them. German copyists have established their easels before the Descent from the Cross, but there is no one before the Elevation of the Cross. This simple fact expresses sufficiently the world's opinion of these two works.

They are much admired, almost without reserve, and the fact is rare for Rubens; but admiration is divided. Great renown has preferred the Descent from the Cross; the Elevation of the Cross has the gift of touching more deeply the passionate or more thoroughly persuaded friends of Rubens. Nothing indeed can be more unlike than these two works, conceived at an interval of two years, inspired by the same effort of mind, and which yet bear so clearly the marks of his two tendencies. The Descent from the Cross is of 1612, the Elevation of the Cross of 1602. I insist upon the dates, for they are important. Rubens had just returned to Antwerp, and it was, so to speak, upon landing that he painted them. His education was completed. At that time he had made an excessive amount of studies, rather too oppressive for him, of which he meant to make use openly, once for all, but of which he was to get rid almost immediately. Each one of the Italian masters whom he had consulted of course advised him differently. The violent masters advised him to dare great things; the severe masters recommended him greatly to restrain himself. Nature, temper, native faculties, former lessons, recent lessons, everything was prepared to divide him; the task itself required him to separate his fine gifts into two parts. He felt the occasion, seized it, treated each subject according to its own spirit, and gave of himself two contrary and yet just ideas, — one the most magnificent example of his wisdom, the other the most astounding revelation ot his dash and ardor. Add to the personal inspiration of the painter a very marked Italian influence, and you will still better understand the extraordinary value that posterity attaches to these pages, which may be considered his masterworks, and which were the first public act of his life as the head of a school.

I will tell you how this influence is manifested and by what character it is recognized. It is enough at first to remark that it exists, that the physiognomy of Rubens's talent loses none of its features at the very moment that we are examining it. It is not that he is positively restrained by the canonical formulas in which others would have been imprisoned. Heaven knows with what ease he moves in them, with what liberty he uses them, with what tact he disguises or avows them, according as it pleases him to permit us to see the learned man or the innovator. However, whatever he does, we feel the *Romanist* who has just passed years on classic ground, who comes home but has not yet changed his atmosphere.

Something remains, which recalls his journey like a strange odor in his garments. Certainly it is to this good Italian odor that the Descent from the Cross owes the exceeding favor it enjoys. Those, in fact, who would have Rubens a little as he is, but very much also as they dream he should be, find here a youthful seriousness, a flower of pure and studious maturity which soon disappears and is unique.

The composition does not need describing. Not one can be cited that is more popular as a work of art and as a page of religious character. There is no one who does not bear in mind the arrangement and effect of the picture, its great central light against a dark background, its grand masses of color, its distinct and massive divisions. It is known that Rubens got the first idea of it in Italy, and that he makes no effort to conceal that he borrowed it. The scene is powerful and grave. It has an effect from a distance, is strongly marked upon the wall; it is serious, and produces seriousness. When the murders are remembered with which the work of Rubens is bloody, the massacres, the torturing executioners, using pincers and exciting roars of anguish, it is evident that this is a noble suffering. Everything is as restrained, concise, and laconic as a page of Scripture.

Here are neither gesticulations, nor cries, nor horrors, nor excessive tears; scarcely one real sob bursts from the Virgin; and thus the intense mournfulness of the drama is expressed by a gesture of the inconsolable mother, by a face bathed in tears, and reddened eyes. The Christ is one of the most elegant figures that Rubens ever imagined in order to paint a God. It has an inexpressible slender grace, pliant and almost meagre, which gives it all the delicacy of nature, and all the distinction of a fine academic study. Its moderation is subtle, its taste perfect, the drawing very nearly equals the sentiment.

You cannot have forgotten the effect of this long body, slightly out of joint, with the little head, so thin and delicate, fallen on one side, so livid and so perfectly limpid in its pallor, neither contracted nor distorted; whence all pain has passed away, and which falls with such blessedness for a moment into the strange beauty of the death of the righteous. Remember how heavy and how precious it is to bear, in what an exhausted attitude it glides along the winding-sheet, with what affectionate anguish it is received by the extended arms and hands of women. Can anything be more touching? One of its feet, livid and scarred with the nails, touches at the foot of the cross the naked shoulder of the Magdalen. It does not bear upon, it lightly brushes it. The contact cannot be perceived; it is divined rather than seen. It would have been profane to emphasize it; it would have been cruel not to let it be believed. All the furtive sensibility of Rubens is in this imperceptible contact, which says so much respecting everything, and touches all with tenderness.

The Magdalen is admirable; it is incontestably the best piece of workmanship in the picture, the most delicate, the most personal, one of the best also that Rubens ever executed in his career so fertile in the invention of feminine beauty. This delicious figure has its legend; how could it fail to have one, its very perfection having become legendary? It is probable that this fair girl with the dark eyes, firm look, and clean-cut profile is a portrait, and that portrait one of Isabel Brandt, whom he had married two years before, and who also served him, perhaps during a pregnancy, as a model for the Virgin of the Visitation in the wing of the triptych. However, in seeing this ampleness of person, the blond hair, and rounded proportions, one thinks of what will be one day the splendid and individual charm of the beautiful Helen Fourment whom he married twenty years after. From the first to the last, a tenacious type seemed to be lodged in the heart of Rubens, a fixed ideal haunted his amorous and constant imagination. He pleases himself with it, completes it, finishes it; he pursues it after a fashion in his two marriages, as he does not cease to pursue it in his works. There is always something of Isabel and Helen in the women that Rubens painted from each of them. In the first he seems to put some preconceived feature of the second; in the second he introduces a sort of ineffaceable memory of the first. At the date we speak of, he possessed one and was inspired by her; the other is not yet born, and still he divines her. Already the future mingles with the present, the real with the ideal divination; when the image appears, it has its double form. Not only is it exquisite, but not a feature is wanting to it. Does it not seem as if, in perpetuating it thus from the first day, Rubens meant that it should be forgotten neither by himself nor by any one?

Moreover, it is the sole mundane grace with which he has embellished this austere picture, slightly monastic, absolutely evangelical, if by that is understood gravity of sentiment and manner, and the rigor be considered with which such a mind must have restrained itself. On this occasion, as you will guess, a large part of his reserve came from his Italian education, as well as the respect he accorded to his subject.

The canvas is dark in spite of its brilliancy and the extraordinary whiteness of the winding-sheet. In spite of its relief, the painting is *flat.* It is a picture with blackish undertones, on which are placed large firm lights, destitute of shades. The coloring is not very rich; it is full, sustained, calculated with precision to have an effect from a distance. He constructs the picture, frames it, expresses the weak points and the strong, and does not seek to embellish it at all. It is composed of a green almost black, of an absolute black, of a rather dull red, and a white. These four tones are set side by side as frankly as four notes of such violence can be. The contact is abrupt, but they do not suffer from it. In the high light the corpse of Christ is drawn with a delicate and supple line, and modelled by its own reliefs, with no effort in the shading, thanks to imperceptible gradations of values. There is nothing shining, not a single division in the lights, hardly a detail in the dark parts. All this is of a singular breadth and rigidity. The edges are narrow, the half-tints simple, except in the Christ, where the undertints of ultramarine have obtruded, and now make some useless spots. The material is smooth, compact, flowing easily and prudently. At the distance from which we examine it, the handiwork disappears, but it is easy to divine that it is excellent, and directed with perfect security by a mind inured to good habits, who conforms to them, applies himself, and is determined to do well. Rubens recollects himself, observes himself, restrains himself, and, taking possession of all his forces, subordinates them, and only half makes use of them.

In spite of this constraint, it is a work singularly original, attractive, and powerful. From it Vandyck will receive his best religious inspiration. Philippe de Champagne will imitate it, I fear, only in its weak portions, and will compose from it his French style. Vœnius must certainly have applauded. What did Van Noort think of it? As to Jordaens, he waited, before following him in these new ways, for his old companion of the studio to become more decidedly Rubens.

One of the wings, that of the Visitation, is delightful in every respect. Nothing can be more severe and charming, richer and more sober, more picturesque and nobly familiar. Never did Flanders clothe itself in the Italian style with so much good feeling, grace, and naturalness. Titian furnished the gamut and partly dictated its tones, colored the architecture in chestnut brown, advised the fine gray cloud which gleams above the cornices, perhaps also the greenish azure which is so effective between the columns; but it was Rubens who discovered the pregnant Virgin with her curved figure, her costume ingeniously combined of red, dark blue, and fawn-color, and her great Flemish hat. It is he who designed, painted, colored, caressed with eye and brush this pretty hand, so luminous and tender, which rests like a rosy flower upon the black iron balustrade; just as he imagined the serving-woman, and intersected her with the frame, showing of this blond girl with blue eyes only her open bodice, her round head with hair turned back, and her lifted arms sustaining a basket of rushes. In short, is Rubens already himself? Yes. Is he entirely himself, and nothing but himself? I think not. Has he ever done better? Not according to foreign methods, but he certainly has, according to his own.

Between the central panel of the Descent from the Cross and the Elevation of the Cross, which decorates the northern transept, everything has changed, — the point of view, tendency, bearing, even a few of the methods, and the influences which the two works feel so differently. A glance suffices to convince you of this. And if one considers the period when these significant pages appeared, it can be understood that if the one was more satisfying and more convincing, the other must have been more astonishing, and consequently have caused the perception of something much more novel. Less perfect, because it is more stirring, and because it contains no figure so perfectly lovely to see as the Magdalen, the Elevation of the Cross conveys much more of the originality of Rubens, more of his impetuosity, his audacity, his happy hits, — in a word, more of the fermentation of that mind full of fervor for novelties and projects. It opens a wider career. It is possible that it is finished in a less masterly manner, but it announces a master of a very different originality, who is both daring and powerful. The drawing is stiffer, less delicate, the forms more violent, the modelling less simple and rougher; but the coloring already shows profound warmth, and that resonance which will be Rubens's great resource when he neglects vivacity of tone for the sake of radiance. Imagine the color more flaming, the outlines less hard, the setting less rough; remove this grain of Italian stiffness, which is only a kind of knowledge of the world, and a gravity of demeanor, contracted during the journey; look only at what is Rubens's own, — the youth, the fire, the already mature convictions, — and little is wanting to have before your eyes Rubens in his best days; in fine, this is the first and last word of his fiery and rapid manner. The slightest latitude would make of this picture, relatively severe, one of the most turbulent that he ever painted. Such as it is, with its sombre amber tints, its strong shadows, the low muttering of its stormy harmonies, it is still one of those in which his ardor bursts forth even more evidently because it is sustained by the most manly effort maintained to the very end by the determination not to fail.

It is a picture of impulse, conceived around a very audacious arabesque, which, in its complication of forms displayed and concealed, of bent bodies, of extended arms, of repeated curves, of rigid lines, preserves throughout the work the instantaneous character of a sketch struck off with sentiment in a few seconds. The first conception, the arrangement, effect, gestures, faces, the caprice of color, the handiwork, — all seem to be the sudden result of an irresistible, lucid, and prompt inspiration. Never will Rubens use greater emphasis to express a page apparently so sudden.

To-day, as in 1610, there may be a difference of opinion about this work, which is absolutely personal in spirit, if not in manner. The question which must have been agitated during the life of the painter is still pending; it consists in deciding which would have been best represented in his country and in history, — Rubens before he was himself, or Rubens as he always was.

The Elevation of the Cross and the Descent from the Cross are the two moments of that drama of Calvary whose prologue we have seen in the triumphal picture at Brussels. At the distance apart that the two pictures are placed, the principal spots of color can be perceived, their dominant tone seized, I might say that their sound might be heard. This is sufficient for briefly understanding their picturesque expression and divining their meaning.

In the other we were present at the ending, and I have told

IESVS NASARENVS
REX

you with what solemn sobriety it is exhibited. All is over. It is night, or at least the horizon is of leaden black. All are silent, in tears ; receiving the august remains, they display most tender care. Hardly are interchanged those words which the lips speak after the death of those who were dear. The mother and the friends are there, and above all, the most loving and the weakest of women, she in whose fragility and grace and repentance are incarnated all the sins of the earth, pardoned, expiated, and now atoned for. Living flesh is opposed to funereal pallor. There is a charm even in the dead body. The Christ seems like a fair flower cut down. He hears no longer those who blasphemed him. He has ceased to hear those who weep for him. He belongs no longer to man, nor to time, nor to anger, nor pity. He is beyond all, even death.

Here there is nothing of that kind. Compassion, tenderness, mother and friends, are far off. In the left wing the painter has assembled all the friendliness of grief in a violent group, in lamenting or despairing attitudes. In the right wing there are only two mounted guards, and on that side there is no mercy. In the centre there are cries, blasphemies, insults, and the trampling of feet. With brute efforts, butcher-like executioners plant the cross, and labor to raise it erect in the canvas. Arms clench, ropes stretch, the cross wavers, and is only half-way up. Death is certain. A Man, nailed by his four members, suffers, agonizes, and forgives with his whole being. Nothing that belongs to him is free, a pitiless fatality has seized his body, the soul alone escapes from it. This is thoroughly felt in this upward glance which turns from earth, and, seeking its certainty elsewhere, goes straight to heaven. All that human ferocity can express of its thirst for slaughter, and its promptness in doing its work, the painter expresses like a man who understands the effect of anger, and knows the workings of savage passions. And all the gentleness of human nature, the bliss in dying of a martyr who gives himself to the sacrifice, — look attentively and see how he translates it!

The Christ is in light; he gathers into a narrow sheaf almost all the lights disseminated in the picture. Plastically he is less excellent than the one in the Descent from the Cross. A Roman painter would certainly have corrected the style of the figure. A Gothic artist would have desired more salient bones, fibres more strained, ligaments more precise, the whole structure more meagre, or perhaps only more delicate. Rubens had, you know, a preference for the full health of form, which belonged to his manner of feeling, and still more to his manner of painting, and without which it would have been necessary for him to change the greater part of his formulas. With that exception the picture is beyond price. No man but Rubens could have imagined it as it is, in the place it occupies, in the highly picturesque acceptation he has given it. And as to that fine head, inspired and suffering, manly and tender, with the hair clinging to the temples, its sweat, its glow, its agony, its eyes reflecting celestial beams, and its ecstasy, — who is the sincere master, even in the palmy days of Italy, who would not have been struck by what force of expression can do when it reaches this degree, and who would not in it have recognized a dramatic ideal of art absolutely novel?

Pure sentiment came, on one day of fever and clear insight, to lead Rubens as far as he could go. Afterwards he will become more free, he will develop still more. There will be, thanks to his flowing and absolutely unfettered manner, more consecutiveness and notably more method in all parts of his work, in the exterior and interior drawing, the color, and the workmanship. He will mark less imperiously the outlines which should disappear; he will arrest less suddenly the shadows which ought to melt away; he will acquire a suppleness which does not exist here; he will gain more agile modes of speech, a language of a more pathetic and personal turn. But will he find anything clearer and more energetic than the inspired diagonal which cuts this composition in two; first makes it hesitate in its perpendicular, then straightens it, and directs it to the top, with the active and resolute flight of a lofty idea? Will he find anything better than these sombre rocks, this faded sky, this great white figure in full brilliancy against the shadows, motionless and yet moving, that a mechanical impulse pushes diagonally across the canvas, with its pierced hands, its oblique arms, and that grand gesture of clemency which makes them balance widely opened over the blind, and black, and wicked world?

If one could doubt the power of a successful line, of the dramatic value of an arabesque, and an effect, — finally, if examples were wanting to prove the moral beauty of a picturesque conception, — one would be convinced of it after this.

It was by this original and masculine picture, that this young man, having been absent ever since the first year of the century, signalized his return from Italy. What he had acquired in his journeys, the nature and the choice of his studies, above all, the human fashion which he intended to use, were known; and no one doubted his destiny, — neither those whom this picture astonished like a revelation, nor those whom it shocked like a scandal; those whose doctrines it overturned and who attacked it, nor those whom it converted and carried away. The name of Rubens was sacred at that day. Even to-day very little is wanting for that first work to appear as accomplished as it seemed, and was, decisive. There is here, too, an inexpressible individuality, like a great breath, that is rarely found elsewhere in Rubens. An enthusiast would write *sublime*, and he would not be wrong if he could determine precisely the signification proper to attach to that term. At Brussels and Mechlin have I not said everything concerning the so diverse gifts of this composer of vast compass, whose fire is a sort of exalted good sense? I have spoken of his ideal, so different from that of others, of the dazzling nature of his palette, of the radiance of his ideas full of illumination, of his persuasive force, of his oratorical clearness, of his leaning towards apotheoses which elevate him, of that heated brain which expands at the risk of inflating him. All this leads us to a still more complete definition, to a word that I am going to say, which says everything, — Rubens is a lyric, and the most lyrical of all painters. His imaginative promptness, the intensity of his style, his sonorous and progressive rhythm, the range of this rhythm, its passage, which might be called vertical, — call all this lyric art, and you will not be far from the truth.

There is in literature a form, the most heroic of all, that it has been agreed to call the *ode*. It is, as you know, the most agile and the most sparkling of the varied forms of metrical language. There never can be too great breadth, nor too much enthusiasm in the ascending movement of the strophes, nor too great light at their summit. Now I might cite for you a picture by Rubens, conceived, conducted, scanned, illuminated like the proudest verses written in Pindaric form. The Elevation of the Cross would furnish me the best example, an example so much the more striking in that everything here is in harmony, and the subject was worthy of being thus expressed. And I shall not merit the reproach of subtlety if I tell you that this page of pure expansion is written from one end to the other in the form rhetorically called *sublime*, — from the leaping lines that cross it, the idea which becomes more luminous as it reaches its culmination, to the inimitable head of Christ which is the dominant and expressive note of the poem, the sparkling note, in the idea it contains, that is, the final strophe.

VI.

RUBENS AT THE ANTWERP MUSEUM.

HARDLY does one set foot in the first hall of the Antwerp Museum before Rubens is encountered. On the right is an Adoration of the Magi, a vast canvas in his rapid and learned manner, painted in thirteen days it is said, about 1624, — that is, in his palmiest years of middle life; on the left is an enormous picture, also celebrated, a Passion, called the Lance Thrust.

Casting a glance along the opposite gallery to the right and left, is seen from far this unique touch, powerful and suave, unctuous and warm, — Rubens — and Rubens again. We begin, catalogue in hand. Do we always admire? Not always. Do we remain cold? Almost never.

I copy my notes: "The Magi, fourth version since the one at Paris, this time with notable changes. The picture is less scrupulously studied than that of Brussels, less finished than that at Mechlin, but of a greater boldness, of a breadth, a fulness, a certainty, and a self-poise that the painter has rarely exceeded in his calm works. It is truly a *tour de force*, especially if the rapidity of this improvised work be considered. Not one gap, nor one violence;

a vast luminous half-tint with lights not too brilliant envelops all the figures, which lean upon each other, all in visible colors, and multiply values of the rarest, the subtlest, the least studied, and at the same time the most distinct character.

"Beside very ugly types cluster finished types. The African king, with his square face, his thick lips, his reddish skin, his great eyes strangely illumined, and his huge body wrapped in a pelisse with sleeves of peacock blue, is a figure entirely unprecedented, before which certainly Tintoretto, Titian, and Veronese would have clapped their hands in applause. On the left two colossal cavaliers pose with solemnity, in a very strange Anglo-Flemish style, — the rarest bit of color in the picture with its dull harmony of black, greenish blue, brown, and white. Add to these the profile of the Nubian camel-drivers, the troops, the men in helmets, the negroes; all in the largest, the most transparent, the most natural reflected lights. Spiders' webs float among the beams, and at the very bottom, the ox's head — rubbed on with a few strokes of the brush in bitumen — has no more importance, and is executed no otherwise than would be a hasty signature. The child is delicious, and can be instanced as one of the most beautiful of the purely picturesque compositions of Rubens, the highest expression of his knowledge of color and of his dexterity of handling, when his vision was clear and instantaneous, his hand rapid and careful, and he was in no difficult humor; it is the triumph of spirit and knowledge, and, in a word, of self-confidence."

The Lance Thrust is a disconnected picture with great blank

spaces, sharpnesses, vast and rather arbitrary masses of color, fine in themselves, but of doubtful relation. Two great reds, too unbroken and badly supported, are astonishing in it because they are out of tone. The Virgin is very beautiful, although her gesture is conventional; the Christ is insignificant; the St. John very ugly, or very much altered, or else repainted. As often happens in Rubens, and other painters of the picturesque and ardent, the best parts are those where the imagination of the artist has been accidentally impressed, such as the expressive head of the Virgin, the two thieves writhing upon their crosses, and perhaps particularly the helmeted soldier in black armor, who is descending the ladder which leans against the gibbet of the impenitent thief, and turns around, raising his head.

The harmony of the bay and gray horses relieved against the sky is magnificent. As a whole, although there are parts of high merit, characteristic of the first order, and at each instant the mark of a master, the Lance Thrust seems to me to be an incoherent work, conceived in fragments, as it were, of which portions taken separately would give an idea of the painter's most beautiful pages.

The Trinity, with its famous foreshortened Christ, is a picture of Rubens's early youth, anterior to his Italian journey. It is a fair beginning, cold, thin, smooth, and colorless, which already contains the germ of his style as to the human figure, its type as to countenances, and his suppleness of hand. All the other merits are to come, so that, though the engraved picture already greatly resembles Rubens, the painting gives no idea of what Rubens will be ten years later.

His Christ in the Manger — very celebrated, too celebrated — is not much stronger nor richer, and does not appear perceptibly more mature, although it belongs to much later years. It is equally smooth, cold, and thin. The abuse of his facility is here felt, — the use of a cursive method not at all rare, of which the formula might be thus dictated: a vast grayish undertone, flesh tones clear and lustrous, much ultramarine in the half-tint, an excess of vermilion in the reflections, a painting lightly made at once upon a drawing of slight consistency. The whole is liquid, flowing, slippery, and careless. When in this cursive style Rubens is not very fine, he is no longer fine at all.

As to the Incredulity of St. Thomas (No. 307), I find in my notes this short and disrespectful observation, "This a Rubens? What a mistake!"

The Education of the Virgin is the most charming decorative fancy ever seen; it is a little panel for an oratory or a room, painted for the eyes more than the mind, but in its sweetness, of an incomparable grace, tenderness, and richness. A fine red, a fine black, and on an azure field, shaded with changing tones of mother-of-pearl and silver, like two flowers, are two rosy angels. Take away the figure of St. Anne and that of St. Joachim, preserve only the Virgin with the two winged figures, which might as well be descending from Olympus as Paradise, and you have one of the most delicious portraits of a woman that Rubens ever conceived and recorded in an allegorical portrait to make an altarpiece.

The Virgin of the Parrot savors of Italy and recalls Venice, both by the scale, the power, the choice, and the intrinsic nature of its colors. The quality of the background, the very arabesque of the picture, the form of the canvas, the square shape, reminds us of a Palma lacking somewhat in severity. It is a fine, almost impersonal picture. I do not know why I think that Vandyck must have been tempted to draw inspiration from it.

I pass by the St. Catherine, and a great Christ on the Cross, a repetition in little of the Descent from the Cross, at Notre Dame. I will neglect even better things than these, to reach, with an emotion that I will not conceal, a picture which has, I believe, only a semi-celebrity, but is none the less a marvellous masterpiece, and possibly the one of all the works of Rubens which does most honor to his genius. I speak of the Communion of St. Francis of Assisi.

The scene represents a dying man, a priest offering him the Host, and monks who surround him, aiding, sustaining, and mourning over him. The saint is naked, the priest in a golden chasuble, faintly tinted with carmine, the two acolytes of the priest in white stoles, the monks in robes of cloth, dark brown or gray. Surrounding them is a strait and sombre architecture, a reddish dais, a bit of blue sky ; and in that azure gap, just above the saint, three rosy angels, flying like heavenly birds, form a soft and radiant crown. The aspect is composed of the most simple elements, the gravest colors, a most severe harmony. To sum up the picture in a rapid glance, you perceive but a vast bituminous canvas of austere style, where everything is in low tone, and where three accidents alone are perfectly evident from afar : the saint in his livid meagreness ; the Host towards which he leans; and above, at the summit of that triangle so tenderly expressive, a vista of rose and silver into a happy eternity,— a smile of the half-opened heaven of which we assuredly have need.

Here is no pomp, no ornament, no turbulence, nor violent gestures, nor grace, nor fine clothing, not one lovely or useless incident, nothing which does not appertain to a cloistral life at its most solemn moment. A dying man, worn with age and a life of sanctity, has left his bed of ashes to be borne to the altar; he longs to die there while he receives the sacred elements, but fears to fail before the Host has touched his lips. He makes an effort to kneel, but cannot. All his movements are over, the chill of the last moments has seized his limbs, his arms make that inward gesture which is the certain sign of approaching death; he is distorted, out of his axis, and would break at all his joints were he not supported by the armpits. The only thing living about him is his small and humid eye, clear, blue, fevered, glassy, with red lids, dilated by the ecstasy of the last vision, and upon his lips, livid with his agony, the wonderful smile of the dying, and the yet more wonderful smile of the righteous believer, who, filled with hope, awaits his end, hastens to meet his salvation, and looks upon the Host as upon his present Lord.

Around the dying man there is weeping, and those who weep are grave men, robust, tried, and resigned. Never was grief more sincere or more sympathetic than this virile tenderness of men of warm blood and great faith. Some restrain themselves, others give way to grief. Some are young, stout, ruddy, and healthy, who strike their breasts with their clenched fists, and whose grief would be noisy if it could be heard. There is one grizzled and bald monk, with a Spanish head, hollow cheeks, thin beard, and pointed mustache, who is sobbing gently within himself, with that tension of feature of a man who restrains himself until his teeth chatter. All these magnificent heads are portraits. The type is admirable in its truthfulness; the design simple, learned, and powerful; the coloring incomparably rich in its shaded, delicate, and beautiful sobriety. Here are clustered heads, joined hands clasped fervently and convulsively, bared foreheads, intense glances, — some reddened by emotion, and others, on the contrary, pale and cold as old ivory; the two acolytes, one of whom holds the censer, and wipes his eyes with the back of his sleeve; — all this group of men, differently moved, sobbing, or masters of themselves, forms a circle around the unique head of the saint, and the little white crescent held like a lunar disk in the pale hand of the priest. It is all inexpressibly fine.

Such is the moral value of this exceptional page of Rubens at Antwerp, and — who knows? — perhaps of all the work of Rubens, that I should almost fear to profane it in speaking of its exterior merits, which are not less eminent. I will only say that this great man has never been more master of his thought, his sentiment, and his hand; his conception has never been more serene or of wider range; his notion of the human soul has never seemed more profound; he has never been more noble or more healthful, richer in color without extravagance, more scrupulous in the drawing of the parts, or more irreproachable, that is to say, more surprising in his execution. This marvel is dated 1619. What noble years! The time in which he painted it is not given, perhaps a few days only. What days! When this unequalled work, in which Rubens is transfigured, has been long examined, it is impossible to look at anything or anybody, — neither others, nor Rubens himself, — we must for to-day leave the museum.

VII.

RUBENS AS A PORTRAIT PAINTER.

Is Rubens a great portrait painter, or merely a good one? Had this great painter of physical and moral life, so skilful in rendering the movement of the body by a gesture, and that of souls by the play of feature; this observer, so prompt, so exact; this mind, so clear that the ideal of human form never for a single instant distracted him from his study of the exterior of things; this painter of the picturesque, of accidents, of individualities, of personal traits; finally, this master, the most universal of all, — had he really all the aptitudes we suppose, and particularly the special faculty of representing the human being in its intimate resemblance?

Are the portraits of Rubens likenesses? I do not think it has ever been said whether they were or not. People have confined themselves to recognizing the universality of his gifts, and because, more than any other, he has employed the portrait as a natural element of his pictures, they take for granted that a man who excelled in painting the human being under all circumstances, acting and thinking, ought from the strongest reasons to paint him well in a portrait. The question is of some moment, for it touches one of the most singular phenomena of this multiplex nature, and consequently offers an opportunity for studying nearer the real organism of his genius.

If one adds to all the portraits he has painted solely to satisfy the desire of his contemporaries — kings, princes, great lords, doctors, abbés, and priors — the incalculable number of living beings whose features he has reproduced in his pictures, it might well be said that Rubens passed his life in painting portraits. Without dispute his best works are those where he yields the greatest part to real life; for instance, his admirable picture of St. George, which is nothing but a family *ex voto*, the most curious document a painter ever left concerning his domestic affections. I do not speak of his own portrait, of which he was lavish, nor those of his two wives, of which he made, as is known, such continual and indiscreet use.

It was Rubens's habit to use nature for every purpose, to take individuals from real life and introduce them into fiction, because it was one of his needs, — a weakness, as well as a power of his mind. Nature was his great and inexhaustible repertory. What were the truths he sought to tell? Subjects? No. His subjects he borrowed from history, from legend, from the gospel, from fables, and always more or less from his fancy. Attitudes, gestures, expressions of countenance? Not at all. The expressions and gestures issued naturally from himself, and were derived by the logic of a well-conceived subject, from the necessities of the action, almost always dramatic, which he had to render. What he asked from nature was what his imagination furnished him but imperfectly, when it was necessary to wholly constitute a living person from head to foot, living as he desired him to live, I mean, in the most personal features, the most precise characteristics both as an individual and a type. His types he accepted rather than chose. He took them as they existed around him in the society of his time, from all ranks, from all classes, if necessary from all races, — princes, soldiers, churchmen, monks, tradesmen, blacksmiths, boatmen, especially hard-working men.

He had in his own town, on the quays of the Scheldt, enough to furnish all the necessities of his great evangelical pages. He had a lively feeling for the relation of these people, continually offered by life itself, to the conventionalities of his subject. When the adaptation is not very rigorous, which often happens, and good sense and good taste also are a little shocked, it is then that his love of individualities gets the better of the conventionalities of taste and good sense. He never denied himself an eccentricity, which in his hands became an evidence of mind, sometimes a happy audacity. It was by his very inconsistencies that he triumphed over subjects most uncongenial to his nature. He put into them the sincerity, the good-humor, the extraordinary unrestraint of his free bursts; the work was nearly always saved by an admirable bit of almost textual imitation.

In this respect he invented but little, — he the great inventor. He looked, informed himself, copied or translated from memory with a security of memory which was equal to direct reproduction. The spectacle of the life of courts, of the life of churches, of monasteries, streets, or of the river, imprinted itself upon this sensitive brain with its most recognizable features, its sharpest accent, its most salient colors, so that beyond this reflected image of things he imagined hardly anything but the frame and the dramatic grouping. His works are (so to speak) a theatre, whose arrangements he regulates, whose decorations he prepares, while he creates the rôles and furnishes life to the actors. Original as he is, affirmative, resolute, and powerful, when he executes a portrait, whether from nature or from the immediate memory of the model, the gallery of his imaginary personages is poorly inspired.

Every man, every woman, who has not lived before him, and to whom he has not succeeded in giving the essential features of human life, are figures that are failures from the beginning. This is why his evangelical personages are more human than they should be, his heroic figures below their fabulous rôle, while his mythological personages exist neither in reality nor in a dream; there is a perpetual contradiction in the action of the muscles, the lustre of the flesh, and the total vacancy of the faces. It is clear that humanity enchants him, Christian dogmas trouble him a little, and Olympus bores him to death. Look at his great allegorical series in the Louvre. It does not take long to discover his indecisions when he creates a type, his infallible certitude when he is informed, and to understand what is strong and what is weak in his mind. There are commonplace parts, there are others absolutely negative which are fictions; the superior parts that you notice are portraits. Whenever Marie de Medici enters the scene she is perfect. The Henri IV. with the Portrait is a masterpiece. No one contests the absolute insignificance of his gods, Mercury, Apollo, Saturn, Jupiter, or Mars.

In the same way, in the Adoration of the Magi, there are principal personages who are always of no account, and supernumeraries who are always admirable. The European king does it harm. He is well known; he is the man in the foreground who figures with the Virgin, either standing or kneeling in the centre of the composition. Rubens may dress him in vain in purple, in ermine or gold, make him hold the censer, offer a cup or a ewer, make him young or make him old, make bald his sacerdotal head or cause it to bristle with dry hairs, give him an air collected or wild, gentle eyes or the glare of an old lion, — whatever he does, he is always a commonplace figure, whose only rôle consists in wearing one of the dominant colors of the picture. It is the same with the Asiatic. On the contrary, the Ethiopian — the grizzled negro with his bony flat-nosed face, livid, and lighted by two shining sparks, the white of his eyes and the pearls of his teeth — is invariably a masterpiece of observation and of nature, because it is a portrait, and a portrait with no alteration whatever from an individual.

What would be the conclusion but that by instinct, necessity, his dominant faculties, his very infirmities (for he had them), Rubens more than any other was destined to make marvellous portraits? It is not so at all. His portraits are feeble, poorly studied, superficially constructed, and of but vague resemblance. When he is compared to Titian, Rembrandt, Raphael, Sebastien del Piombo, Velasquez, Vandyck, Holbein, Antonio Moro, — I might exhaust the list of the most diverse and great, and descend many degrees to Philippe de Champagne in the seventeenth century, and to the excellent portrait painters of the eighteenth, — it is perceived that Rubens was wanting in that attentive simplicity, at once submissive and powerful, that the study of the human face requires, to be perfect.

Do you know one portrait of his which satisfies you as the result of faithful and profound observation, which edifies you with the personality of its model, which instructs, and I may say reassures you? Of all the men of age and rank, of such diverse character and temperament, whose portraits he has left us, is there a single one who impresses himself upon the mind as a particular and very distinct person, and whom one remembers as one does a striking countenance? At a distance they are forgotten; seen together, they might almost be confounded. The individualities of their existence have not clearly separated them in the mind of the painter, and separate them still less in the memory of those who only know them from him. Are they like? Yes, almost. Are they living? They live rather than are living. I will not say that they are commonplace, but they are not precise. I will not say either that the painter has failed to see them properly, but I think he has looked at them lightly, only skin deep, perhaps through the medium of habit, doubtless according to a formula, and that he has treated them, whatever their sex or their age, as women love, it is said, to be painted, — as handsome first, and after that with a likeness. They are good for their time, and not bad for their rank, although Vandyck, to take an example beside the master, puts them still more decidedly at their date and in their social surrounding; but they have the same blood, they have especially the same moral character, and all the exterior features modelled on a uniform type. They have the same clear eye, wide open, with a direct glance, the same complexion, the same mustache, delicately curled up, lifting by two black or blond slits the corner of a manly mouth, that is to say, one that is a little conventional. There is red enough in the lips, carnation enough in the cheeks, roundness enough in the oval, to proclaim, with the want of youth, a man in his normal condition, whose constitution is robust, whose body is healthful, and whose soul is at rest.

It is the same for the women, — a clear complexion, a round forehead, large temples, small chins, eyes prominent, the same coloring, almost the identical expression, the style of beauty peculiar to the time, a breadth befitting the races of the North, with a sort of grace peculiar to Rubens, which is felt as the mingling of several types, — Marie de Medici, the Infanta Isabella, Isabel Brandt, Helen Fourment. All the women that he has painted seem to have contracted, in spite of themselves and in spite of him, an inexplicable familiar air, resulting from the contact of his persistent memories; and all of them partake more or less of one or another of these four celebrated personages, less surely immortalized by history than by his brush. They themselves have together a sort of family air which is largely owing to Rubens.

Can you picture to yourself the women of the courts of Louis XIII. and Louis XIV.? Have you a very clear idea of Mesdames de Longueville, de Montbazon, de Chevreuse, de Sablé, of that beautiful Duchesse de Guémenée, to whom Rubens, interrogated by the Queen, dared to give the prize of beauty as the most charming goddess of the Luxembourg Olympus; of that incomparable Mademoiselle du Vigean, the idol of society at Chantilly, who inspired so great a passion, and such a quantity of little verses? Can you see any more distinctly Mademoiselle de la Vallière, or Mesdames de Montespan, de Fontanges, de Sévigné, and de Grignan? And if you cannot perceive them as you would wish, whose fault is it?

Is it the fault of that epoch of display, of politeness, of artificial manners, both pompous and forced? Is it the fault of the women themselves, who all sought a certain court ideal? Have they been ill-observed, unscrupulously painted? Or was it agreed that among so many kinds of grace or beauty, there was but one that was in good style and good taste and according to etiquette? One hardly knows just what nose, what mouth, what oval, what complexion, what glance, what degree of seriousness or freedom, of delicacy or plumpness, or indeed what soul, should be given to each of these celebrated people, become so alike in their imposing rôles of favorites, Frondeuses, princesses, and great ladies. We know what they thought of themselves, and how they painted themselves or how they were painted, according as they made their own literary portraits or allowed them to be made by others. From the sister of Condé to Madame d'Epinay, that is, through the whole seventeenth century and the larger half of the eighteenth, we have only fine complexions, pretty mouths, superb teeth and shoulders, and admirable arms and throats. They undressed themselves a good deal, or let themselves be undressed, without displaying anything but rather cold perfections modelled on an absolutely handsome type according to the fashion and ideal of the time. Neither Mademoiselle de Scudery, nor Voiture, nor Chapelain, nor Desmarets, nor any of the witty writers who occupied themselves with their charms, have had the idea of leaving us a portrait of them perhaps less flattered but more faithful. It is with difficulty that one perceives, here and there in the gallery of the Hôtel de Rambouillet, a complexion less divine, lips less purely outlined or of a less perfect carnation.

The most truthful and the greatest portrait painter of his time, St. Simon, was necessary to teach us that a woman might be charming without being perfect, and that the Duchesse de Maine and the Duchess of Burgundy, for instance, had many attractions of physiognomy, quite natural grace and fire, the one with her limp, and the other with her dark complexion, her thin figure, her turbulent expression and imperfect teeth. Up to that time the hand of the image-maker was directed by the neither too much nor too little principle. An inexpressible impressiveness, a solemnity, something like the three scenic unities, the perfection of a fine phrase, had clothed them all with the same impersonal, almost royal aspect, which for us moderns is the opposite of charming. Times changed; the eighteenth century destroyed many formulas, and consequently treated the human countenance with no more respect than the other unities. But our age has restored, with other tastes and other fashions, the same tradition of portraits without type, and the same ostentation, less solemn, but yet more objectionable. Recall the portraits of the Directory, of the Empire and the Restoration, those of Girodet and of Gérard. I except the portraits of David, but not all, and a few of those of Prudhon. Form a gallery of the great actresses and great ladies, — Mars, Duchesnois, Georges, the Empress Josephine, Madame Tallien, also that unique head of Madame de Staël, and even that pretty Madame Recamier, — and tell me whether it lives, is as characteristic and diversified as a series of portraits by Latour, Houdon, and Caffieri.

Well! all the proportions being maintained, this is what I find in Rubens's portraits, — great uncertainty and conventionality, the same chivalrous air in the men and the same princess-like beauty in the women, but nothing individual, which arrests the attention, impresses, causes reflection, and is not forgotten. Not one plainness of feature, not one meagreness of contour, not one inharmonious eccentricity of any feature.

Have you ever perceived in his world of thinkers, of politicians, of men of war, any characteristic accident wholly personal, like Condé's falcon head, the wild eyes and nocturnal mien of Descartes, the fine and adorable countenance of Rotrou, the angular and pensive face of Pascal, and the never to be forgotten glance of Richelieu? How is it that these human types swarmed before the great observers, and not one really original type sat to Rubens? Must I finish explaining myself at one blow by the most rigorous of examples? Imagine Holbein with the personages of Rubens, and you see at once appear a new human gallery, very interesting for the moralist, equally admirable for the history of life and the history of art, which Rubens, we must agree, would not have enriched by one single type.

The Brussels Museum possesses four portraits by Rubens, and it is precisely in remembering them that these reflections come to me afterwards. These four portraits represent justly enough the powerful and the mediocre side of his talent as a portrait painter. Two of them are very fine, the Archduke Albert and the Infanta Isabella. They were both ordered to adorn the Arch of Triumph erected in the Place de Meïr, on the occasion of the entry of Ferdinand of Austria, and it is said that each was executed in a day. They are larger than life, conceived, designed, and treated in the Italian manner, ample and decorative, a little theatrical, but very ingeniously appropriate to their destination. There is in them so much Veronese melted into the Flemish manner that Rubens never had more style, and yet was never more completely himself. There is here seen a way of filling a canvas, of composing a grand arabesque with a bust, two arms and two hands diversely occupied, of increasing a border, and rendering a doublet majestically severe, of giving boldness to the contour, of painting thickly and flatly, which is not habitual in his portraits, and which recalls, on the other hand, the best parts of his pictures. The likeness is of the kind which impresses from afar by a few just and brief accents that might be called a resemblance of effect. The work is of extraordinary rapidity, assurance, and seriousness, and, for the style, of remarkable beauty.

It is quite superb. Rubens is there with his habits, on his own ground, in his element of fancy, and of very lucid, but hasty and emphatic observation. He would not have proceeded otherwise for a picture: success was certain.

The two others, bought recently, are very celebrated, and a great price is attached to them. Dare I say that they are among his weakest works? They are two portraits of familiar order, two little busts, rather short and rather scanty, presented in full face, with no arrangement, cut in the canvas with no more preparation than if they were studies of heads.

With much brilliancy, relief, and apparent life, of extremely skilful but succinct rendering, they have precisely this fault of being seen from near and seen lightly, made with application and little studied, — in a word, they are treated by surfaces. The putting together is correct, the drawing insignificant. The painter has given accents which resemble life; the observer has not marked a single trait which intimately resembles his model. Everything is on the epidermis. From the physical point of view we look for something beneath, which has not been observed; from the moral point we seek an inwardness that has not been divined. The painting is flat upon the canvas, the life is but skin deep. The man is young, about thirty years of age; his mouth is mobile, his eye moist, his glance direct and clear, — nothing more, nothing beyond, nothing below. Who is this young man? What has he done? Has he thought? Has he suffered? Has he himself lived on the surface of things as he is represented without consistency on the surface of a canvas? These are the characteristic indications that a Holbein would give us before thinking of the rest, which cannot be expressed by a spark in an eye or a red touch on a nostril.

The art of painting is perhaps more indiscreet than any other. It is the indisputable witness of the mental state of the painter at the moment he held the brush. What he intended to do he did; that which he desired but feebly is seen in his indecisions; what he did not wish for is, with even better reason, absent from his work, whatever he or others may say. An abstraction, a forgetfulness, a warmer sensation, a less profound insight, application wanting, a less hearty love for what he is studying, whether he is tired of painting or has a passion for painting, — all the shades of his nature, even to the intermittent character of his sensitiveness, are manifest in the works of the painter as clearly as if he took us into his confidence. One can say with certainty what is the deportment of a scrupulous portrait painter to his models, and in the same way one can fancy what Rubens was to his.

When one looks, a few paces from the portraits of which I am speaking, at the portrait of the Duke of Alva by Antonio Moro, he is certain that, grand nobleman as he was, and wholly accustomed to painting great lords, Antonio Moro was very serious, very attentive, and a good deal moved at the moment when he seated himself before this tragic personage, dry, angular, choked in his dark armor, jointed like an automaton, with an eye which looks sidelong up and down, cold, hard, and black, as if the light of heaven had never touched its surface.

On the contrary, on the day when Rubens painted, to please them, the Seigneur Charles de Cordes and Jacqueline his wife, he was undoubtedly in a good humor, but absent-minded, sure of his work, and in a hurry as he always was. It was in 1618, the year of the Miraculous Draught. He was forty-one years old, in the full tide of his talent, his glory, and his success. He did everything rapidly. The Miraculous Draught had just cost him ten days' labor. The two young people had been married October 30, 1617; the portrait of the husband was made to please the wife, that of the wife to please the husband, so you can see under what conditions the work was done, and you can imagine the time he took for it; the result was a painting hasty and brilliant, an agreeable likeness, — an ephemeral work.

Many, I may say the greater part, of Rubens's portraits are the same. Look in the Louvre at that of the Baron de Vicq. (No. 458 of the catalogue), in the same style, the same quality, almost of the same period as the portrait of the Seigneur de Cordes of which I speak; look too at that of Elizabeth of France, and the one of a lady of the Boonen family (No. 461), — all agreeable, brilliant, light, alert works, forgotten as soon as seen. See, on the other hand, the portrait sketch of his second wife, Helen, with her two children, — that admirable sketch, that scarcely indicated dream, left there by chance or purposely; and if you look over the three works preceding this with a little reflection, I shall not need to persist to make myself understood.

To resume, Rubens, to consider him only as a portrait painter, is a man who dreamed in his own way when he had the time, with an eye admirably true, of slight depth of insight, which was a mirror rather than a penetrating instrument, a man who occupied himself little with others, much with himself; morally and physically a man of the exterior, and outwardly, marvellously but exclusively, fitted to seize the exterior of things. This is why it is proper to distinguish in Rubens two observers of very unequal power, of hardly comparable artistic value, — one who made the life of others serve the needs of his conceptions, subordinates his models, taking from them only what he needs; and the other, who remains inferior to his task, because he ought, and does not know how, to subordinate himself to his model.

This is why he has sometimes magnificently observed and again greatly neglected the human face. This is why his portraits are all a little alike, and a little like him; why they are wanting in a life of their own, and in that lack moral resemblance and interior life, while his portrait personages have just that degree of striking personality which increases still more the effect of their rôle, a force of expression which does not permit you to doubt that they have lived; and as to their mental calibre, it is evident that they all have an active soul, ardent and prompt to spring forth, just upon their lips, the one that Rubens has put into them, — almost the same in all, for it is his own.

VIII.

THE TOMB OF RUBENS.

I HAVE not yet taken you to Rubens's tomb at St. Jacques. The sepulchral stone is placed before the altar, and the inscription on the tomb reads thus: *Non sui tantum sæculi, sed et omnis ævi Apelles dici meruit.*

With this approach to an hyperbole, which neither adds to nor detracts from the universal glory nor the very certain immortality of Rubens, these two lines of funereal eulogium make one remember that a few feet below these flags lie the ashes of this great man. He was placed there the first day of June, 1640. Two years later, by an authorization of March 14, 1642, his widow finally consecrated to him the little chapel behind the choir, and placed in it the fine picture of St. George, one of the most charming works of the master, — a work wholly formed, says tradition, of the portraits of members of his family, that is to say, of his affections, his dead loves, his living loves, his regrets, his hopes, the past, present, and future of his house.

You know, in fact, that to all the personages who compose this so-called *Holy Family* are attributed resemblances of priceless value.

Side by side in it are his two wives, first, the fair Helen Fourment, a child of sixteen when he married her in 1630, a quite young woman of twenty-six when he died, fair, plump, amiable, and gentle, *en grand déshabillé*, naked to the waist.

There also is his daughter, his niece, the celebrated girl of the *Chapeau de Paille*, his father, his grandfather, — finally, his younger son under the features of an angel, a youthful and delicious babe, perhaps the most adorable child he ever painted. As to Rubens himself, he figures there in armor shining with sombre steel and silver, holding in his hand the banner of St. George. He is growing old and is thinner, his hair is grizzled, he is dishevelled, a little worn, but superb with inward fire. Without posturing or emphasis he has conquered the dragon, and planted upon him his mailed foot. How old was he then? If the date of his second marriage is recalled, and the age of his wife and the child born of this marriage, Rubens must have been fifty-six or fifty-eight years of age. Almost forty years before the brilliant combat had begun which, impossible for others, but easy for him who was always successful, he had waged against life. In what enterprises, in what order of activity, of struggle, and success, had he not triumphed?

If ever, at the solemn hour of self-examination, after the lapse of years and the accomplishment of a career, at that moment of absolute certainty, a man had a right to paint himself as a victor, it was certainly he.

The thought, as you see, is most simple; it needs not to be sought after. If the picture conceals an emotion, that emotion can easily be communicated to any man who has any warmth of heart, who can be moved by glory, and who makes for himself a second religion of the memory of such men.

One day, towards the end of his career, in full glory, perhaps in deep repose, under an august title, invoking the Virgin and the sole saint whose own image he would have permitted himself to assume, it pleased him to paint within a very small frame (about two metres) whatever there had been that was venerable and seductive in the beings he had loved. He owed this last glorification to those who had borne him, to those who had shared, beautified, charmed, ennobled with their perfume of grace, tenderness, and excellence his noble and laborious career. He gave it to them as fully, in as masterly a way, as could be expected from his affectionate hand, his genius, and his great power. He put into it his science, his piety, his most rare carefulness. He made of the work what you know, — an infinitely touching marvel as the work of a son, a father, and a husband ; forever admirable as a work of art.

Shall I describe it to you ? The arrangement is one of those that a catalogue note is sufficient to indicate. Shall I tell you its particular merits ? They are all the painter's qualities in their familiar acceptation, under their most precious form. They do not give of him a new or a more lofty idea, but one that is finer and more exquisite.

It is the Rubens of his best days, with more naturalness, precision, caprice, richness of coloring, and power without effort ; with a more tender eye, a more caressing hand ; a more loving labor, at once more intimate and more profound. If I used technical terms, I should spoil the greater part of those subtle things which should be rendered with the pure language of idea in order to preserve their character and their value.

Little as it cost me to study the mechanician in such a practical picture as the Miraculous Draught of Fishes, at Mechlin, it is equally befitting to ease and purify the manner of speech when the conception of Rubens is elevated, as it is in the Communion of St. Francis of Assisi, or when his manner of painting is penetrated at once by spirit, feeling, ardor, conscientiousness, affection for those he is painting, and attachment to what he does, — the ideal, in a word, as in the St. George.

Has Rubens ever been more perfect? I think not. Has he been as perfect? I have nowhere observed it. There are in the lives of the great artists these works of predestination, not the largest, nor always exhibiting the greatest knowledge, sometimes the very humblest, which, by a fortuitous conjunction of all the gifts of the man and the artist, have expressed unconsciously to themselves, the pure essence of their genius; — of this number is the St. George.

This picture, moreover, marks, if not the end, at least the last five years of Rubens's life, and by a sort of grand coquetry which is not unbefitting the things of the spirit, he manifests that this magnificent organization knew neither fatigue nor relaxation nor decline. Thirty-five years, at least, had elapsed between the Trinity in the Antwerp Museum and the St. George. Which is the younger of the two pictures? At which moment had he the most fire, the most vivid love of all things, and the most suppleness in all the organs of his genius?

His life had almost made its revolution; it could be closed and measured. It seemed as if he foresaw the end on the day when he glorified himself and his family. He also had erected and nearly finished his monument; he could say this to himself with as much assurance as others, without self-glorification. Only five or six years more of life remained to him. He was happy, peaceable, a little weary of politics; retired from ambassadorial life, and more his own than ever. Had he well spent his life? had he deserved well of his country, his time, and himself? He had unique faculties; how did he use them? Destiny heaped honors upon him; did he ever fail to merit his destiny? In this grand life, so distinct, so clear, so brilliant, so adventurous and yet so pure, so correct in its most astonishing events, so luxurious and so simple, so troubled and so exempt from all littleness, so divided and so fruitful, can you discover one stain that causes regret? He was fortunate; was he ungrateful? He had his trials; was he ever bitter? He loved much and warmly; was he forgetful?

He was born at Spiegen, in exile, on the threshold of a prison, of a mother admirably upright and generous, of a cultivated father, who was a learned doctor, but a man of slight feeling, of tolerably weak conscience, and of a character without great consistency. When Rubens was fourteen, he was among the pages of a princess; at seventeen he was in the studios; at twenty years he is mature, and a master. At twenty-nine he returned from a journey of study as from a foreign victory, and he entered his home in triumph. They asked to see his studies, and, so to speak, he could show nothing but works. He left behind him strange pictures which were at once understood and relished. He had taken possession of Italy in the name of Flanders, planted from city to city the marks of his passage, founding on the way his own renown, that of his country, and something more still, an art unknown to Italy. He brought back, as trophies, marbles, engravings, pictures, fine works by the best masters, and, above all, a new and national art, the most vast in surface and the most extraordinary in resources of all the arts known.

In proportion as his fame increased and radiated, and his talent was noised abroad, his personality seemed to enlarge, his brain to dilate, his faculties to multiply with the demands made upon him, and those he made of them. Was he an astute politician? His policy appears to me to have clearly, faithfully, and nobly comprehended and transmitted the desires or wishes of his masters; he pleased by his noble mien, charmed all who approached him by his wit, his cultivation, his conversation, his character, and seems to have been still more seductive by the indefatigable presence of mind of his painter's genius. He would arrive, often with great pomp, present his letters of credence, converse and paint. He made portraits of princes and kings, mythological pictures for palaces, religious ones for cathedrals. It can hardly be told which has the most distinction, — Peter Paul Rubens *pictor*, or the Chevalier Rubens, accredited plenipotentiary; but we have every reason to believe that the artist was a singular help to the diplomate. He succeeded in all things to the satisfaction of those whom he served with his speech and his talent. The sole embarrassments, the sole delays, and the rare annoyances perceived in his journeys, so picturesquely divided between business, galas, cavalcades, and painting, never came from sovereigns. The real statesmen were more punctilious and less easy, — witness his quarrel with Philippe d'Arenberg, Duke of Aerschot, concerning the last mission with which he was charged in Holland. Was this the only wound he received in the discharge of his delicate functions? It was at least the sole cloud observed from a distance, that casts the slightest bitterness over a radiant existence. In everything else he was fortunate. His life from one end to the other was one of those that make life lovable. In every circumstance he was a man who was an honor to mankind.

He was handsome, perfectly well-bred, and cultivated. He retained from his hasty early education the taste for languages, and facility in speaking them. He wrote and spoke Latin, he was fond of healthy and strong reading; they amused him with Plutarch and Seneca while he was painting, and "he was equally attentive to both reading and painting." He lived in the greatest luxury, inhabited a princely dwelling; he had valuable horses which he rode every evening, a unique collection of works of art with which he delighted his hours of repose. He was regular, methodical, and cold in the discipline of his private life, in the administration of his work, in the government of his mind, in a certain way, in the fortifying and healthful hygiene of his genius. He was simple and plain, of an exemplary fidelity in his relations with his friends, sympathetic with all talent, inexhaustible in encouragements to those who were making a beginning. There was no success which he did not aid with his purse or his praise. His magnanimity with regard to Brauwer is a celebrated episode of his benevolent life, and one of the most living witnesses that he has furnished of his spirit of fraternity. He adored everything that was beautiful, and never separated from it what was good.

He experienced the accidents of his grand official life without being either dazzled by them, or lessened in character, or sensibly troubled in his domestic habits. Fortune spoiled him as little as did honors. Women no more demoralized him than princes. No well-known gallantries are attributed to him; on the contrary, he was always seen at home, with regular habits, in his domestic surroundings from 1609 to 1626 with his first wife, from 1630 with the second, with numerous fine children, assiduous friends, — that is to say, amusements, affections, and duties, all things which kept his mind in repose, and helped him to bear with the natural ease of a Colossus the daily burden of a superhuman labor. Everything was simple in his occupations; whether complicated, agreeable, or overwhelming, everything is honest in this untroubled home. His life is in full light; it is broad daylight there as in his pictures; not the shadow of a mystery, not one grief, except the sincere sorrow of his first widowhood; no suspicious circumstances, nothing which one is obliged to imply, nor which is a matter of conjecture, except one thing, the mystery of this incomprehensible fecundity.

"He solaced himself," writes Taine, "by creating worlds;"* in which ingenious definition I see but one word to correct. Solace would suggest tension, the malady of over-fulness, that is never to be remarked in this thoroughly healthy mind, which is never troubled. He created, as a tree bears fruit, with no more uneasiness or effort. When did he think? *Diu noctuque incubando,* — such was his Latin device, which means that he reflected before painting, as can be seen from his sketches, projects, and draughts. In truth, the improvisation of the hand was the successor of improvisations of mind; there was the same certainty and the same facility of utterance in one case as in the other. His was a soul without storms, or languors, or torments, or chimeras. If ever the melancholy of toil left its trace anywhere, it was neither on the features nor in the pictures of Rubens. By his birth, in the midst of the sixteenth century, he belonged to that mighty race of thinkers and men of action in whom action and thought were one. He was a painter as he would have been a soldier; he made his pictures as he would have made war, with as much coolness as ardor, combining skilfully, deciding quickly, and trusting, besides, to the surety of his glance on the field. He takes things as they are, his fine faculties just as he has received them; he exercises them as fully as a man can, pushes them to their full extent, asks of them nothing beyond, and with a clear conscience in this regard he pursues his labor with the help of God.

His painted work comprises about fifteen hundred productions,

* H. Taine, Philosophy of Art in the Netherlands.

the most immense result that ever issued from one brain. To approach such a figure, we must add together the lives of several of the men most fertile in productiveness. If, independently of the number, the importance, the dimensions, and the complicated character of his works be considered, it is an astonishing spectacle, giving of human faculties the most lofty, even, we might say, the most religious idea.

Such is the teaching which seems to me to result from the amplitude and power of a soul. In this respect he is unique, and in every way he is one of the grandest specimens of humanity. We must in art go back to Raphael, Leonardo, and Michael Angelo, to the demigods themselves, to find his equals, and in certain things still his masters. Nothing, it is said, was wanting to him "except the very pure instincts and the very noble." It is true that in the world of the beautiful two or three spirits can be found, who have gone farther, with a more lofty flight, who consequently have seen more nearly the divine Light and the Eternal Truths. There are also in the moral world, in that of sentiments, visions, and dreams, depths into which Rembrandt alone has descended, which Rubens has not penetrated and has not even perceived.

On the other hand, he has taken possession of the earth as no other man has. Spectacles are his domain. His eye is the most marvellous prism that has ever been given us, of the light and color of objects, of true and magnificent ideas. Dramas, passions, attitudes of the body, expressions of countenance, that is to say, the whole man in the multifarious incidents of human life, pass through his brain, take from it stronger features, more robust forms, become amplified but not purified, and are transfigured into some unknown heroic appearance. Everywhere he stamps them with the directness of his character, the warmth of his blood, the admirable equilibrium of his nerves, and the magnificence of his ordinary visions. He is unequal, and oversteps moderation; he lacks taste when he draws, but never when he colors. He is forgetful, even careless; but from the first day to the last, he atones for a fault by a masterpiece; he redeems a want of care, of seriousness, or of taste by the instantaneous testimony of self-respect, an almost touching application, and supreme taste.

His grace is that of a man who sees grandly and powerfully, and the smile of such a man is delicious. When he puts his hand upon a very rare subject, when he touches a deep and manifest sentiment, when his heart beats with a lofty and sincere emotion, he paints the Communion of St. Francis of Assisi, and then, in the rank of purely moral conceptions, he attains the utmost beauty in truth, and in that is as great as any one in the world.

He does not look back, nor does he fear what is to be done. He accepts overwhelming tasks, and accomplishes them. He suspends his labor, abandons it, lets his mind wander from it, turns aside from it altogether. He returns to it, after a long and distant embassy, as if he had not left it for an hour. One day is sufficient for him to paint The Kermis, — thirteen for the Magi of Antwerp, perhaps seven or eight for the Communion, judging from the price which was paid him for them.

Did he love money as much as was said? Did he, as has also been said, commit the wrong of being helped by his pupils, and did he treat with too much disdain an art to which he has done such great honor, because he estimated his pictures at the rate of a hundred florins a day? The truth is, that at that time the craft of a painter was indeed a craft, nor was it less nobly nor less well practised because it was treated almost like a high profession. The truth is, there were apprentices, masters, corporations, and a school which was very decidedly a studio, and the pupils were co-laborers with the master, while neither scholars nor master had any reason to complain of this salutary and useful exchange of lessons and services.

More than any one Rubens had the right to hold to the ancient usages. With Rembrandt he is the last great head of a school, and, better than Rembrandt, whose genius is untransmissible, he has determined new, numerous, and fixed laws of æsthetics. He leaves a double inheritance of good teaching and superb examples. His studio recalls, with as much renown as any, the finest habits of the Italian schools. He formed disciples who are the envy of other schools, the glory of his own. He can always be seen surrounded by this bevy of original minds and great talents, over whom he exercises a sort of paternal authority full of gentleness, solicitude, and majesty.

He had no wearisome old age, nor heavy infirmity, nor decrepitude. The last picture that he signed, and which he never had time to deliver, his Crucifixion of St. Peter, is one of his very best.

He speaks of it in a letter in 1638, as of a work of predilection which charms him, and which he desires to treat at leisure. Hardly had he been warned, by some little suffering, that our forces have limits, than he suddenly died at the age of sixty-three, leaving to his son, with a very wealthy patrimony, the most solid inheritance of glory that ever a thinker, at least in Flanders, had acquired by the labor of his mind.

Such is this exemplary life that I would wish to see written by some man of great learning and deep heart for the honor of our art, and the perpetual edification of those who practise it. It is here that it should be written, if possible, if it could be done, with one's feet upon his tomb, and before the St. George. Having before his eyes that part of us which passes away and that which endures, that which perishes and that which abides, a man might weigh with more moderation, certainty, and respect what there is in the life of a great man and in his works that is ephemeral, perishable, and truly immortal!

Who knows, too, but that if the work were meditated upon in the chapel where Rubens sleeps, this miracle of genius, taken in himself, might not become a little more clear, and this supernatural being, as we call him, be better explained?

IX.

VANDYCK.

It is thus I should imagine a portrait of Vandyck, made as it were by a rapid sketch with a broad pencil:—

A young prince of royal race, with everything in his favor,—beauty, elegance, magnificent gifts, precocious genius, a rare education,—and owing all these things to the advantages of birth; cherished by his master, himself a master among his fellow-students, everywhere distinguished, everywhere sought for, fêted everywhere, in foreign parts even more than at home; the favorite and friend of kings, entering thus by right into the most enviable things of the world, such as talent, renown, honors, luxury, passions, and adventures; ever young even at a ripe age, never steady even in his last days, a libertine, a gamester, eager, prodigal, dissipated, playing the devil, and, as they would have said in his time, selling himself to the devil for golden guineas, then spending them wildly on horses, in display, on ruinous gallantries; as much as possible a lover of his art, but ready to sacrifice it to passions less noble, to loves less faithful, to attachments far less fortunate; charming, of powerful origin, of elegant stature, such as one sees in the second generation of great races, of a complexion less virile than delicate, the air of a Don Juan rather than of a hero, with a flavor of melancholy and an undercurrent of sadness penetrating through the gayeties of his life; the tenderness of a heart prompt to fall in love, and that indefinable disillusionment of a heart too often moved; a nature more inflammable than burning, with, at bottom, more sensuality than true ardor, less fire than freedom, less capable of seizing things than of being seized by them and abandoning himself to them; a being exquisite in attraction, sensitive to all attraction, consumed by the two most absorbing things in the world, the muse and women; a man who abused everything, his seductions, his health, his dignity, his talent; crushed by necessities, worn out with pleasure, exhausted in resources; an insatiable being, who ended, says the legend, by keeping low company with Italian knaves, and by seeking gold secretly in alembics; a seeker of adventures, who at the end of his career married to order, as it were, a charming, well-born maiden, when he could no longer give her either strength, or much money, or great charm, or a secure life; a wreck of a man who, up to his last hour, had the good fortune, the most extraordinary of all, to preserve his greatness when painting; in fine, a *mauvais sujet*, adored, decried, calumniated at length, better in reality than his reputation; a man who was forgiven for everything on account of one supreme gift, one of the forms of genius, — grace; — to sum up all, a Prince of Wales dying upon his accession to the throne, who was by no means fitted to reign.

With his important work, his immortal portraits, his soul open to the most delicate sensations, his individual style, his personal distinction, his taste, his restraint, and his charm in everything he touched, one may ask what Vandyck would be without Rubens.

How would he have seen nature, how conceived painting? What sort of palette would he have created, what would have been his modelling, what laws of color would he have fixed, what would he have adopted that was poetic? Would he have been more Italian, or would he have bent more decidedly towards Correggio or towards Veronese? If the revolution made by Rubens had been retarded for a few years, or had not taken place, what would have been the fate of those charming spirits for whom the master had prepared the way, who only had to see him live to live a little like him, only to watch him paint to paint as none had ever painted before him, and only to consider as a whole his works such as he had imagined them, and the society of their time such as it had become, to perceive, in their definite relations henceforth bound to each other, two worlds equally new, — a modern society, a modern art? Who among them could have undertaken such discoveries?

There was an empire to found: could they found it? Jordaens, Crayer, Gérard, Zeghers, Rombouts, Van Thulden, Cornelis Schutt, Boyermanns, Jan van Oost of Bruges, Teniers, Van Uden, Snyders, Johann Fyt, all those whom Rubens inspired, enlightened, formed, and employed, — his co-laborers, his pupils, or his friends, — could at the utmost divide among themselves certain provinces, small or great; and Vandyck, the most gifted of all, deserved the finest and most important among them. Deprive them of that which they owed directly or indirectly to Rubens, take from them the central planet, and imagine what would remain of these luminous satellites. Take from Vandyck the original type from which his issued, the style whence he drew his own, the feeling for form, the choice of subject, the movement of mind, the manner and the method which served him for example, and see what he would lack. At Antwerp, at Brussels, everywhere in Belgium, Vandyck follows in the footsteps of Rubens. His Silenus, and his Martyrdom of St. Peter, are like a delicate and almost poetical Jordaens, — that is to say, Rubens preserved in his nobility by a more curious hand. His Sanctities, Passions, Crucifixions, Descents from the Cross, beautiful dead Christs, fair women in mourning and tears, would not exist, or would be different, if Rubens, once for all, in his two triptychs at Antwerp, had not revealed the Flemish formula of the Gospel, and determined the local type of the Virgin, the Christ, the Magdalen, and the disciples.

There is always more sentimentality, and sometimes even more profound sentiment, in the fine Vandyck than in the great Rubens; but is one quite certain of that? It is a matter of temperament and complexion. All sons like Vandyck have a feminine trait added to the father's features. It is by this that the paternal type is sometimes made more beautiful; it is softened, altered, diminished. Between these two souls, elsewhere so unequal, there is something like this influence of the woman. In the first place there is something which we may call a difference of sex. Vandyck heightens the statures that Rubens made too stout; he indicates less muscle, less relief, fewer bones, and not so much blood. He is less turbulent, never brutal; his expressions are less gross; he laughs but little, has often a vein of tenderness, but he knows not the strong sob of violent men. He never startles; he often corrects the roughnesses of his master; he is easy, because his talent is prodigiously natural and facile; he is free and alert, but he never is carried away.

Taking work for work, there are some that he would draw better than his master, especially when the work is choice; an idle hand, a woman's wrist, a slender finger circled by a ring. He has more restraint, more polish; one might say he is better bred. He is more refined than his master, because in fact his master formed himself alone, and the sovereignty of rank dispenses with, and takes the place of many things.

He was twenty-four years younger than Rubens. Nothing of the sixteenth century remained in him. He belonged to the first generation of the seventeenth, and that makes itself felt. It is felt physically and morally, in the man and in the painter, in his own handsome face and in his taste for other handsome faces. It is especially felt in his portraits. On this ground he belongs wonderfully to the world, — the world of his day and hour.

Never having created an imperious type to distract him from the real, he is true, he is exact, he sees correctly, he sees the likeness. Possibly he gives to all the personages who sat for him something of the graces of his own person, — an air more habitually noble, a more elegant undress, a finer attraction and style in garments, hands more regularly handsome, pure, and white. In every case he has, more than his master, a feeling for draperies well put on, for fashion;

he has a taste for silky stuffs, for satins, for ribbons, for points, for plumes and ornamental swords.

These gentlemen are no longer cavaliers, they are chevaliers. The men of war have laid aside their armor and their casques; they have become courtiers and men of the world in loose doublets and flowing linen, in silk hose and loose breeches and high-heeled satin shoes, — all fashions and habits which were his own, and which he was fitted better than any one to reproduce in their perfect mundane ideal.

In his manner, his style, by the unique conformity of his nature with the spirit, the needs, and the elegances of his epoch, he is, in the art of painting his contemporaries, the equal of anybody. His Charles I., from its profound feeling for model and subject, the familiarity and nobility of its style, the beauty of everything in this exquisite work, the drawing of the face, the coloring, the unrivalled rarity and justness of the values, the quality of the handling, — the Charles I., I say, to choose from his work an example well known in France, will bear comparison with the greatest.

His triple portrait at Turin is of the same order and of the same significance. Under this head he has done better than any one since Rubens. He has completed Rubens by adding to his work portraits wholly worthy of him, better than his. He has created in his country an original art, and consequently has his part in the creation of a new art.

Elsewhere he has done still more; he has engendered a whole foreign school, the English school. Reynolds, Lawrence, Gainsborough, I might add almost all the genre painters faithful to the English traditions, and the best landscape painters, are the direct issue of Vandyck, and indirectly of Rubens through Vandyck. These are worthy titles. Thus posterity, ever very just in its instincts, makes for Vandyck a place of his own between men of the first order and men of the second. The order of precedence which should be accorded to him in the procession of great men has never been accurately determined ; and since his death, as during his life, he seems to have preserved the privilege of being placed near the throne, and there being a distinguished presence.

However, I return to my statement that, in spite of his personal genius, his personal grace, his personal talent, Vandyck as a whole would be inexplicable if we had not before our eyes the solar light from which issue so many brilliant reflections. One would seek to know who had taught him these new manners, this liberal language which bears no trace of the ancient tongue ; one would detect in him gleams from elsewhere, which did not issue from his own genius ; and finally one would suspect that somewhere in his neighborhood some mighty planet must have disappeared.

No longer would Vandyck be called the son of Rubens, but to his name would be added, *His master is unknown*, and the mystery of his birth would well deserve to occupy the attention of historiographers.

PART II.

HOLLAND.

HOLLAND.

I.

THE HAGUE AND SCHEVENINGEN.

THE Hague is unquestionably one of the least Dutch towns there is in Holland, and one of the most singular towns in all Europe.

It has just the degree of local eccentricity necessary to give it that individual charm and that shade of cosmopolitan elegance which adapt it especially for a place of meeting. There is a little of everything, too, in this city of composite manners, and yet of very individual physiognomy, whose space, cleanness, stylish picturesqueness, and rather haughty grace seem to be a perfectly polite manner of showing hospitality. Here is met an indigenous aristocracy which travels, a foreign aristocracy which enjoys the place, imposing fortunes made in the depths of Asiatic colonies that establish themselves here in great comfort, finally envoys extraordinary on occasion, perhaps oftener than is necessary for the peace of the world. It is an abode that I would recommend to those whom the ugliness, the platitude, the confusion, the meanness, or the vain luxury of things, have disgusted with great cities but not with towns. And as for me, if I had to choose a place for work, a pleasant spot where I could be comfortable, breathe a delicate atmosphere, see beautiful things and dream of more beautiful ones, especially if I were disturbed by cares, contentions, or difficulties with myself, and I needed tranquillity to solve them, and something very agreeable about me to calm them, I would do as Europe does after its storms; I would here establish my Congress.

The Hague is a capital, as can plainly be seen, even a royal city; and one might say it has always been one. It only lacks a palace worthy of its rank to have all the features of its physiognomy accord with its final destiny. One feels that it had princes for stadtholders, and that these princes were in their way De Medicis, that they had a taste for the throne, and ought to have reigned somewhere, and that it only depended upon them to have their kingdom here. The Hague is then a city royally distinguished; it is so by right, for it is very wealthy, and by duty, for fine manners and opulence are all one when everything is as it should be. It might be dull, but it is only regular, correct, and peaceable. It might be arrogant, but it is only ostentatious and grand-mannered. It is clean, as would be expected, but not, as one would suppose, solely because it has well-kept streets paved with brick, painted houses, unbroken glasses, varnished doors, shining coppers; but because its waters, perfectly green and beautiful, green with the reflections of their banks, are never soiled by the muddy wake of the canal boats and the open-air cooking of the sailors.

The Wood is admirable. The Hague, born of a prince's caprice, formerly a hunting-seat of the counts of Holland, has for trees a secular passion, which comes from the natal forest which was its cradle. It promenades there, gives festivities and concerts, has races and military reviews ; and when its fine forest is no longer of any use, it has constantly under its eyes this green, dark, compact curtain of oaks, beeches, ashes, and maples, that the perpetual moisture of its ponds seems every morning to paint with a newer and more intense green.

Its great domestic luxury — the sole which it ostensibly parades with the beauty of its waters and the splendor of its parks, that with which it decorates its gardens, its winter and summer drawing-rooms, its bamboo verandas, its doorsteps, and its balconies — is its unrivalled abundance of rare plants and flowers. These flowers come from everywhere, and go everywhere. Here India is acclimated before it goes to make Europe blossom. The Hague, as an heritage of the Nassau family, has preserved a taste for the country, for drives under the trees, for menageries, sheepfolds, fine animals at large upon lawns. By its architectural style it is connected with the seventeenth century in France. Its fancies, some of its habits, its exotic adornments, and its odor come from Asia. Its actual comfort passed to England and came back again, so that at the present time it is impossible to say whether the original type is at London or at the Hague. In short, it is a town worth seeing, for it has much without; but what is within is worth more than what is without, for it contains besides a great deal of art concealed under its elegances.

To-day I was driven to Scheveningen. The road is a long,

narrow shaded avenue, leading in a straight line through the heart of the woods. It is cool and dark, whatever may be the warmth of the sky and the blue of the atmosphere. The sun leaves you at the beginning and meets you at the end. The exit is upon the rear of the downs, — a vast wavy desert, sparsely sown with thin grass and sand, such as are found at the edge of great beaches. Traversing the village, you find casinos, bath palaces, and princely pavilions, adorned with the colors and arms of Holland. You climb the downs, and heavily descend them to reach the shore. Before you, flat, gray, wind-blown, and white-capped, lies the North Sea. Who has not been there? and who has not seen it? One thinks of Ruysdael, Van Goyen, and of Van de Velde. Their point of view is easily found. I could tell you, as if their trace had been imprinted there for two centuries, the exact spot where they sat; the sea is on the right; the terraced downs grow dark upon the left, taper, grow small, and softly melt into the pallid horizon. The grass is dry, the downs are pale, the beach colorless, the sea milky, the sky silky, cloudy, wonderfully aerial, well drawn, well modelled, and well painted, as they used to paint it in old times.

Even at high tide the beach is interminable. As formerly, the promenaders make upon it spots that are soft or vivid and sometimes piercing. The darks are solid; the lights, tasteful, simple, and soft. The daylight is excessive, and the picture is in low tone; nothing can be more variegated, and the whole effect is dreary. Red is the only vivid color that preserves its activity in this astonishingly subdued scale, of which the notes are so rich, while the tone remains grave. There are children playing and stamping, wading, making holes and wells in the sand; women in light costumes, made of white shaded with pale blue or tender pink, not at all as they are painted nowadays, but much more as they would be painted, wisely and soberly, if Ruysdael and Van de Velde were there to give their advice. Dripping boats lie near the shore, with their delicate rigging, their black masts, their massive hulls, recalling feature for feature the ancient sketches colored with bistre of the best marine draughtsmen; and when a rolling car passes by, we think of the *Chariot with Six Dapple-Gray Horses of the Prince of Orange.* If you remember certain simple pictures of the Dutch School, you know Scheveningen, — it is now what it was then. Modern life has changed its accessories; each era renews the personages, and introduces its fashions and habits, — but what of that? It is hardly a special accent in an outline. Whether burghers of the olden time or tourists of to-day, they are only little picturesque spots, moving and changing, ephemeral points succeeding each other from age to age, between the great heaven, the great sea, the immense downs, and the ashy-white beach.

However, as if better to prove the permanence of things in this grand scenic picture, the same wave, studied so many times, was beating with regularity the shore imperceptibly sloping towards it. It gathered, rolled and broke, continuing that intermittent sound that has not varied a note since this world was a world. The sea was empty. A storm was forming in the offing and circled the horizon with banks of clouds gray and fixed. In the evening there would be lightning from them; and on the morrow, if they were only alive, William van de Velde, Ruysdael, who did not fear the wind, and Bakhuysen, who expressed nothing well but the wind, might come to watch the downs at their moment of melancholy, and the North Sea in its wrath.

I came home by another route, along the new canal to the Princessen-gracht. There had been races in the Maliebaan.* The crowd was still standing in the shelter of the trees, massed against the sombre background of foliage, as if the perfect turf of the hippodrome were a carpet of rare quality that must not be trampled upon.

A little smaller crowd, a few black landaus under the forest shade, and I could describe to you, because I have just had it under my eyes, one of those pretty pictures by Paul Potter, so patiently worked with the needle, so ingeniously bathed with light green half-tints, such as he painted in the days when he was only half working.

* The mall, — an open field in the Wood, where reviews are held.

II.

ORIGIN AND CHARACTER OF THE DUTCH SCHOOL.

THE Dutch School begins with the first years of the seventeenth century. By taking a slight liberty with dates, the very day of its birth might be fixed.

It is the last of the great schools, perhaps the most original, certainly the most local. At the same hour, under the same circumstances, are seen to appear in conjunction two events, — a new state and a new art. The origin of Dutch art has often been narrated pertinently and admirably, with its character, purpose, methods, appropriateness, its rapid growth, its unprecedented physiognomy, and particularly the sudden manner in which it was born, on the morrow of an armistice, with the nation itself, like the quick and natural blossoming of a people glad to live, and in haste to understand itself. I will touch upon the historical part only as a reminder, so as to come more quickly to what is of import to my subject.

Holland had never possessed many national painters, and possibly to this destitution she owes the fact of counting so many in later days that belonged entirely to herself. While she was confounded with Flanders, it was Flanders that undertook to think, invent, and paint for her. She had neither her Van Eyck nor her Memling, nor even a Roger van der Weiden. She had a momentary gleam from the school of Bruges. She can congratulate herself upon having seen the birth, about the beginning of the sixteenth century, of a native genius, in the painter engraver, Lucas van Leyden; but Lucas van Leyden formed no school, that flash of Dutch life died with him. Just as Stuerbout (Bouts van Harlem) disappeared almost, in the style and manner of the primitive Flemish school, so Mostaert, Schoreel, Hemskerk, in spite of all their worth, are not individual talents which illustrate and characterize a country.

Moreover, the Italian influence had reached all who held a brush, from Antwerp to Haarlem, and this reason was added to others to efface boundaries, mingle schools, and denationalize painters. Jan Schoreel did not even leave living pupils. The last and most illustrious of them, the greatest portrait painter of whom Holland can boast next to Rembrandt, and by the side of Rembrandt, that cosmopolitan of such supple nature, of such virile organization, of such a fine education, and so changeable a style, but of such great talent, who preserved no trace of its origin even in his name, Antonio Moro, *Hispaniarum regis pictor*, as he was called, had died in 1588. Those who lived were scarcely any longer Dutchmen, nor were they better grouped, nor more capable of renewing the school. They were the engraver Golzius; Cornelis van Harlem, in the style of Michael Angelo; Bloemaert, the Correggian; Mierevelt, a good characteristic painter, learned, correct, and concise, a little cold, but savoring of his time, though not much of his country, —

the only one, however, who was not an Italian, and who was, take notice, a portrait painter.

It was the destiny of Holland to love *what is like*, to return to it from time to time, to survive and save itself by the portrait.

However, the end of the sixteenth century approached, and, taking the portrait painters as a foundation, other painters were born or were formed. From 1560 to 1597 quite a number of these new births may be observed ; already there was a half-awakening. Thanks to many dissimilarities, and consequently to many aptitudes in different directions, the attempts were designed according to the tendency, and the roads to be pursued multiplied. They compelled themselves to try all things and all scales; there was a division between the *light* manner and the *brown* manner; the light was defended by the draughtsmen, the brown inaugurated by the colorists and advised by the Italian Caravaggio. They entered into the picturesque, they undertook to regulate chiaroscuro. The palette and the hand became emancipated. Rembrandt already had direct forerunners. Genre painting, properly so called, released itself from the obligations of history ; very nearly the final expression of modern landscape was approached. Finally, a style almost historical and profoundly national was created, the civic picture, and it was with this acquisition, the most decided of all, that the sixteenth century ended and the seventeenth began.

In that order of great canvases with numerous portraits, like the *doelen* or *regentenstukken*,* to follow the rigorous appellation of these

* Corporation or Regents' pictures. — Tr.

particularly Dutch works, other things may be found, but none better.

Here, as we see, are the germs of a school, but not yet a school. Talent is not wanting; it abounds. Among these painters on the high road to acquire and decide, were learned artists, even one or two great painters. Moreelze, issue of Mierevelt, Jan Ravesteyn, Lastman, Pinas, Frans Hals, an incontestable master, Poelemburg, Van Schotten, Van de Venne, Theodore de Keyser, Honthorst, the elder Cuyp, finally, Esaias van de Velde and Van Goyen, had their names on the birth register of this year, 1697. I quote their names without other explanation. You will easily recognize in this list those whom history was to remember, and you will especially distinguish the attempts they individually represent, the future masters whom they foretell, and you will understand what Holland still lacked, and what it was indispensably necessary she should possess, under penalty of letting her high hopes be lost.

The moment was critical. Here there was no assured political existence, and as a result everything else was in the hands of chance; in Flanders, on the contrary, was the same awakening, with a certainty of life that Holland was far from having acquired. Flanders was crammed with painters ready made or nearly so. At this very hour she was about to found another school, the second in a little more than a century, as brilliant as the first, and as a neighbor quite otherwise dangerous, for it was extraordinarily novel and dominant. It had a supportable, better inspired government, old habits, a definite and more compact organization, traditions, and a society. To the impulses received from above were added the needs of luxury, and consequently artistic needs more exciting than ever. In a word, the most energetic stimulus and the most powerful reasons were driving Flanders into becoming for the second time a great centre of art. It was about to have some years of peace; and a master to constitute the school was found.

In this very year 1609, which was to decide the fate of Holland, Rubens entered upon the scene.

Everything depended upon a political or military accident. Beaten and submissive, Holland was subject in every sense. Why should there be two distinct arts among the same people under one rule? Why should there be a school at Amsterdam, and what was to be its rôle in a country vowed henceforth to Italo-Flemish inspiration? What was to become of its vocation, so spontaneous, free, and provincial, so little fitted for a state art? Admitting that Rembrandt would have persisted in a style very difficult to practise away from its own home, can you imagine him belonging to the Antwerp school, which had not ceased to reign from Brabant to Friesland, a pupil of Rubens painting for cathedrals, decorating palaces, and pensioned by archdukes?

In order that the Dutch people might come into the world, and that Dutch art might be born on the same day with it, it was necessary — and this is why their two histories are so united — that there should be a revolution that should be profound and successful. It was necessary, besides, — and this was the most marked claim of Holland to the favors of fortune, — that this revolution should have for itself right, reason, and necessity, and that the people should deserve what they wished to obtain ; that they should be resolute, convinced, laborious, patient, heroic, wise, and without useless turbulence ; and that in every respect they should show that they were worthy to own themselves.

It might be said that Providence had its eye upon this little nation, — that it examined its complaints, weighed its claims, became persuaded of its force, judged that all was according to its design, and performed, when the day came, in its favor a unique miracle. War, instead of impoverishing it, enriched it ; struggles, instead of enervating, fortified, exalted, and tempered it. That which it had accomplished against so many physical obstacles, — the sea, the inundated land, the climate, — it did against the enemy. It succeeded. That which ought to have destroyed it, aided it. It had anxiety on but one point, the certainty of its existence, and it signed, thirty years apart, two treaties which first set it free and then consolidated it. There only remained, to confirm its own existence and to give to it the lustre of other prosperous civilizations, the instantaneous production of an art which consecrates it, honors and intimately represents it, and this was found to be the result of the twelve years' armistice. This result is so prompt, so decidedly the issue of the political incident to which it corresponds, that the right of having a free and national school of painting, and the certainty of having it on the morrow of the peace, seem to form a part of the stipulations of the treaty of 1609.

At that very moment a lull is felt. A breath of more propitious temperature has passed over men's minds, revived the soil, found germs ready to burst, and made them sprout. As always happens in spring at the North, with its sudden vegetation, and quick expansion after the mortal cold of its long winter, it is truly an unlooked for spectacle to see appear, in so little time, — hardly thirty years, — in such a small space, upon this ungrateful and desert soil, in this dreary spot, amid the rigor of all things, such a growth of painters, and great painters.

They were born everywhere at once, — at Amsterdam, at Dordrecht, at Leyden, Delft, Utrecht, Rotterdam, Enkhuysen, Haarlem, sometimes even beyond the frontiers, like a seed that has fallen outside the field. Two alone preceded the hour, — Van Goyen, born in 1596, and Wynants in 1600. Cuyp came in 1605. The year 1608, one of the most fruitful, saw the birth of Terburg, Brouwer, and Rembrandt, within a few months. Adrian van Ostade, the two Boths, and Ferdinand Bol were born in 1610; Van der Helst and Gerhard Douw, in 1613; Metzu, in 1615; Aart van der Neer, from 1613 to 1619; Wouvermans, in 1620; Weenix, Everdingen, and Pynaker, in 1621; Berghem, in 1624; Paul Potter illustrates the year 1625; Jan Steen, the year 1626; and the year 1630 became forever memorable for having produced, next to Claude Lorraine, the greatest landscape painter in the world, Jacob Ruysdael.

Is the stem exhausted? Not yet. Pieter de Hoogh's birth is uncertain, but it can be placed between 1630 and 1635; Hobbema is a contemporary of Ruysdael; Van der Heyden was born in 1637; and, finally, Adrian van de Velde, the last of all the great ones, was born in 1639. The very year that this late shoot sprouted, Rembrandt was thirty years old; and, taking for a central date the year in which appeared his Lesson in Anatomy, 1632, you can state that twenty-three years after the official recognition of the United Provinces, with the exception of a few tardy members, the Dutch School attained its first blossoming. Taking history from this moment, we know what to expect from the aims, character, and future destiny of the school; but before Van Goyen and Wynants had opened the way, before Terburg, Metzu, Cuyp, Ostade, and Rembrandt had shown what they meant to do, it might well be asked what painters were going to paint at such a time, in such a country.

The revolution which had just rendered the Dutch people free, rich, and prompt for all undertakings, had despoiled them of what elsewhere formed the vital element of the great schools. It changed beliefs, suppressed needs, reduced habits, stripped walls, abolished the representation of antique fables as well as the gospel; cut short those vast enterprises of mind and hand, — church pictures, decorative pictures, and large pictures. Never did a country set before artists so singular an alternative by constraining them expressly to be original, under penalty of not existing.

This was the problem: Given a nation of burghers, practical, unimaginative, busy, not in the least mystical, of anti-Latin mind, with traditions destroyed, with a worship without images, and parsimonious habits, — to find an art which should please it, that should seize its conventionalities, and represent it. A writer of our time, very enlightened in such matters, has wittily replied that such a people had but one thing to propose, — a very simple and very bold thing, and moreover the only one in which their artists had constantly succeeded for fifty years, and that was to require that they should paint its *portrait*.

This phrase says everything. Dutch painting, it is quickly perceived, was and could be only the portrait of Holland, its exterior image, faithful, exact, complete, and like, with no embellishment. Portraits of men and places, citizen habits, squares, streets, country places, the sea and sky, — such was to be, reduced to its primitive elements, the programme followed by the Dutch School, and such it was from its first day to the day of its decline. In appearance nothing can be more simple than the discovery of this art of earthly aim; but until they tried to paint it, nothing had been imagined equally vast and more novel.

At a blow everything was changed in the manner of conceiving, seeing, and rendering, — point of view, ideal, poetry, choice of subject, style, and method. Italian painting in its finest moments, Flemish painting in its noblest efforts, were not a sealed letter, for they were still enjoyed; but they were a dead letter because they were to be no longer consulted.

There existed a habit of high thinking, of thinking grandly, an art that consisted in the choice of things, and in embellishing and rectifying them, which lived in the absolute rather than in the relative, perceiving nature as it is, but preferring to exhibit it as it is not. Everything related more or less to the human being, depended upon it, was subordinate to it, or imitated from it, because, in fact, certain laws of proportion and certain attributes, such as grace, force, nobility, and beauty, intelligently studied in man and reduced into a body of doctrines, could be applied equally to what was not man. Thence resulted a sort of universal humanity, or humanized universe, of which the human body, in its ideal proportions, was the prototype. In history, visions, beliefs, dogmas, myths, symbols, and emblems, the human form almost alone expressed everything that could be expressed by itself. Nature existed vaguely around this absorbing being. It was barely considered as a frame which would diminish and disappear of itself when man should take his place in it. Everything was elimination and synthesis. As it was necessary that each object should borrow its plastic form from the same ideal, nothing modified it. Then, by virtue of these laws of the historical style, it was agreed that planes should be reduced, horizons abridged; that trees should be expressed broadly; that the sky should be less changeable, the atmosphere more limpid and equable; and that man should be more like himself, oftener naked than clothed, more habitually of lofty stature and fair countenance, to play his rôle in the most sovereign manner.

Now the theme had become more simple. It was necessary to give everything its own interest, to restore man to his proper place, and at need to dispense with him altogether. The moment had come for thinking less, for aiming less high, for more closely examining, for observing better, and for painting as well, but differently. It was painting for the crowd, consisting of the citizen, the working-man, the upstart, and the first comer, entirely made for them and made of them. It was necessary to become humble for humble things, little for little things, subtle for subtleties; to welcome all without omission or disdain; to enter into their intimacy familiarly, and affectionately into their habits; it was to be a matter of sympathy, of attentive curiosity, and patience. Henceforth genius was to consist of lack of prejudice, of not knowing what one knows, of letting the model be a surprise, and only asking him how he wished to be represented. As to embellishing, never; ennobling, never; correcting, never; — they would but be so many lies or so much useless labor. Was there not, in every artist worthy of the name, an indescribable something which would undertake this care naturally and without effort?

Even within the boundaries of the Seven Provinces the field of observation is unlimited. A corner of land in the North, with its waters, woods, and maritime horizon, may be called an abridgment of the universe. In its relations to the tastes and the instincts of the observer, the smallest country, scrupulously studied, becomes an inexhaustible repertory, as crowded as life, as fertile in sensations as the heart of man is fertile in ways of feeling. The Dutch School might grow and work for a hundred years, and Holland would still have enough to satisfy the indefatigable curiosity of her painters, so long as their love for her was unextinguished.

There is enough there, without going out of the pastures and polders, to gratify all inclinations. There are things made for the delicate as well as the coarse, for the melancholy, the ardent, for those who love laughing and those who care to dream. There are dark days and joyous sunshine, level and shining seas, and black and stormy ones; there are pastures and farms, seacoasts with their ships, and almost always the visible movement of the air through space, and ever the great winds of the Zuyder Zee, piling up clouds, bending trees, driving before them lights and shadows, and turning windmills. Add to these the towns and their exteriors, existence within doors and without, the fairs, intemperance and debauchery, good-breeding and elegance; the distresses of poverty, the horrors of winter, the disarray of taverns with tobacco, pots of beer, and laughing waiting-maids, trades and suspicious places on every floor, — on one side the security of home, the benefits of labor, abundance in fertile fields, the charm of living out of doors, with business affairs, cavalcades, siestas, and hunts. Add to these public life, civic ceremonies, and civic banquets, and you will have the elements of a wholly new art with subjects as old as the world.

Thence comes a most harmonious unity in the spirit of the school, and the most surprising diversity yet produced in the same spirit.

The school in its entirety is called the school of genre painting. Dissect it, and you will find painters of *conversations*, of landscapes, animals, marines, official pictures, still life, flowers; and in each category, almost as many subgenera as temperaments, from the picturesque to the ideal painters, from the copyists to the arrangers, from travellers to sedentaries, from the humorists who are amused and captivated by the human comedy, to those who flee from it; from Brouwer and Van Ostade to Ruysdael; from the impassive Paul Potter to the turbulent and riotous Jan Steen; from the gay and witty Van de Velde, to that morose and mighty dreamer, who without living apart had no relations with any of them, repeated none of them, but was the summing up of them all; who seemed to be painting his epoch, his country, his friends and himself, but who at bottom painted only one of the unknown recesses of the human soul. I speak, as you must know, of Rembrandt.

From such a point of view, such a style; and from such a style, such a method. If you omit Rembrandt, who is an exception at home as elsewhere, in his own time as in all times, you perceive but one style and one method in all the studios in Holland. The aim is to imitate what is, to make what is imitated charming, to clearly express simple, lively, and true sensations. Thus the style has the simplicity and clearness of the principle. It has for law, sincerity; for obligation, truth. Its first condition is to be familiar, natural, and characteristic, whence results a whole of moral qualities, innocent simplicity, patient will, and directness. It might be called the transportation of domestic virtues from private life into the practice of art, serving equally well for good conduct and good painting.

Remove from Dutch art what might be called probity, and you would no longer comprehend its vital element; it would be impossible afterwards to define either its morality or its style. But, even as in the most practical life there are springs of action which elevate behavior, thus in this art, reputed so positive, among these painters considered for the most part as near-sighted copyists, you feel a loftiness and goodness of soul, a tenderness for the true, a cordiality for the real, which give to their works a value that the things themselves do not seem to have. Hence their ideality, an ideal a little misunderstood, rather despised, but indisputable for him who can seize it, and very attractive to him who knows how to relish it. At times a grain of warmer sensibility makes of them thinkers, even poets, on occasion, and I will tell you in what rank in our history of art I place the style and inspiration of Ruysdael.

The basis of this sincere style and the first effect of this probity is the drawing, the perfect drawing. Every Dutch painter who does not draw faultlessly is to be despised. There are some, like Paul Potter, whose genius consists in taking measures, in following a feature. Elsewhere, and in his own manner, Holbein did nothing else, which constitutes for him, within and outside of all the schools, an almost unique glory, entirely his own. Every object, thanks to the interest it offers, must be examined in its form, and drawn before it is painted. Nothing is secondary in this connection. A bit of ground with its vanishing points, a cloud with its movement, architecture with its laws of perspective, a face with its expression, distinctive features, passing changes, a hand with its gesture, a garment with its habitual look, an animal, with its bearing, its frame, the intimate character of its race and instincts, — all these, with equal rights, form a part of this levelling art, and play, so to speak, the same part in the design.

For ages it was believed, and it is still believed in many schools, that it is sufficient to extend aerial tints, to shade them sometimes with azure and sometimes with gray, to express the grandeur of spaces, the height of the zenith, and the ordinary changes of the atmosphere. Now, consider that in Holland the sky is often half, and sometimes the whole picture, and that here the interest must be divided or misplaced. The sky must move and transport us, lift and excite us; the sun must set, the moon must rise; it must be actually day, or evening, or night; it must be warm or cold; one must shiver, or rejoice, or meditate in it. If the drawing applied to such problems be not the noblest of all, at least we can easily be convinced that it is neither without depth nor without merit.

And if the science and the genius of Ruysdael and Van de Veer were doubted, the whole world might be searched in vain for a painter who could paint a sky as they did, or express so many things, and express them so well. Everywhere we find the same drawing, strict, concise, precise, natural, and simple, seemingly the fruit of daily observation, which, as I have made you understand, is skilled labor, not known to all the world.

The particular charm of this ingenuous knowledge, of this experience without self-conscious airs, the ordinary merit and the true style of these kindly souls, may be summed up in a word. More or less skilful they may be, but there is not one pedant among them.

As to their palette, it is as good as their drawing; it is worth neither more nor less, whence results the perfect unity of their method. All the Dutch painters paint in the same way, and nobody has painted or can paint as they did. If you examine closely a Teniers, a Breughel, or a Paul Bril, it can be seen, in spite of a certain analogy of character and aim which are nearly similar, that neither Paul Bril, nor Breughel, nor even Teniers, the most Dutch of all the Flemings, had the Dutch education.

It is a painting made with application, with order, which denotes a well-poised hand, and labor executed while sitting, which presupposes perfect composure, and inspires it in those who study it. The mind meditated to conceive it; the mind meditates to comprehend it. There is a certain action, easy to follow, of exterior objects upon the painter's eye, and through it upon his brain. No painting gives a clearer idea of the triple and silent operation of feeling, reflecting, and expressing. Nor is any other more condensed, because none contains more things in so little space, nor is obliged to express so much in so small a frame.

From that, everything takes a more precise, more concise form, and a greater density. The color is stronger, the drawing more intimate, the effect more central, the interest better circumscribed. Never do these pictures spread out, nor do they risk being confounded with the frame or escaping from it. The ignorance or the perfect ingenuousness of Paul Potter must be possessed, to take so little care about the organization of a picture by effect, which seems to be a fundamental law in the art of his country.

All Dutch painting is concave; that is, it is composed of curves described around a point determined by the interest, — circular shadows around a dominant light. It is drawn, colored, and lighted like an orb with a heavy base, a tapering summit, and rounded corners converging to the centre, — whence result its depth and the distance from the eye of the objects reproduced in it. No painting leads with greater certainty from the foreground to the distance, from the frame to the horizon. It can be dwelt in, moved about in; you look into its depths, and lift your eyes to measure its sky. Everything contributes to this illusion, — the severity of the aerial perspective, the perfect relation of color and values to the plane occupied by the object. All painting foreign to this school of open sky, of aerial surroundings, of distant effects, produces pictures which seem flat upon the canvas. With rare exceptions, Teniers, in his open-air pictures with bright scales of color, derives his style from Rubens; he has his spirit and ardor, his rather superficial touch, his work, more elaborate than intimate; or, to force the expression, it might be said that he decorates, and does not paint profoundly.

I have not said all, but I must stop. To be complete, every one of the elements of this art, so simple and so complex, should be examined one after the other. The Dutch palette should be studied, and an examination made of its basis, its resources, extent, and use, to know and say why it is so reduced, almost monochromatic, and yet so rich in its results, common to all and yet varied; why its lights are so rare and narrow, the shadows dominant; what is the most ordinary law of that lighting which is so contrary to natural laws, especially out of doors. And it would be interesting to determine how much this conscientious painting contains of art, of combinations, of necessary measures, of systems almost always ingenious.

Finally would come the handiwork, the skill with tools, the care, the extraordinary care; the use of smooth surfaces, the thinness of the paints, their radiant quality, the gleam of metal and precious stones. It would be necessary to seek out how these excellent masters divided their labor, — if they painted on light or dark under-tints, or if, according to the example of the primitive schools, they colored solidly or glazed.

All these questions, especially the last, have been the subject of many conjectures, and have never been elucidated nor solved.

But these running notes are neither a profound study, nor a treatise, nor a course of lectures. The idea that is commonly held of Dutch painting, and that I have tried to sum up, suffices to wholly distinguish it from others, and the idea of the Dutch painter at his easel is equally true and expressive in all points. One imagines an attentive man, a little bent, with a fresh palette, clear oil, brushes clean and fine, a reflective air, and a prudent hand, painting in a half-light, and this man is an especial enemy of dust. If they may all be judged by Gerhard Douw and Mieris, that is about what they were; the picture is like. They were possibly less fastidious than is believed, and laughed more freely than is supposed. Genius did not radiate otherwise in the professional order of their good habits. Van Goyen and Wynants, from the beginning of the century, had fixed certain laws. These lessons were transmitted from masters to pupils, and for a hundred years, with no variation, they lived on this fund.

III.

THE VIJVER.

THIS evening, weary of reviewing so many painted canvases, of admiring and disputing with myself, I took a walk along the edge of the Vijver, or Pond.

Reaching it towards the end of the day, I remained until a late hour. It is a peculiar place, very solitary, and not without melancholy at such an hour, when one is a stranger abandoned by the escort of joyous years. Imagine a great basin between straight quays and black palaces, — on the right, a deserted promenade shaded with trees; beyond, closed houses; on the left, the *Binnenhof*, with its foundation in the water, its brick façade, slate roof, morose aspect, its physiognomy of another age and yet of all ages, its tragic memories, and, finally, I know not what, — something that belongs to certain places inhabited by history. Far away is the spire of the cathedral, hidden towards the north, already chilled by night, and drawn like a light wash of colorless tint; in the pond a green island, and two swans swimming softly in the shadow of the banks, and tracing only very slight ripples in it; above are swallows flying high and swiftly in the evening air. There is perfect silence, profound repose, a total forgetfulness of things present or past. Exact, but colorless reflections sink to the very bottom of the slumbering water, like the half-dead immobility of reminiscence that a far removed life has fixed in a memory three quarters extinct.

I looked at the Museum, the Mauritshuis, which forms the southern angle of the Vijver, and terminates at this point the taciturn line of the Binnenhof, whose purple brickwork is this evening full of gloom. The same silence, the same shadow, the same desolation, envelop all the phantoms shut up in the Palace of the Stadtholders, or in the Museum. I thought of what the Mauritshuis contained, I thought of what had passed in the Binnenhof. In the first were Rembrandt and Paul Potter; but here abode William of Orange, Barneveldt, the brothers De Witt, Maurice of Nassau, Heinsius,— all memorable names. Add to them the memory of the States General,— that assembly chosen by the country, within the country, from those citizens who were most enlightened, most vigilant, most resisting, most heroic; that living part, that soul of the Dutch people which lived within these walls, and there renewed itself, ever equable and constant, holding its sittings there during the stormiest fifty years that Holland ever knew, holding its own against Spain and England, dictating conditions to Louis XIV., and without which neither William nor Maurice nor the grand Pensionaries would have been aught.

To-morrow, at ten o'clock, a few pilgrims will knock at the door of the Museum. At the same hour there will be no one in the Binnenhof nor in the Buitenhof, and no one, I fancy, will visit the

Knights' Hall, where there are so many spiders, showing how great is its ordinary solitude.

Admitting that Fame, who, it is said, watches night and day over all glory, descends here, and rests somewhere, where do you think that she arrests her flight? Over which palace does she fold her golden wings, her weary pinions? Over the palace of the States General, or over the house of Potter and of Rembrandt? What a singular distribution of favor and forgetfulness! Why such curiosity to see a picture, and so little interest in a great public life? Here were mighty statesmen, great citizens, revolutions, coups-d'état, tortures, martyrdoms, controversies, intestine commotions, — all those things which combine at the birth of a people, when this people belongs to another people from which it tears itself away, to a religion that it transforms, to an European political state from which it separates, and which it seems to condemn by the very fact of separation. All this history recounts; does the country remember it? Where do you find living echoes of these extraordinary emotions?

At the same moment a very young man was painting a bull in a pasture; and another, to make himself agreeable to a physician, one of his friends, was representing him in a dissecting-room surrounded by his pupils with the scalpel in the arm of a corpse. By so doing they gave immortality to their name, their school, their century, and their country.

To whom then belongs our gratitude? To what is worthiest, to what is truest? No. To what is greatest? Sometimes. To what is most beautiful? Always. What then is the beautiful, —

this great lever, this powerful moving spring, this mighty magnet, that may almost be called the sole attraction of history? Is it nearer than any ideal on which in spite of himself man has cast his eyes? Is the *great* so seductive only because it is more easy to confound it with the beautiful? It is necessary to be very advanced in morals, or very learned in metaphysics, to say of a good action or of a truth that it is beautiful. The most simple man says it of a grand deed. At bottom, we naturally love only what is beautiful. Imagination turns thither, sensibility is excited by it, all hearts precipitate themselves towards it. If we seek carefully for what the mass of mankind loves most voluntarily, it may be seen that it is not what touches, nor what convinces, nor what edifies it; it is what charms it, and excites its wonder.

Thus, when an historical personage has not in his life this element of powerful attraction, we say that he lacks something. He is understood by moralists and learned men, unknown to others. If the contrary happens, his memory is safe. A people disappears, with its laws, morals, its policy, and its conquests; there remains of its history but one piece of marble or bronze, and that witness survives. There was a man, — a very great man by his lights, his courage, his political judgment, by his public acts; but perhaps his name might not have been known if he had not been embalmed in literature, and if some sculptor friend had not been employed by him to adorn the pediment of a temple. Another was a coxcomb, light, dissipated, witty, a libertine, valiant at times; but he is spoken of oftener and more universally than Solon or Plato, Socrates or

Themistocles. Was he wiser or braver? Did he better serve truth, justice, and the interests of his country? He had, above all, the charm of having passionately loved the beautiful, — women, books, pictures, and statues. Another was an unfortunate general, a mediocre statesman, a heedless chief of an empire; but he had the good luck to love one of the most seductive women in history, — a woman who was, it is said, beauty itself.

About ten o'clock the rain fell. It was night; the pond gleamed almost imperceptibly, like a remnant of aerial twilight forgotten in a corner of the town. Fame did not appear. I know what may be the objections to her preferences, and it is not my purpose to judge them.

IV.

THE SUBJECT IN DUTCH PAINTING.

ONE thing strikes you in studying the moral foundation of Dutch art, and that is the total absence of what we call now a *subject*.

From the day when painting ceased to borrow from Italy its style, its poetry, its taste for history, for mythology and Christian legends, up to the moment of decadence, when it returned thither, — from Bloemaert and De Poelemburg to Lairesse, Philippe Vandyck, and later Troost, — more than a century elapsed, during which the great Dutch School appeared to think of nothing but painting well. It was content to look around it, and to dispense with imagination. Nudities, which were out of place in this representation of real life, disappeared. Ancient history was forgotten, and contemporaneous history too, which is the most singular phenomenon. There is hardly to be perceived, drowned in this vast sea of genre scenes, one picture like Terburg's Peace of Munster, or some few deeds of the maritime wars, represented by vessels cannonading each other, — for instance, an Arrival of Maurice of Nassau at Scheveningen (Cuyp, Six Museum); a Departure of Charles II., from

Scheveningen (June 2, 1660), by Lingelbach, and this Lingelbach is a sorry painter. The great artists hardly treated such subjects. And apart from the painters of marines, or of exclusively military pictures, not even one of them seemed to have any aptitude for treating them. Van der Meulen, that fine painter, issue by Snayers of the School of Antwerp, a thorough Fleming, though adopted by France, pensioned by Louis XIV., and the historiographer of our French glories, gave to the Dutch anecdote painters a very seductive example, followed by nobody. The great civic representations of Ravesteyn, Hals, Van der Helst, Flinck, Karel Dujardin, and others, are, as is well known, portrait pictures, where the action is unimportant, and which, although historical documents of great interest, take no place in the history of the time.

In thinking of the events contained in the history of the seventeenth century in Holland, the gravity of the military deeds, the energy of this people of soldiers and sailors in their fights, and what they suffered, — in imagining the spectacle that the country must have offered in those terrible times, one is filled with surprise to see their painting thus indifferent to what was the very life of the people.

There was fighting abroad by land and by sea, on the frontiers and in the heart of the country; at home they were tearing each other to pieces. Barneveldt was decapitated in 1619; the brothers De Witt were beheaded in 1672; fifty-three years apart, the struggle between the Republicans and the Orangemen was complicated with the same religious or philosophical discords, — here Arminians against Gomarites, there Voetians against Cocceians,* bringing about the same tragedies. There was a permanent war with Spain, with England, with Louis XIV. Holland was invaded; how she defended herself is known: the peace of Munster was signed in 1648; the peace of Nimeguen, in 1678; the peace of Ryswick, in 1698. The war of the Spanish Succession opened with the new century, and it can be said that all the painters of the grand and pacific school of which I treat, died, having hardly ceased for a single day to hear the cannon. What they were doing at that time, their works show. The portrait painters painted their great warriors, their princes, their most illustrious citizens, their poets, their writers, themselves or their friends. The landscape painters inhabited the fields, dreaming, drawing animals, copying huts, living a farm-life, painting trees, canals, and skies, or they travelled; they went to Italy and established a colony there, met Claude Lorraine, forgot themselves at Rome, forgot their country, and died like Karel, without recrossing the Alps. Others scarcely came out of their studios but to frequent taverns, to prowl about places of ill-fame, to study their manners when they did not enter into them on their own account, which rarely happened.

The war did not prevent peaceful life somewhere, and into that tranquil and as it were indifferent corner they bore their easels, and pursued, with a placidity that may well surprise, their meditations,

* F. Gomar, a celebrated Protestant minister of Bruges, 1563–1609, founded this sect. J. Cocceius, an Orientalist and theologian of Bremen, 1603–1669, invented a very singular system for the interpretation of the Bible. Gilbert Voet, Dutch theologian and controversialist, 1593–1680, rendered himself odious by his persecutions of Descartes. — Tr.

their studies, and their charming, smiling industry. And as every-day life went on all the same, it was domestic habits, private, rustic, or urban, that they undertook to paint in spite of everything, through everything, to the exclusion of everything that caused the emotion, anguish, patriotic effort, and grandeur of their country. Not a trouble, not an anxiety, existed in this world so strangely sheltered, that this might be taken for the golden age of Holland, if history did not inform us to the contrary.

Their woods are tranquil, the highways secure, boats come and go along the course of the canals; rustic festivities have not ceased; on the threshold of beer-shops men smoke, while dancing goes on within. There is hunting and fishing and promenading. A faint still smoke issues from the roof of the little farmhouses, where nothing savors of danger. Children go to school, and within the dwellings there are the order, peace, and imperturbable security of happy days. The seasons succeed each other; there is skating on the waters that were navigated, fire on the hearth; doors are closed, curtains drawn; the asperities come from the climate and not from man. It is always the regular course of things that nothing deranges, and a permanent foundation of little daily facts with which they take so much delight in composing their excellent pictures.

When a skilful painter of equestrian scenes shows us by chance a canvas where horses are charging, men fighting with pistols and swords, where they are stamping, struggling, and exterminating each other quite fiercely, all this takes place in spots where war is out of place, and danger not at home. These murders savor of fantastic anecdote, and it is perceived that the painter was not greatly moved by them himself. It was the Italians, Berghem, Wouvermans, Lingelbach, the not over truthful painters of the picturesque, who perchance amused themselves by painting these things. Where did they see these fights ?— on this side of, or beyond the mountains ?

There is something of Salvator Rosa, minus the style, in these simulated skirmishes or grand battles, whose cause, moment, and theatre are unknown ; nor is it very clear who are the parties engaged. The titles of the pictures themselves indicate sufficiently the part played by the imagination of the painters. The Hague Museum possesses two great pages, very fine and very bloody, where the blows fall thick, and wounds are not spared. One, by Berghem, — a very rare picture, astonishingly well executed, — a *tour de force* in action, tumult, the admirable order of the effect, and the perfection of the details, — a canvas not at all historical, — bears for title, A Convoy Attacked in a Mountain Pass. The other, one of the largest pictures that Wouvermans has signed, is entitled A Great Battle. It recalls the picture at the Munich Pinacothek, known as the Battle of Nordlingen ; but there is nothing more decided in this, and the historically national value of this very remarkable work is no better established than the veracity of Berghem's picture.

Everywhere, besides, there are episodes of brigandage or anonymous fights which certainly were not lacking among them, and yet they all have the appearance of being painted from hearsay, during or after their journeys in the Apennines.

Dutch history has not marked at all — or so little that it amounts to nothing — the painting of those troubled times, and seems not to have agitated the mind of the painters for a single moment. Note, moreover, that even in such of their painting as is properly picturesque and anecdotic, there is not the slightest anecdote to be perceived.

There is no well-determined subject, not one action that requires reflection upon the composition or is expressive or particularly significant. No invention, no scene which trenches upon the uniformity of this existence of the fields or the town, commonplace, vulgar, devoid of pursuits, of passions, one might almost say of sentiment. Drinking, smoking, dancing, and kissing maids cannot be called very rare or attractive incidents. Nor are milking cows, taking them to water, and loading haycarts, notable accidents in a life of husbandry.

One is forever tempted to question these indifferent and phlegmatic painters, and to ask them, Is there then nothing new? nothing in your barns and farms, nothing in your houses? There has been a high wind; has it destroyed nothing? There has been a thunderstorm; has the lightning struck nothing, — neither your fields, nor roofs, nor laborers? Children are born; are there no birthdays? They die; is there no mourning? You marry; are there no decent rejoicings? Do they never weep among you? You have all been lovers, but how do we know it? You have suffered, you have pitied the misery of others, — you have had before your eyes all the wounds, the pains, the calamities of human life; where can it be discovered that you have had one day of tenderness, of sorrow, or true pity? Your time, like all others, has seen quarrels, passions, jealousies, gallant intrigues, and duels; what do you show us of all those? Plenty of libertine behavior, drunkenness, coarseness, sordid idleness; people who embrace as if they were fighting, and here and there fisticuffs and kicks exchanged in the exasperation of wine and love. You love children, you flog them, they do mischief in a corner, and such are your family pictures.

Compare epochs and countries. I do not speak of the contemporary German School, nor of the English School, where everything was subject, art, intention, as in their dramas, comedies, and farces, — where painting is too impregnated with literature, since it lives but for that and in the eyes of certain people dies of it, — but take a catalogue of a French exhibition, read the titles of the pictures, and then look over those of the museums at Amsterdam and the Hague.

In France every picture which has not a title, and consequently contains no subject, runs a great risk of being reckoned as a work neither considered nor serious; and that is not only for to-day, it has been so for a hundred years. Since the day when Greuze imagined the picture of sentiment, and with the great applause of Diderot conceived a picture as a scene in a theatre is conceived, and put into painting the homely dramas of the family, — since that day what do we see? Has genre painting in France done anything but invent scenes, compel history, illustrate literature, paint the past, paint the present but little, contemporary France very little indeed, and give us a great many curiosities of foreign manners and climates?

It suffices to cite names to revive a long series of piquant and beautiful works, ephemeral or ever celebrated, all signifying something, representing all sorts of facts and sentiments, expressing passions or relating anecdotes, all having their principal person and their hero, — Granet, Bonington, Léopold Robert, Delaroche, Ary Scheffer, Roqueplan, Decamps, Delacroix, — I stop with the dead artists. Do you remember the Francis I., Charles V., the Duc de Guise, Mignon, Margaret, The Lion Lover, the Vandyck at London; all the pages borrowed from Goethe, Shakespeare, Byron, and Walter Scott, and from the history of Venice; the Hamlets, Yoricks, Macbeths, Mephistopheles, Polonius, The Giaour, Lara, Goetz de Berlichingen, The Prisoner of Chillon, Ivanhoe, Quentin Durward, The Bishop of Liége, and then The Foscari, Marino Faliero and The Boat of Don Juan, and yet again The History of Samson, The Cimbri, preceding the oriental curiosities? And since, if we prepare a list of the genre pictures that have year by year charmed, moved, and impressed us, from the Scenes of the Inquisition, and the Colloquy of Poissy, to Charles V. at St. Just, — if we recall, I say, in these last thirty years, whatever the French School has produced most striking and honorable in genre painting, we shall find that the dramatic, pathetic, romantic, historical, or sentimental element has contributed almost as much as the painters' talent to the success of their works.

Do you perceive anything like this in Holland? The catalogues are desperately insignificant and vague. The Spinner with Cattle at the Hague, of Dujardin; — of Wouvermans, The Arrival at the Inn, The Halt of the Hunters, The Country Riding School, The Hay Wagon (a celebrated picture), A Camp, The Hunters' Rest, etc.; —

of Berghem, A Boar Hunt, An Italian Ford, A Pastoral, etc.; — of Metzu, we have The Hunter, The Lovers of Music; — of Terburg, The Despatch; — and so on with Gerhard Douw, Ostade, Mieris, even with Jan Steen, the most wide-awake of all, and the only one who, by the profound or gross meaning of his anecdotes, is an inventor, an ingenious caricaturist, a humorist of the family of Hogarth, and a literary painter, almost a comic author in his facetiousness. The finest works are concealed under titles of the same platitude. The fine Metzu of the Van der Hoop Museum is called The Hunter's Gift, and no one would suspect that the Rest by the Farm designates an incomparable Paul Potter, the pearl of the d'Aremberg Gallery. We know what is meant by the Bull of Paul Potter, and the still more celebrated Cow Admiring Herself, or the Cow of St. Petersburg. As to the Anatomical Lecture, and the Night Watch, I may be permitted to think that the significance of the subject is not what assures to these two works the immortality which they have acquired.

It seems, then, that everywhere but in the Dutch School are to be found gifts of the heart and mind, sensibility, tenderness, generous sympathy for the dramas of history, extreme experience of those of life, pathos, power to move, interest, unexpectedness, and instruction. And the school which has most exclusively occupied itself with the real world seems the one of all that has most despised moral interest, and while it is also the one which has most passionately devoted itself to the study of the picturesque, it seems less than any other to have discovered its living springs.

What reason had a Dutch painter to make a picture? None; and observe that no one ever asked him to do it. A peasant with a nose swollen with wine looks at you with his big eye, and laughs with all his teeth showing, while he lifts his jug; — if the thing is well painted, it has its price. With us, if a subject is lacking, there must be at least a true and lively sentiment and a perceptible emotion in the painter to take its place. A landscape not strongly tinted with the colors of a man is a failure. We do not know, as Ruysdael did, how to make a picture of the rarest beauty, of a stream of foaming water falling between brown rocks. An animal in the pasture *which has not its idea,* as peasants say of the instinct of brutes, is a thing not to be painted.

A very original painter of our time, an elevated soul, a sorrowful spirit, a good heart, and a truly rural nature, has spoken of the country and its country folk, of the asperity, the melancholy, and the nobility of their labor, — things that no Hollander would ever have thought of finding.* He has said them in a slightly barbarous language, and in formulas where the thought has more vigor and clearness than the hand. We have been infinitely grateful to him for his tendencies; we have seen in him in French painting something like the sensibility of a Burns less skilful in making himself understood. To sum up the account, has he, or has he not made and left fine pictures? Have his form and his language, — I mean the exterior envelope without which the works of the spirit neither are nor live, — have they the qualities necessary to consecrate

* Jean François Millet. — Tr.

him as a fine painter, and assure his living for a long time? He is a profound thinker beside Paul Potter and Cuyp, he is an attractive dreamer compared to Terburg and Metzu; he has something incontestably noble when we think of the trivialities of Steen, of Ostade, and of Brouwer; as a man he can put them all to the blush, but as a painter does he equal them?

What is the conclusion? you ask.

First, is it necessary to conclude? France has shown much inventive genius, but few of the truly pictorial faculties. Holland has imagined nothing, but she has painted miraculously well. This is certainly a great difference. Does it follow that we must absolutely choose between the qualities which are opposite in two peoples, as if there were between them a certain contradiction which would render them irreconcilable? I really do not know exactly. Till now the thought has truly sustained only great plastic works. In reducing itself to enter into works of medium order, it seems to have lost its virtue.

Sensibility has saved some of them; curiousness has destroyed a great number; mind has ruined them all.

Is this the conclusion to be drawn from the preceding observations? Certainly another might be found, but to-day I do not perceive it.

V.

PAUL POTTER.

With the Anatomical Lecture and the Night Watch, Paul Potter's Bull is the most celebrated thing in Holland. The Hague Museum owes to it a large part of the curiosity of which it is the object. It is not the largest of Paul Potter's canvases, but it is at least the only one of his large pictures which merits serious attention. The Bear Hunt in the Amsterdam Museum, supposing it to be authentic, and separating it from the repainting which disfigures it, was never anything but the extravagance of a youth, — the grossest error he ever committed. The Bull is priceless. Estimating it according to the actual value of the works of Paul Potter, no one doubts that if it were put up for sale it would attain in the markets of Europe a fabulous price. Is it, then, a fine picture? Not at all. Does it deserve the importance attached to it? Unquestionably. Is Paul Potter, then, a very great painter? Very great. Does it follow that he paints as well as is supposed? Not precisely. There is in this a misunderstanding that it would be well to dispel.

On the day when the fictitious markets of which I speak shall be opened, and consequently one will have the right to discuss without regard to merits this famous work, if any one dared to express the truth, he would say about what follows:—

"The reputation of the picture is at once very much exaggerated and very legitimate; it results from an ambiguity. It is considered as an exceptional page of painting, which is an error. It is thought to be an example to be followed, a model to copy, in which ignorant generations can learn the technical secrets of their art. In that there is also a mistake, the greatest mistake of all. The work is ugly, and unconsidered; the painting is monotonous, thick, heavy, pale, and dry. The arrangement is of the utmost poverty. Unity is wanting in this picture which begins nobody knows where, has no end, receives the light without being illuminated, distributes it at random, escapes everywhere, and comes out of the frame, so entirely does it seem to be painted flat upon the canvas. It is too full without being entirely occupied. Neither lines, nor color, nor distribution of effect give it those first conditions of existence indispensable to every well-regulated work. The animals are ridiculous in form. The dun cow with a white head is built of some hard substance. The sheep and the ram are modelled in plaster. As to the shepherd, no one defends him. Two parts only of the picture seem made to be understood, the wide sky and the huge bull. The cloud is in its true place; it is lighted and colored as it should be, where it is appropriate to the needs of the principal object, which it is made to accompany, to give value to its relief. By a wise understanding of the law of contrasts, the painter has greatly lowered the tone of the light colors and the dark shadows of the animal. The darkest part is opposed to the light part of the sky, and that which is most energetic and most trenchant in the brute to what is most limpid in the atmosphere; but this is hardly a merit, given the simplicity of the problem. The rest is an accompaniment that might be cut out without regret, greatly to the advantage of the picture."

This may seem a rough criticism, but it is exact. And yet public opinion, less punctilious or more clairvoyant, would say that the signature was well worth the price.

Public opinion is never wholly mistaken. By uncertain roads, often by the best selected ones, it arrives finally at the expression of a true sentiment. When it is given to some one, the motives, by virtue of which it is given, are not always the best, but there are always other good reasons found, by virtue of which it has been given wisely. It makes mistakes in titles, sometimes it takes faults for merits; it prizes a man for his way of working, which is the least of his merits; it may believe that a painter paints well when he paints badly, because he paints minutely. What amazes in Paul Potter is the imitation of objects pushed to an extreme. It is ignored or it is not noticed in such a case that the painter's soul is worth more than the work, and his manner of feeling infinitely superior to the result.

When he painted the Bull in 1647, Paul Potter was only twenty-three years old. He was a very young man, and according to what is common among men of twenty-three, he was a mere child. To what school did he belong? To none. Had he had masters? No other teachers of his are known but his father, Pieter Simonsz

Potter, an obscure painter, and Jacob de Weth, of Haarlem, who also had not knowledge enough to act upon a pupil either for good or evil. Paul Potter found then, either around his cradle or in the studio of his second master, nothing but simple advice and no doctrines; but, strange to say, the pupil asked nothing further. Till 1647 Paul Potter lived between Amsterdam and Haarlem, that is between Frans Hals and Rembrandt, in the heart of the most active, the most stirring art, the richest in celebrated masters, that the world has ever known, except in Italy in the preceding century. Teachers were not wanting; there was only the embarrassment of choice. Wynants was forty-six years old; Cuyp forty-two; Terburg thirty-nine; Ostade thirty-seven; Metzu thirty-two; Wouvermans twenty-seven; Berghem, who was about his own age, was twenty-three. Many of them, even the youngest, were members of the brotherhood of St. Luke. Finally, the greatest of all, and the most illustrious, Rembrandt, had already produced the Night Watch, and he was a master who might have been a temptation. But what did Paul Potter do? How did he isolate himself in the heart of this rich and crowded school, where practical skill was extreme, talent universal, the manner of rendering rather similar, and yet, an exquisite thing in those beautiful days, the manner of feeling so very individual? Had he co-disciples? None are seen. His friends are unknown. He was born, but we hardly know the year with exactitude. He awoke early; at fourteen years signed a charming etching; at twenty-two, though ignorant on many points, he was of unexampled maturity in others. He labored, and produced work upon work, and some of them were admirable. He accumulated them in a few years with haste and abundance, as if death was at his heels, and yet with an application and a patience which make this prodigious labor seem a miracle. He was married at an age young for another, very late for him, for it was on July 3, 1650, and on August 4, 1654, four years after, death took him, possessing all his glory, but before he had learned his trade. What could be simpler, briefer, more complete? Take genius and no lessons, brave study, an ingenuous and learned production resulting from attentive observation and reflection, add to this a great natural charm, the gentleness of a meditative mind, the application of a conscience burdened with scruples, the melancholy inseparable from solitary labor, and possibly the sadness of a man out of health, and you have nearly imagined Paul Potter.

With the exception of the charm, in this respect the Bull at the Hague represents him wonderfully. It is a great *study*, too great from the point of view of good sense, but not too great for the research which was its object, and for the instruction the painter derived from it.

Remember that Paul Potter, when compared with his brilliant contemporaries, was ignorant of all the cleverness of his trade. I do not speak of the tricks which his candor never suspected. He studied especially forms and their aspects, in their absolute simplicity. The least artifice was an embarrassment that would have disturbed him because it would have altered the clear sight of things. A great bull in a vast plain, a wide sky, and, so to speak, no horizon, — what could be a better occasion for a student to learn once for all a crowd of very difficult things, and to know them, as they say, by rule and measure? The movement is simple, — none was necessary, — the gesture true, the head admirably living. The animal shows its age, its type, its character, temperament, length, height, joints, bones, muscles, its hide rough or smooth, tangled or curled, its loose or tight skin, all in perfection. The head, the eye, the shoulders, the fore quarters, are from the point of view of a very simple and powerful observer, and are a very rare piece of work, perhaps unequalled. I do not say that the subject is beautiful, or the color well chosen; but matter and color are here too visibly subordinate to the preoccupation of form, for much to be expected in this regard, when the draughtsman has given us almost everything in another. There is more; the very tone, and the work upon those parts that are violently observed, result in rendering nature as it really is, in its relief, its shadows, its power, almost its mysteries themselves. It is not possible to have a more circumscribed but most decided aim, or to attain it with more success. It is called Paul Potter's Bull, but I affirm that that is not enough; it might be called the Bull, and in my idea that would be the greatest eulogium that could be pronounced upon this work so commonplace in its weak parts, and yet so conclusive.

Almost all the pictures of Paul Potter have the same quality. In most of them he proposes to himself to study some characteristic accident of nature, or some new part of his art, and you can be certain that on that day he succeeded in knowing, and instantaneously

rendering what he had learned. The Field, in the Louvre, of which the principal object, the rusty gray ox, is the reproduction of a study which was often to serve him, is also a very weak or a very strong picture, according as it is taken for a page from a master or for a magnificent exercise by a scholar. The Field with Cattle, of the Hague Museum, Shepherds and their Flock, and Orpheus charming the Animals, of the Amsterdam Museum, are, each in its own kind, an occasion of study, a pretext for study, and not, as one might be tempted to believe, one of those conceptions in which imagination plays the least rôle. They are animals closely examined, grouped without much art, drawn in simple attitudes, or in difficult foreshortening, never in a very complicated or very striking effect.

The labor is thin, hesitating, sometimes painful. The touch is a little infantine. Paul Potter's eye, of a singular exactness, and a penetration that nothing wearies, details, scrutinizes, expresses to excess, never is fatigued, and never stops. Paul Potter ignores the art of sacrifices, and he has not yet learned that things must be sometimes understood and but half expressed. You recognize the urgency of his brush, and the distracting embroidery which he employs to render the compact foliage and thick grass of the fields. His talent as a painter is the result of his talent as an engraver. To the end of his life, in his most perfect works, he never ceased to paint as one works with a burin. The tool becomes more supple, and lends itself to other uses, but under the thickest paint one continues to feel the fine point, the sharp-edged notches, and the biting touch.

It is only gradually, with effort, by a progressive and entirely personal education, that he learns to manage his palette like other people; but as soon as he succeeds he is superior.

By choosing certain pictures, of dates comprised between 1647 and 1652, the movement of his mind can be followed, as well as the meaning of his studies and the nature of his investigations, and nearly to a moment the almost exclusive preoccupation in which he was plunged.

Thus the painter may be seen separating himself little by little from the draughtsman, his color becoming more decided, his palette taking on a more learned arrangement; finally, chiaroscuro is born of itself in it, like a discovery for which this innocent spirit is indebted to no one.

The extensive menagerie collected around a charmer in doublet and boots, who is playing the lute, and is called Orpheus, is the ingenious effort of a young man who is a stranger to all the secrets of his school, but who is studying the varied effects of half-tint upon the hair of animals. It is weak, but learned; the observation is just, the workmanship timid, the design charming.

In the Field with Cattle the result is still better; the atmosphere is excellent, the method alone has persisted in its infantine equality.

The Cow Admiring Herself is a study of light, of full light, made about noon of a summer day. It is a very celebrated picture, and, believe me, extremely weak, disconnected, complicated with a yellowish light, which, although studied with unheard-of patience, has on that account neither more interest nor more truth. It is full of uncertainty in its effect, and executed with an application which betrays difficulty. I would omit this student's exercise, one of the least successful he has attempted, if even in this unfruitful effort one did not recognize the admirable sincerity of a mind which is seeking something, which does not know everything, but wants to know everything, and becomes all the more fierce in the pursuit because his days are numbered.

On the other hand, without leaving the Louvre and the Netherlands, I will mention two of Paul Potter's pictures that are by a consummate painter, and which are also decidedly *works* in the highest and rarest acceptation of the word; and, what is remarkable, one of them is dated 1647, the very year in which he signed the Bull.

I mean the Little Inn at the Louvre, catalogued under the title, Horses at the Door of a Cottage, No. 399. It is an evening effect. Two horses loosened from the vehicle, but harnessed, have stopped before a trough; one is bay, the other white; the white one is exhausted. The carter has just drawn water from the river; he climbs the bank with one arm lifted, while the other is holding a bucket, and he is relieved in soft outline against a sky whence gleams are cast by the setting sun. It is unique in sentiment and design, in the mystery of the effect, in the beauty of the tone, in the delicious and spiritual intimacy of the work.

The other, painted in 1653, the year that preceded Paul Potter's death, is a wonderful masterpiece from every point of view, — arrangement, picturesque touches, acquired knowledge, persistent simplicity, firmness of drawing, force in workmanship, clearness of eye, and charm of hand. The d'Aremberg Gallery, which owns this precious jewel, contains nothing more valuable. These two incomparable works prove, if they alone are regarded, what Paul Potter intended to do, and what he certainly would have done with more breadth if he had had the time.

This, then, is what may be said, that what experience Paul Potter acquired, he owed only to himself. He learned from day to day, — every day; let us not forget that the end came before he had done learning. As he had no master he had no pupils. His life was too short to permit any teaching. Moreover, what would he have taught? His way of drawing? That is an art which recommends itself, but which can hardly be taught. Arrangement and the knowledge of effect? He was hardly sure of them in his last days. Chiaroscuro? It was taught in all the studios of Amsterdam much better than he practised it himself, for it was the one thing, as I have said, that the sight of Dutch fields had revealed to him only after a long time, and very rarely. The art of composing a palette? It can be seen how much trouble it caused him to become master of his own. And as to practical skill, he was no better able to recommend it than his works were made to give a proof of it.

Paul Potter painted fine pictures which were not all fine models; or rather he gave good examples, and his whole life was but a piece of excellent advice.

More than any painter of that honest school, he spoke of simplicity, patience, circumspection, persevering love for truth. His precepts were perhaps the only ones that he had received, certainly they were the only ones that he could transmit. All his originality came from them, and his grandeur also.

With a lively taste for country life, a soul very frank, tranquil, and unbeset by storms, no nerves, a profound and healthy sensibility, an admirable eye, a feeling for proportion, a taste for things clearly defined and well established, he was learned in the equilibrium of forms, understanding the exact relation between quantities, and possessing the instinct of anatomy; finally, he was a constructor of the first order; in everything he showed that virtue which one of the masters of our day calls the probity of talent. He had a native preference for drawing, but such an appetite for perfection, that later he meant to paint well, and had already succeeded in painting excellently; he showed an astonishing division in his labor, an imperturbable coolness in effort, and was of an exquisite nature, to judge from his sad and suffering countenance, — such was this young man, unique in his time, always unique whatever may happen; and thus he appeared from his gropings till he reached his masterpieces.

How rare it is to surprise a genius, sometimes without talent; and what happiness to thus admire an ingenuous being who had only one good fortune at his birth, the love of the true and a passion for the best!

VI.

TERBURG, METZU, AND PIETER DE HOOGH AT THE LOUVRE.

When Holland has not been visited, but the Louvre is well known, is it possible to form a just idea of Dutch art? Certainly it is. With here and there a rare hiatus, — a painter almost wholly wanting, and another whose best works are not present (and this list would be a short one), — the Louvre offers us, concerning the school as a whole, its spirit, its character, its perfections, the diversity of its styles, with one exception, — the Corporation or Regent pictures, — an historical compendium nearly complete, and consequently an inexhaustible fund of study.

Haarlem possesses for its own a painter whom we knew only by name before he was revealed to us, quite recently, by a hearty and very merited favor. This man is Frans Hals; and the tardy enthusiasm of which he is the object would hardly be understood outside of Haarlem and Amsterdam.

Jan Steen is hardly more familiar to us. He is an unattractive spirit who must be visited at home, cultivated near at hand, with whom one must converse often not to be too shocked by his rough sallies and by his licenses. He is, however, less rash than he seems, less coarse than one would believe; very unequal, because he paints at random, after drinking as well as before. In short, it is well to know the value of Jan Steen when he is sober, and the Louvre gives but a very imperfect idea of his temperance and his great talent.

Van de Meer is almost unrepresented in France; and as he has phases of observation strange even in his own country, the journey would not be useless if one desired to be well informed upon this individuality in Dutch art. Apart from these discoveries, and several others of not much importance, there are no very notable ones to be made outside of the Louvre and its annexes, — I mean by that, certain French collections which have the value of a museum in their choiceness of names and in the beauty of their specimens. It might be said that Ruysdael has painted for France, so numerous are his works in that country, and so evident is it that he is enjoyed and respected. To divine the native genius of Paul Potter or the broad power of Cuyp, some effort of induction would be necessary, but it might be accomplished. Hobbema might have confined himself to painting the Mill at the Louvre; and he would certainly gain if he were only known by this masterly page. As to Metzu, Terburg, the two Ostades, and especially Pieter de Hoogh, one might well be content to see them at Paris, and nowhere else.

I have also long believed — and it is an opinion here confirmed — that some one of us would render a great service in writing a Journey through the Louvre, or even less, a Journey through the Salon Carré, or still less, a simple Journey through several pictures, among which would be chosen, I suppose, Metzu's Visit, Terburg's Soldier and Young Woman, and Pieter de Hoogh's Dutch Interior.

Assuredly this would be, without going very far, a curious exploration, and for our day important in instruction. I believe that an enlightened critic who would undertake to reveal all that these three pictures contain would astonish us greatly by the abundance and novelty of his observations. We should be convinced that the most modest work of art might serve as a text for a long analysis, that study is a labor rather in depth than extent, that it is not necessary to enlarge its boundaries to increase its penetrating force, and that very great laws exist in a very little object.

Who has ever defined, in its intimate character, the manner of these three painters, the best, the most learned draughtsmen of their school, at least as regards figures? The German Foot-Soldier of Terburg, for instance, this stout man in his harness, with his cuirass, his doublet of buff, his great sword, his funnel-shaped boots, his felt hat thrown on the ground, his fat face illumined, ill-shaved, and sweaty, with his sleek hair, his little moist eyes, and his large hand dimpled and sensual, offering some pieces of gold, the gesture of which enlightens us sufficiently upon the sentiments of this personage and the object of his visit, — this figure, one of the finest Dutch works that the Louvre owns, what do we know about it? Certainly it has been said that it was lifelike, that the expression was most true, and that the painting was excellent. Excellent is not very conclusive, we must admit, when we want to know the why and wherefore of things. Why excellent? Is it because

Nature is imitated in it in such a way that one seems to surprise her in the very act? Is it because no detail is omitted? Is it because the painting is smooth, simple, clean, limpid, charming to see, easy to understand, and that it is faulty neither from minuteness nor by negligence? How does it happen that since the beginning of the practice of painting figures costumed in their ordinary way, in a fixed attitude, and certainly posing before the painter, no one has ever drawn, modelled, or painted like this?

Where do you perceive the drawing, if not in the result, which is quite extraordinary in its naturalness, truth, breadth, and reality without excess? Can you find a feature, a contour, an accent, a single mark, which denotes the rule or measure? Those shoulders, diminishing in their perspective and curve; that long arm, poised on the thigh, so perfectly within its sleeve; that stout round body, belted high, so exact in its thickness, so vague in its exterior limits; those two supple hands, which, increased to the natural size, would have the astonishing appearance of being modelled, — do you not find that all this is poured at once into a mould which does not at all resemble the angular accents, timid or presumptuous, uncertain or geometrical, in which modern design is ordinarily enclosed?

Our time is rightly honored for possessing observers of merit who draw strongly, delicately, and well. I could cite one who characteristically draws an attitude, a movement, a gesture, a hand with its planes, its bones, its action and contraction, so that for this merit alone — and he has greater ones — he would be incontestably a master in our present school. Compare his sharp, clever, expressive, energetic point to the almost impersonal drawing of Terburg. In the former you perceive formulas, a science thoroughly possessed, an acquired knowledge that comes to the aid of study, supports it, if necessary could supply its place, and which, so to speak, dictates to the eye what it should see and to the mind what it ought to feel. In the latter there is nothing of the kind, but an art which bends itself to the character of things, a knowledge which forgets itself before the individualities of life, nothing preconceived, nothing which takes precedence of the simple, powerful, and sensitive observation of what exists, so that it might be said that the eminent painter * of whom I speak has a design, while it is impossible to perceive at a glance what is that of Terburg, Metzu, or Pieter de Hoogh.

Go from one to the other. After having examined the gallant soldier of Terburg, pass on to this thin personage, a trifle affected in his gravity, of another society, and already of another age, who presents himself with some ceremony, standing and saluting like a person of quality this delicate woman with the thin arms and nervous hands, who receives him in her house without thought of offence. Then stop before the Interior, by Pieter de Hoogh; enter into this deep, stifled picture, so shut up, where the light sifts through, where there is fire, silence, a charming comfort, a lovely mystery; and examine closely the woman with the shining eyes, red lips, dainty teeth, and this great boy, a sort of blockhead, who makes you think of Molière, an emancipated son of M. Diaforus, standing straight upon his spindle legs, awkward in his fine stiff clothes, quite unused to his rapier,

* Meissonier (?). — Tr.

maladroit in his false perpendicular, occupied entirely with what he is doing, so marvellously created that he can never be forgotten. Here, too, is the same hidden knowledge, the same anonymous design, the same incomprehensible mixture of nature and art. Not a shade of preconceived ideas in this expression of things so ingenuously sincere that the formula cannot be grasped, no "*chic*" at all, — which means, in studio phrase, no bad habits, — no ignorance affecting knowing airs, and not one mania.

Make an attempt if you know how to hold a pencil; copy the features of these three figures, try to *put them in their place,* set yourself the difficult task of making from this indecipherable picture an extract which shall contain its drawing. Try to do the same with modern designers, and perhaps, without other information, you will yourself discover, as you succeed with the moderns and fail with the old masters, that there is a whole abyss of art between them.

The same astonishment seizes you when the other parts of this model art are studied. The color, the chiaroscuro, the modelling of the well-filled surfaces, the play of the surrounding air, finally, the workmanship, that is to say, the operations of the hand, — all are perfection and mystery.

Taking the execution superficially alone, do you find that it resembles what has been done since? and do you think that our way of painting has advanced or is behind that? In our days — and should I be the one to say it? — we have one of two things: either a man paints with care, and does not always paint very well; or he puts more cleverness into it, and scarcely paints at all. The work is either heavy and abridged, clever and careless, sensitive and very much shirked, or it is conscientious, thoroughly explained, rendered according to the laws of imitation; and no one, not even those who practise it, would venture to declare that this painting is more perfect on account of its scrupulosity. Each one plies his trade according to his own taste, degree of ignorance or education, the heaviness or subtlety of his nature, according to his moral and physical complexion, his blood, and his nerves. We have execution that is lymphatic, nervous, robust, weak, fiery or orderly, impertinent or timid, simply good, which is called tiresome, or exclusively sensitive, which is called without depth. In short, there are as many styles and formulas as there are individuals, as to drawing, color, and the expression of everything else by the action of the hand.

There are discussions of some vivacity to know which of these so diverse executions is correct. Conscientiously speaking, no one is exactly wrong, but the facts testify that no one is fully right.

The truth which would harmonize us all remains to be demonstrated, and would consist in establishing that painting is a craft to be learned, and consequently can be and ought to be taught, — an elementary method which also can and ought to be transmitted; that this craft and method are as necessary in painting as the art of good expression or good writing is necessary to those who use speech or the pen; that there is no reason why these elements should not be common to us all; that to pretend to be distinguished by the garment, when in person people are undistinguished, is a poor and vain fashion of proving that one is somebody. Formerly it was quite the contrary; and the proof of it is in the perfect unity of the schools, where the same family air belonged to such distinct and lofty personalities. This family air resulted from an education, simple, uniform, well understood, and, as can be seen, extremely salutary. Now, what was this education of which we have not preserved a single trace?

This is what I would wish should be taught, and this I have never heard said from the rostrum, nor in a book, nor in lectures on æsthetics, nor in oral lessons. It would be one way of professional teaching in an epoch when almost all professional teachings are given except this particular one.

Let us not weary of studying together these beautiful models. Look at this flesh, these heads, these hands, these bare throats; remark their suppleness, their amplitude, their truth of coloring almost without color, their compact thin tissue so dense and yet so little loaded. Examine in the same way their appointments, the satins, furs, cloths, velvets, silks, felts, plumes, swords, the gold, the embroideries, the carpets, backgrounds, beds with hangings, the floors so perfectly smooth and so perfectly solid. See how alike all this is in Terburg and Pieter de Hoogh, and yet how everything differs, — how the hand works in the same way, how the coloring has the same elements, and yet how the subject of the latter is enveloped, receding, veiled, profound; how the half-tint transforms, darkens, and makes distant all the parts of this admirable canvas; how it gives to objects their mystery, their spirit, a sense still more moving, a warmer and more inviting intimacy; — while in Terburg, things pass with less concealment, true daylight is everywhere; the bed is hardly hidden by the sombre color of the hangings; the modelling is like nature, firm, full, shaded with simple tones, but slightly transformed, only selected, so that color, execution, evidence of tone, evidence of fact, are all in accord to express that with such people as these there were necessary neither roundabout ways, nor circumlocutions, nor half-tints. And observe that in Pieter de Hoogh as in Metzu, in the most reserved as in the most communicative of these three famous painters, you can always distinguish one part of sentiment, which is their own and is their secret, and another part of method and education received, which is common to them and is the secret of the school.

Do you find that they color well, though one colors principally in gray and the other in brown or dark gold? and do you not decide that their color has more brilliancy than ours, at the same time that it is duller in hue; that it has more richness, though it is more neutral; that it has far more power, while containing much less visible force?

When by chance you perceive in an ancient collection a modern genre picture, even one of the best, and in every relation the most strongly conceived, answer me, is it not something like an *image*, — that is to say, a painting which makes an effort to be colored and is not sufficiently so, to be painted and yet is airy and empty, to have consistency and yet does not attain it always, either by its heaviness when it is thick, or by the enamel of its surfaces when by chance it is thin? On what does this depend? — for it is enough to fill with consternation the men of instinct, sense, and talent, who may be struck with these differences.

Are we much less gifted? Perhaps. Less faithful seekers? Quite the contrary. We are, above all, less well educated.

Suppose that by a miracle which is not sufficiently prayed for, and which, even if it were implored as it should be, will probably not happen in France, a Metzu or a Pieter de Hoogh should be resuscitated among us, what a seed he would cast into the studios, and what rich and generous soil he would find to raise fine painters and good works! Our ignorance then is extreme. It may be said that the art of painting has for a long time been a lost secret, and that the last masters who were at all expert in its practice carried off the key with them. We want it; it is asked for, but no one has it; we seek it, but it is not to be found. Hence it results that individuality of method is, to speak truly, but the effort of each to imagine what he has not learned; that in a certain practical skill we feel the laborious expedients of a mind in difficulties; and that almost always the so-called originality of modern processes conceals at bottom an incurable uneasiness. Do you want me to give you an idea of the investigations of those who are seeking, and the truths which are brought to light after long efforts? I will give but one example.

Our picturesque art, whether historical, genre, landscape, or still-life, has been for some time complicated with a question much in fashion, which merits in fact our attention, for it aims to restore to painting one of its most delicate and most necessary means of expression. I mean to speak of what we have agreed to call *values.*

By this word, of rather vague origin and obscure meaning, is understood the quantity of light or dark which is found contained in a tone. Expressed by drawing and engraving, the shade is easy to seize; such a black will have, in relation to the paper which represents the unity of the light, more value than such a gray. Expressed by color it is not less positively an abstraction, but it is less easy to define. Thanks to a series of observations, of no great profundity, and by an analytical observation familiar to chemists, we separate from any given color that element of light or dark which is combined with its coloring principle, and arrive scientifically at considering a tone under the double aspect of color and value, so that in a violet, for instance, we have not only to estimate the quantity of red or blue which can multiply its shades infinitely, but to keep an account also of the quantity of light or strength which approaches it to the unit of light or the unit of dark.

The interest of the examination is this: a color does not exist in itself, since it is, as is known, modified by the influence of a neighboring color. For still better reasons, it has in itself neither virtue nor beauty. Its quality comes from its surrounding, or what are also called its complementary colors. Thus by contrast or by favorable association very diverse acceptations may be given to it. To color well — I shall say this more particularly elsewhere — is either to know or to feel thoroughly by instinct the necessity of these associations; but to color well is especially and beyond all things to know how to skilfully bring into connection the values of tones. If you take from a Veronese, a Titian, or a Rubens this just relation of values in their colors, you would have only a discordant coloring without force, delicacy, or preciousness. In proportion as the coloring principle diminishes in a tone, the element of values predominates. If it happens, as in the half-tints, where all color grows pale, or as in the pictures of extravagant chiaroscuro, where all shading vanishes, like Rembrandt's for instance, or sometimes where everything is monochromatic, — if it happens, I say, that the coloring element disappears almost entirely, there remains upon the palette a neutral principle, subtle and yet real, the abstract value, it may be called, of the vanished things; and it is with this negative, colorless principle of an infinite delicacy that the rarest pictures are sometimes made.

These things, terrible to announce in French, and the explanation of which is really only permissible in a studio with closed doors, I have been forced to say, because without that I should not have been understood. Now, this law, which we are trying to-day to put in practice, you must not imagine that we have invented; it has been rediscovered, among the much forgotten portions, in the archives of the art of painting. Few painters in France have had a very marked feeling for it. There were whole schools who never thought of it, did without it, and were none the better for that, as has now been discovered. If I were writing the history of French art in the nineteenth century, I would tell you how this law was in turn observed and misunderstood, what painter used it, and who ignored it, and you would find no difficulty in agreeing that he was wrong to ignore it.

An eminent painter, too much admired for his technicalities, who will live, if he does live, by the depth of his sentiment, his very original impulses, a rare instinct for the picturesque, and especially by the tenacity of his efforts, Decamps, never took the trouble to find out there were values on a palette. This is an infirmity which begins to strike people who are well informed, and from which delicate spirits suffer greatly. I will tell you, too, to what sagacious observer contemporaneous landscape painters owe the best lessons that they have received, — how by a charming state of grace Corot, that sincere spirit, a simplifier in his essence, had a natural sentiment for the values in all things, studied them better than any one, established their rules, formulated them in his works, and day by day gave of them more successful demonstrations.

Henceforth this is the principal care of all who are seeking, from those who seek in silence to those who seek most noisily and under eccentric names. The so-called realistic doctrine has no other serious foundation than a more healthy observation of the law of coloring. We must yield to evidence, and recognize that there is something good in these aims, and that if the realists knew more and painted better, there are some of them who would paint exceedingly well. Their eye in general has very just perceptions, their sensations are particularly delicate, and, what is singular, the other parts of their craft are no longer so at all. They have one of the rarest faculties, but they lack what should be the most common, so that their merits, which are great, lose their worth by not being employed as they should be ; they seem to be revolutionary because they affect to admit only half of the necessary truths, and they lack at the same time very little and very much of being perfectly right. All that was the A B C of Dutch art, and ought to be the A B C of ours. I do not know, doctrinally speaking, what was the opinion of Pieter de Hoogh, of Terburg, and of Metzu upon *values*, nor how they called them, nor even if they had a name to express what colors should have of shade, relativeness, sweetness, suavity, or subtlety in their relations. Perhaps coloring as a whole allows all these qualities, whether positive or impalpable. But always the life of their works and the beauty of their art result precisely from the learned use of this principle.

The difference which separates them from modern attempts is this: in their time great value was attached to chiaroscuro, and there was a great feeling for it only because it appeared to be the vital element of all well-conceived art. Without this artifice, in which imagination plays the first part, there was, so to speak, no more fiction in the reproduction of things, and hence the man was absent from his work, or at least participated in it no longer at that moment of the labor when his sensibility should especially intervene. The delicacy of a Metzu, the mystery of a Pieter de Hoogh result, as I have told you, from much atmosphere around the objects, much shadow around the lights, much quietness in the receding colors, many transpositions of tones, many purely imaginary transformations in the aspect of things, — in a word, the most marvellous use that ever was made of chiaroscuro, and also, in other terms, the most judicious application of the law of values.

To-day it is the other way. Every value a little rare, every color delicately observed, seems to have for an aim the abolition of chiaroscuro, and the suppression of the atmosphere. What served to bind now serves to loosen. Every painting called original is a veneering, a mosaic. The abuse of useless roundness has driven into excess flat surfaces, and bodies without thickness. Modelling disappeared the very day when the means of expression seemed best, and ought to have rendered it more intelligent, so that what was a progress among the Hollanders is for us a step backward; and after issuing from archaic art, under pretext of a new innovation, we return thither.

What shall be said about that? Who is there to demonstrate the error into which we are falling? Who shall give us clear and striking lessons? There would be one sure expedient, — the construction of a new work which should contain all the old art with the modern spirit, which, while belonging to the nineteenth century and France, should resemble a Metzu, feature by feature, and yet never permit one to see that he had been remembered.

VII.

RUYSDAEL.

Of all the Dutch painters, Ruysdael is the one who most nobly resembles his country. He has its breadth, its sadness, its rather dreary placidity, and its monotonous and tranquil charm.

With vanishing lines, a severe palette, in two grand traits expressly belonging to its physiognomy, — gray and limitless horizons, and a gray heaven by which the infinite is measured, — he has left us of Holland a portrait which I will not call familiar, but intimate, lovable, admirably faithful, which never grows old. By still other claims Ruysdael is, as I fully believe, the most distinguished figure in the school after Rembrandt, and this is no small glory for a painter who has painted only so-called inanimate landscapes, and not one living being, at least without the aid of some one.

Remember that, taking him in detail, Ruysdael would perhaps be inferior to many of his compatriots. In the first place he is not adroit at a moment and in a style where address was the current money of talent; and perhaps it was owing to this lack of dexterity that he owes the character and the ordinary weight of his thought. Neither is he precisely skilful. He paints well, and affects no singularity in his craft. What he wants to say he says clearly with truth, but as if slowly, without hidden meaning, vivacity or archness. His drawing has not certainly the incisive, sharp character, and the eccentric accent belonging to certain pictures by Hobbema.

I do not forget that at the Louvre, before the Watermill, the floodgate of Hobbema, — a superior work which has not, as I have told you, its equal in Holland, — it has sometimes happened that I have cooled towards Ruysdael. This Mill is so charming a work, — it is so precise, so firm in its construction, so resolute in its method from one end to the other; of such strong, fine coloring; its sky is of so rare a quality; and everything in it seems so delicately engraved before being painted, and so well painted over this severe engraving; finally, to use an expression which will be understood in the studios, it is framed in so piquant a fashion, and *suits the gold so well,* — that sometimes, seeing two paces off the little Bush by Ruysdael, and finding it yellowish, woolly, a little round in treatment, I have almost decided in favor of Hobbema, and thus nearly committed an error which would not have lasted, but which would be unpardonable if it had existed but for an instant.

Ruysdael never knew how to put a figure in his pictures, and in that respect the aptitude of Adrian van de Velde would be very different; nor an animal, and in this Paul Potter would have had great advantage over him, as soon as Paul Potter succeeded in being perfect. He has not the pale golden atmosphere of Cuyp, and the ingenious habit of placing in a bath of light, boats, towns, horses, and riders, all well drawn, as we know, for Cuyp is excellent in all points.

His modelling, although most learned when applied either to vegetation or to aerial surfaces, does not offer the extreme difficulties of the human modelling of Terburg and Metzu. However trained is the sagacity of his eye, it is less so on account of the subjects which he treats. Whatever may be the value of moving water, of a flying cloud, a bushy tree tormented by the wind, a cascade rolling between rocks, — all these things, when one thinks of the complicated character of the undertakings, of the number of the problems, and of their subtlety, are not equal in difficulty of solution to the Intérieur Galant of Terburg, the Visit of Metzu, the Dutch Interior of Pieter de Hoogh, the School and the Family of Van Ostade, that are seen at the Louvre, or the marvellous Metzu of the Van der Hoop Museum, at Amsterdam. Ruysdael shows no liveliness, and also in that respect the sprightly masters of Holland make him appear a little morose.

Considered in his normal habits, he is simple, serious, and robust, very calm and grave, almost habitually the same, to such a degree that his merits end by ceasing to impress, they are so sustained ; and before this mask which seldom is without a frown, before these pictures of almost equal merit, one is sometimes confounded by the beauty of the work, but rarely surprised. Certain marines by Cuyp, for instance the Moonlight in the Six Museum, are works of sudden impulse, absolutely unforeseen, and make us regret that there are not in Ruysdael some outbursts of the same kind. Finally, his color is monotonous, strong, harmonious, and not very rich. It varies from green to brown, and an undertone of bitumen is its basis. It has slight brilliancy, is not always pleasing, and in its first essence is not of very exquisite quality. A painter of refined interiors would not find it difficult to reprove him for the parsimony of his means, and would judge his palette sometimes too limited.

With all that, in spite of everything, Ruysdael is unique; it is easy to be convinced of it at the Louvre, from his Gleam of Sunshine, the Bush, the Tempest, the Little Landscape (No. 474). I except the Forest, which was never very beautiful, and which he compromised by getting Berghem to paint the figures.

At the Retrospective Exhibition held for the benefit of the inhabitants of Alsace-Lorraine, it may be said that Ruysdael reigned manifestly supreme, although the exhibition was most rich in Dutch and Flemish masters; for in it there were specimens of Van Goyen, Wynants, Paul Potter, Cuyp, Van de Velde, Van der Neer, Van der Meer, Hals, Teniers, Bol, Solomon Ruysdael, and two priceless works of Van der Heyden. I appeal to the memory of all those for whom that exhibition of excellent works was a gleam of light, if Jacob Ruysdael was not there remarked as a master, and what is more estimable still, as a great mind. At Brussels, at Antwerp, at the Hague, and Amsterdam, the effect is the same; everywhere that Ruysdael appears, he maintains himself by a manner of his own; he is imposing, he impresses us with respect and attracts attention, which warns us that before us is a man's soul, that this man is of grand race, and that he always has something important to say. Such is the sole cause of Ruysdael's superiority, and this cause suffices; there is in the painter a man who thinks, and in each one of his works a conception. As learned in his way as the most learned of his compatriots, as highly endowed by nature, more thoughtful and more feeling, more than any other he adds to his gifts an equilibrium which makes the unity of the work and the perfection of work. You perceive in his pictures an air of plenitude, certainty, and profound peace, which is his distinctive characteristic, and which proves that not for a single moment has harmony ceased to reign among his fine native faculties, his great experience, his always lively sensibility, and ever present reflectiveness. Ruysdael paints as he thinks, healthily, strongly, largely. The exterior quality of the labor indicates quite plainly the ordinary condition of his mind. There is in this sober, careful, rather proud painting an inexpressible, sad haughtiness, which is recognized from far, and at hand captivates by a charm of natural simplicity and noble familiarity wholly his own. A canvas by Ruysdael is a whole, wherein are felt an arrangement, a comprehensive view, and a master-intention, — the determination to paint once for all one of the features of his country, perhaps also the desire to fix the memory of a moment of his life. A solid foundation; a need of constructing and organizing, of subordinating details to the whole, color to effect, interest in objects to the plane that they occupy; a perfect knowledge of natural and technical laws, and with all that a certain disdain for the useless, the too agreeable, or the superfluous; great taste combined with great good sense; a strong hand calm with the calmly beating heart, — such is nearly what one discovers in analyzing a picture by Ruysdael.

I do not say that everything pales beside this painting of mediocre brilliancy, of discreet coloring, of methods constantly veiled;

but everything becomes disorganized, unconnected, and empty. Place one of Ruysdael's canvases beside the best landscapes of the school, and you will at once see appear, in the neighboring works, gaps, weaknesses, digressions, an absence of design where it is necessary, flashes of cleverness when none are necessary, ill-disguised ignorance, and a fading away which foretells oblivion. Beside Ruysdael a fine Adrian van de Velde is thin, pretty, studied, never very virile nor very mature; a Willem van de Velde is dry, cold, and thin, almost always well drawn, rarely well painted, quickly observed but little meditated. Isaac van Ostade is too red, his skies too insignificant. Van Goyen is too uncertain, volatile, airy, and woolly; one feels in him the light and rapid trace of a fine intention; the sketch is charming; the work did not succeed because it was not substantially nourished by preparatory studies, patience, and labor. Cuyp himself, so strong and so healthy, suffers sensibly from this severe neighbor. His perpetual gold has a gayety of which one tires beside the sombre and bluish verdure of his great rival, and as to that luxury of atmosphere which seems a reflection taken from the South to embellish the pictures of the North, one ceases to believe in it if he knows ever so little the shores of the Meuse and the Zuyder Zee. It can generally be remarked in Dutch pictures — I mean open-air pictures — that there is a determined force in the lights which gives them much relief, and, in painters' language, a particular authority. The sky plays the aerial part, — that which is colorless, infinite, impalpable. Practically it serves to measure the powerful values of the ground, and consequently to designate more sharply and firmly the outline of the subject. Whether this sky be golden, as in Cuyp; silver, as in Van de Velde and Solomon Ruysdael; or fleecy, gray, melting in light washes, as in Isaac van Ostade, Van Goyen, or Wynants, — it makes an opening in the picture, rarely preserves a general value which is its own, and almost always fails to have a decided relation to the gold of the frame. Estimate the strength of the ground, and it is extreme. Try to estimate the value of the sky, and the sky will surprise you by the exceeding light which is its basis.

I could cite to you certain pictures in which the atmosphere is forgotten, and some aerial backgrounds that might be repainted as an afterthought, without the picture, which is otherwise finished, losing anything by the change. Many modern works are in this condition. It can even be remarked, that with some exceptions, which I do not need to signalize if I am well understood, our modern school, as a whole, appears to have adopted for principle that, the atmosphere being the emptiest and most unseizable part of the picture, there is no objection to its being the most colorless and negative.

Ruysdael felt things differently, and fixed once for all a very different principle, both audacious and truthful. He considered the immense vault which arches over the country or the sea as the real, compact, and dense ceiling of his pictures. He curves it, unfolds it, measures it, determines its value by its relation to the accidents of light sown in the terrestrial horizon; he shades its great surfaces, models them, and executes them, in a word, as a work of the greatest interest. He discovers lines in it which continue those of the subject, arranges the masses of color in it, makes the light descend from it, and only puts it there in case of necessity.

His great eye, well opened to observe everything living, — that eye accustomed to the height of objects as well as their extent, — travels constantly from the soil to the zenith, never looks upon an object without observing the corresponding point in the atmosphere, and thus, omitting nothing, makes the circuit of the round field of vision. Far from losing himself in analysis, he constantly employs synthesis and makes abstracts. What nature disseminates, he concentrates into a total of lines, colors, values, and effects. He frames all that in his thought, as he means it to be framed in the four angles of his canvas. His eye has the properties of a camera-obscura; it reduces, diminishes the light, and preserves things in the exact proportion of their forms and colors. A picture by Ruysdael, whatever it may be, — the finest are, of course, the most significant, — is an entire painting, full and strong, in its principle grayish above, brown or greenish below, which rests solidly with its four corners upon the shining flutings of the frame; it seems dark at a distance, but is penetrated with light when approached; it is beautiful in itself, with no vacancy, with few digressions, like a lofty and sustained thought which has for language a tongue of the most powerful kind.

I have heard it said that nothing was more difficult to copy than a picture by Ruysdael, and I believe it, — just as nothing is more difficult to imitate than the manner of expression of the great writers of our seventeenth century in France. Here we have the same turns, the same styles, something of the same spirit, I had almost said the same genius. I do not know why I imagine that if Ruysdael had not been a Hollander and a Protestant, he would have been a Port-Royalist.

You will notice at the Hague and Amsterdam two landscapes which are the repetition of the same subject, one large, the other small. Is the little canvas the study which served for a text for the larger one? Did Ruysdael draw or paint from nature? Was he inspired, or did he copy directly? That is his secret, as it is of most of the Dutch masters, except perhaps Van de Velde, who certainly painted out of doors, excelled in direct studies, and in the studio lost much of his skill, whatever people may say. But it is certain that these two works are charming, and demonstrate what I have been saying about Ruysdael's habits. It is a view taken at some distance from Amsterdam, with the little city of Haarlem, dark and bluish, visible through the trees, under the vast rolling waves of a cloudy sky, in the rainy dimness of a low horizon; in front, for the foreground, is a laundry with red roofs, and the bleaching linen spread out flat over the fields. Nothing could be simpler or poorer than this point of departure, but nothing either could be more true. This canvas, one foot eight inches high, ought to be seen to learn, from a master who never feared to degrade himself because he was not a man to stoop, how a subject can be elevated when a man is himself a lofty spirit, — to learn that there is nothing ugly for an eye which sees beauty, no littleness for a great sensitiveness, — to learn, in a word, what the art of painting becomes when practised by a noble mind.

The River View, in the Van der Hoop Museum, is the highest expression of this haughty and magnificent manner. This picture would be better named the Windmill, and under this title no one would be able to treat without disadvantage a subject which in the hands of Ruysdael has found its incomparable typical expression.

Briefly, this is the rendering. A part of the Meuse probably; on the right, terraced ground with trees and houses, and on the summit the black mill with wide-spread arms, rising high in the canvas; a palisade against which the water of the river softly undulates, — a sluggish water, soft and admirable; a little corner of a vague horizon, very slight and very firm, very pale and very distinct, on which rises the white sail of a boat, — a flat sail with no wind in its canvas, of a soft and perfectly exquisite value. Above it a wide sky loaded with clouds, with openings of pale blue, gray clouds scaling to the top of the canvas, — no light, so to speak, anywhere in this powerful tone, composed of dark browns and dark-slate colors, but a single gleam in the middle of the picture, which comes from the far distance, like a smile, to illumine the disk of a cloud. It is a great square picture, *grave* (we need not fear to make too great use of this word with Ruysdael), of extreme sonorousness in the lowest register, and, as my notes add, *marvellous in the gold.* In fact, I describe it and insist upon it only to arrive at this conclusion, — beyond the value of the details, the beauty of form, the grandeur of expression, the intimate nature of its sentiment, it is a task singularly impressive to consider it as a simple decoration.

All Ruysdael is here, — his noble way of working, little charm, except by chance, a great attractiveness, an inwardness which is revealed little by little, accomplished science, very simple means. Imagine him in conformity with his painting, try to represent him to yourself beside his picture, and if I am not mistaken you will have the double and very harmonious image of an austere dreamer, of warm heart, and laconic and taciturn spirit.

I have read somewhere, so evident is it that a poet reveals himself through all the restraints of form and in spite of the conciseness of his language, that his work had the character of an elegiac poem in an infinity of songs. This is much to say when we think how little relation literature bears to this art, in which technicalities have so much importance, and where matter has such weight and value.

Elegiac or not, but surely a poet, if Ruysdael had written instead of painted, I think he would have written in prose instead of verse. Verse admits of too much fancy and stratagem, prose compels too great sincerity, for this clear mind not to have preferred its language to the other. As to the depths of his nature, he was a dreamer, — one of those men of whom there are many in our time, though they were rare at the epoch in which Ruysdael was born, — one of those *solitary ramblers* who fly from towns, frequent the suburbs, sincerely love the country, feel it without emphasis, relate it without phrasing, who are made restless by far-off horizons, charmed by level expanses, affected by a shadow, and enchanted by a gleam of sunshine.

We imagine Ruysdael neither very young nor very old; we do not see that he had a period of youth, nor do we feel in him the enfeebling weight of advancing years. If we did not know that he died before the age of fifty-two years, we should imagine him between two ages, as a mature man or one of precocious maturity, very serious, master of himself early, with sad memories, regrets, and the reveries of a mind which looks back, whose youth has not known the overwhelming unrest of hope. I believe he had no heart to cry, "Rise! longed-for storms!" His melancholy, of which he is full, has something manly and reasonable, in which appears neither the tumultuous childishness of early years nor the nervous tearfulness of later ones; it only tinges his painting with a sombre hue, as it would have tinged the thought of a Jansenist.

What has life done for him that he should have for it a sentiment so bitter and disdainful? What have men done to him that he should retire into deep solitude, and so avoid meeting them, even in his painting? Nothing or almost nothing is known of his existence except that he was born about 1630, that he died in 1681; that he was the friend of Berghem; that he had Solomon Ruysdael for an elder brother, and probably for his first adviser. As to his journeys, they are supposed and they are doubted; his cascades, mountain regions well wooded, with rocky declivities, would lead one to believe either that he must have studied in Germany, Switzerland, or Norway, or that he utilized the studies of Everdingen,* and was inspired by them. His great labor did not enrich him, and

* A fine painter of Norwegian scenery. Alkmaar, 1621–1675.

his title of burgher of Haarlem did not prevent him, it appears, from being almost forgotten.

Of this we should have a truly harrowing proof, if it is true that, in commiseration of his distress, more than from respect to his genius, which was hardly suspected by any one, they were obliged to admit him to the hospital at Haarlem, his native town, and that there he died. But before reaching this point what happened to him? Had he joys as he certainly had bitterness? Did his destiny give him an opportunity to love anything but clouds; and from what did he suffer most, if he did suffer, — from the torment of painting well or of living? All these questions remain without answer, and yet posterity would be glad to know.

Would you ever think of asking as much about Berghem, Karel Dujardin, Wouvermans, Goyen, Terburg, Metzu, Pieter de Hoogh himself? All these brilliant or charming painters painted, and it seems as if that was enough. Ruysdael painted; but he lived, and this is why it would be of so much importance to know how he lived. In the Dutch School I know but three or four men whose personality is thus interesting, — Rembrandt, Ruysdael, Paul Potter, perhaps Cuyp, — and this is already more than is necessary to class them.

VIII.

CUYP.

Cuyp also was not much recognized during his life, which did not prevent him from painting as he understood the business, applying himself or being negligent quite at his ease, and following his free career according to the inspiration of the moment. Besides, he shared this disfavor, natural enough when one thinks of the taste which reigned at that time for extreme finish, with Ruysdael; he shared it even with Rembrandt, when about 1650 Rembrandt suddenly ceased to be understood. He was, as may be seen, in good company. Since then he has been avenged, first by the English, afterwards by all Europe. In any case, Cuyp is a very beautiful painter.

In the first place, he has the merit of universality. His work is so complete a repertory of Dutch life, especially in its rural surroundings, that its extent and variety would suffice to give it considerable interest. Landscapes, marines, horses, cattle, people of every condition, from men of fortune and leisure to shepherds, small and large figures, portraits, and pictures of poultry yards, — such are the curiosities and aptitudes of his talent that he more than any other has contributed to enlarge the list of local observations in which the art of his country was displayed. Born, one of the first in 1605, belonging to his age in every respect, — by the diversity of his investigations, by the vigor and independence of his way of proceeding, — he must have been one of the most active promoters of the school.

A painter who on one side touches Hondekoeter, and on the other Ferdinand Bol, and who without imitating Rembrandt paints animals as easily as Van de Velde, skies better than Both, horses, and great horses, more severely than Wouvermans or Berghem painted their little ones; who feels the sea keenly, as well as rivers and their banks; who paints cities, boats at anchor, and great maritime scenes, with a breadth and authority that William Van de Velde did not possess, — a painter who, moreover, had a manner of his own of seeing, an appropriate and very beautiful coloring, an easy, powerful hand, a taste for rich, thick, abundant stuffs, — a man who expands, grows, renews himself, and is fortified by age, — such a person is a very great man. If it is remembered, beside, that he lived until 1691; that he thus survived the greater part of those whom he had seen born; and that during that long career of eighty-six years, with the exception of a trace of his father very strongly marked in his works, and afterwards a reflection of the Italian sky which came to him perhaps from the Boths and his friends the travellers, he remains himself, without alloy, without admixture, moreover without signs of weakness, — we must admit that he had a very powerful brain.

If our Louvre gives a tolerably complete idea of the diverse forms of his talent, his manner, and his coloring, it does not give his full measure, and does not mark the point of perfection that he could attain, and which he sometimes did attain.

His great landscape is a beautiful work, which is more valuable as a whole than in its details. No one could go farther in the art of painting light, of rendering the pleasing and restful sensations with which a warm atmosphere envelops and penetrates one. It is a picture. It is true without being too true; it shows observation without being a copy. The air that bathes it, the amber warmth with which it is soaked, that gold which is but a veil, those colors which are only the result of the light which inundates them, of the air which circulates around, and of the sentiment of the painter which transforms them, those values so tender in a whole which is so strong, — all these things come both from nature and from a conception; it would be a masterpiece if there had not slipped into it some insufficiencies which seem the work of a young man or of an absent-minded designer.

His Départ pour la Promenade, and the Promenade, two equestrian pictures of beautiful form and noble workmanship, are also full of his finest qualities, — all bathed in sunlight, and steeped in those golden waves which are, as it were, the ordinary color of his mind.

However, he has done better, and we are indebted to him for even rarer things. I do not speak of those little pictures, too much boasted of, which have been shown at different times in our French Retrospective exhibitions. Without leaving France, there may have been seen, in sales of private collections, works of Cuyp, not more delicate, but more powerful and profound. A true, fine Cuyp is a painting at once subtile and gross, tender and robust, aerial and massive. That which belongs to the impalpable, as the background, the surroundings, the shadows, the effect of the air upon the distances, and broad daylight upon the colors, all corresponds to the lighter parts of his mind; and to render it his palette becomes volatile, and his art grows supple. As to the objects of more solid substance, of more defined contours, of more evident and consistent color, he does not fear to enlarge planes, to fill out forms, to insist upon robust features, and to be a little heavy, in order never to be weak in touch, tone, or execution. In such a case he is no longer refined, and, like all the good masters at the beginning of strong schools, it costs him nothing to be wanting in charm when the charm is not the essential character of the object he represents. This is why the Cavalcades at the Louvre are not, to my idea, the highest expression of his fine sober manner, — a little gross and abundant, but wholly masculine. There is in them an excess of gilding, of sun, and of all that follows, — redness, gleams, reflections, shadows cast. Add to these an inexpressible mingling of open air and studio light, of textual truth and of combinations, finally, something improbable in the costumes and suspicious in the elegance, and it results that in spite of exceptional merits these two pictures are not absolutely satisfactory.

The Hague Museum has a Portrait of the Sire de Roover, directing the salmon-fishing in the neighborhood of Dordrecht, which reproduces with less brilliancy and still more manifest defects the mannerism of the two celebrated pictures of which I speak. The figure is one of those we know. He is in a deep scarlet gown embroidered with gold, bordered with fur, wearing a black cap with red plumes, and a short sword with a gilded handle. He bestrides one of those great brown bay horses, whose arching head, rather heavy body, stiff legs, and mule hoofs we know of old. There is the same golden tint in the sky, in the background, on the waters, on the faces; the same too distinct reflections, that are seen in a vivid light when the atmosphere modifies neither the color nor the exterior edge of objects. The picture is simple and well set, ingeniously planned, original, personal, full of conviction; but, from the force of truth, the excess of light makes one believe in errors of knowledge and taste.

Now see Cuyp at Amsterdam in the Six Museum, and consult the two great canvases which figure in this unique collection.

One represents the Arrival of Maurice of Nassau at Scheveningen. It is an important marine work with boats loaded with figures. Neither Backhuysen, do I need to say? nor Van de Velde, nor any one, would have had the power to construct, conceive, or color in this way a showy picture of this kind and of such insignificance. The first boat, on the left, opposite the light, is an admirable bit.

As to the second picture, the very famous effect of moonlight on the sea, I copy from my notes the succinctly formulated trace of the surprise and pleasure that it caused me. "A wonder and a marvel; large, square; the sea, a rugged coast, a boat on the right, in front a fishing-boat with a figure spotted with red, on the left two sail-boats, no wind, a tranquil serene night, the water quite calm, the full moon half-way up the picture a little to the left, absolutely clear in a large opening of cloudless sky; the whole incomparably true and fine in color, force, transparency, and limpidity. A night Claude Lorraine, graver, simpler, fuller, more naturally executed from a true sensation, a veritable deceit of the eye (*trompe l'œil*) by the most cultivated art.

As may be seen, Cuyp succeeds in each new enterprise; and if one undertook to follow him, I do not say in his variations, but in the variety of his attempts, it would be perceived that in every kind of art he has excelled at times, if only for once, all those of his contemporaries who shared around him the so singularly extended domain of his art. It would have needed great lack of comprehension, or very little self-knowledge, to paint after him a Moonlight, a Disembarkation of a Prince in grand naval array, or Dordrecht and its Environs. What he has said is said, because he has expressed it in his own manner, and his manner upon a given subject is worth all the others. He has the method of a master, and a master's eye. He has created—and that suffices in art—a wholly personal, fictitious formula of light and its effects. He has had the very uncommon power of imagining, first, an atmosphere, and then making of it not only the flying, fluid element that can be breathed, but the law, and, as it were, the regulating principle of his pictures. It is by this sign that he is recognizable. If it is not perceived that he has influenced his school, with still more reason one can be assured that he has undergone the influence of no one. He is alone; various, but himself.

However, — for, according to my idea, there is an *however* with this fine painter, — he is wanting in that something which makes the indispensable masters. He has practised all kinds of art in a superior manner, but he has created neither a kind nor an art; he does not personify in his name a complete way of seeing, feeling, and painting, — as we say, "It is like Rembrandt, Paul Potter, Ruysdael." He reaches a very high rank, but certainly in the fourth line, in that just classing of talents where Rembrandt is throned apart, where Ruysdael is first. If Cuyp were absent, the Dutch School would lose superb works, but perhaps there would be no great void to fill in the inventions of the art of Holland.

IX.

THE INFLUENCE OF HOLLAND UPON FRENCH LANDSCAPE.

One question presents itself, among many others, when Dutch landscape is studied, and the corresponding movement that took place in France about forty-five years ago is remembered. One asks himself, what was the influence of Holland upon this novelty; if it acted upon us, how, in what measure, and at what moment; what it could teach us; finally, for what reason, without ceasing to please, it has ceased to instruct us. This very interesting question never has been, so far as I know, studied to the purpose, and I shall not attempt to treat it. It touches matters too near us, our contemporaries, living artists. It may easily be understood that I should not be at my ease; but I would like simply to express its terms.

It is clear that for two centuries we had in France but one landscape painter, Claude Lorraine. This very great painter — very French, though very Roman; a true poet, but with much of that clear good sense which for a long time has produced doubts as to whether we were a race of poets; good-natured enough at bottom, though solemn — is, with more naturalness and less purpose, the match, in his style, to Poussin in historical painting. His painting is an art which marvellously well represents the value of our mind, the aptitudes of our eye; it does us honor, and will one day become one of the classic arts. It is consulted, admired, but not used; we especially do not confine ourselves to it, nor return to it, any more than we return to the art of *Esther* and *Bérénice.*

The eighteenth century occupied itself very little with landscape, except to introduce into it gallantries, masquerades, festivals, so-called rural or amusing mythologies. The whole school of David visibly disdained it, and neither Valenciennes,* nor Bertin,† nor their successors in our time, were of a humor to make it attractive. They sincerely adored Virgil, and also nature; but in truth it may be said that they had a delicate sense of neither one nor the other. They were Latin scholars who nobly scanned hexameters, painters who saw things in an amphitheatre, rounded a tree pompously, and gave the detail of a leaf. At bottom they perhaps enjoyed Delille ‡ better than Virgil, made some good studies, and painted badly. With much more mind than they, with fancy and real gifts, the elder Vernet, § whom I had nearly forgotten, is not what I should call a very penetrating landscape painter, and I will class him, before Hubert Robert, || but with him, among the good decorators of mu-

* A French landscape painter, pupil of Doyen. Toulouse, 1750–1819. — TR.

† The painter employed by Louis XIV. at the Trianon. Member of the Academy at Paris, 1667–1736. — TR.

‡ Jacques Delille, a didactic poet, member of the French Academy, 1738–1813, who enjoyed an immense reputation at the end of the last century, and under the Empire. — TR.

§ Claude Joseph Vernet, an eminent French marine painter, 1714–1789. He was commissioned by Louis XV. to paint the seaports of France, and fifteen of these pictures are now in the Louvre. He was the grandfather of Horace Vernet. — TR.

|| Hubert Robert, architectural and landscape painter. Paris, 1733–1808. — TR.

seums and royal vestibules. I do not speak of Demarne,* half Frenchman, half Fleming, about whom Belgium and France have no desire to warmly dispute; and I think I could omit Lantara † without great harm to French painting.

It was necessary for the school of David to be at the end of its credit, for everything to have run short, and for people to be ready to reverse everything as a nation does when it changes its taste, in order to see appear at the same time, in letters and the arts, a sincere passion for rural things.

The awakening began with the prose writers; from 1816 to 1825 it passed into verse; finally, from 1824 to 1830, the painters became aware of it and began to follow. The first impulse came to us from English painting, and consequently, when Géricault and Bonington acclimated in France the painting of Constable and Gainsborough, it was at first an Anglo-Flemish influence that prevailed. The coloring of Vandyck in the backgrounds of portraits, the audacity and the fantastic palette of Rubens, are what served to release us from the coldness and conventionalities of the preceding school. The palette gained much thereby, poetry lost nothing, but truth was but half satisfied with the result.

Remark that at the same time, in consequence of a love of the marvellous which corresponded to the literary fashion of ballads and legends, and to the rather rosy color of the imaginations of those

* J. L. Demarne, a Flemish painter, pupil of Nicasius. Brussels, 1752; Paris, 1829.

† Simon Mathurin Lantara, a celebrated landscape painter, born near Montargis, 1745; died 1778. He excelled in moonlights and sunsets.

days, the first Hollander who whispered in the ear of the painters was Rembrandt. In a visible state or in a latent state, a little of the Rembrandt of warm mists is everywhere, at the beginning of our modern school; and it is precisely because Rubens and Rembrandt were vaguely felt to be hidden behind the scenes, that what was called the Romantic School was received with doubtful enthusiasm when it came upon the stage.

About 1828 there was a new life. Some very young men — there were even children among them — exhibited one day some very small pictures that were at once found eccentric and charming. Of those eminent painters I will name only two who are dead; or rather I will name them all, saving my right to speak only of those who can no longer hear me. The masters of French contemporary landscape presented themselves together; they were Messieurs Flers, Cabat, Dupré, Rousseau, and Corot.

Where were they formed? Whence did they come? What drove them to the Louvre rather than elsewhere? Who led them, some to Italy, and others to Normandy? One might really think, so uncertain is their origin, their talents being to all appearance fortuitous, that we find in them the painters who disappeared two centuries before, whose history has never been well known.

However it may be with the education of those children of Paris, born upon the quays of the Seine, formed in the suburbs, learning one can hardly say how; two things appeared at the same time in them, — landscapes simply and truly rustic, and Dutch formulas. This time Holland found the right hearers; she taught us to see, to feel, and to paint. Such was the surprise, that the intimate originality of the discoveries was not too closely examined. The invention seemed as new in all points as fortunate. People admired; and the same day Ruysdael entered France, a little hidden for the time being behind the glory of these young men. At the same moment it was discovered that there was a French country, a French landscape art, and museums with old pictures that could teach us something.

Two of the men of whom I speak remained nearly faithful to their first affections, or if they wandered from them for a moment, it was but to return at last. Corot detached himself from them from the beginning. The road he followed is known. He cultivated Italy early, and brought back from it something that was indelible. He was more lyrical, equally rural, less rustic. He loved woods and waters, but differently. He invented a style; he employed less exactitude in seeing things than subtlety in seizing what he could extract from them, and what might be separated from them. Hence his quite individual mythology and his paganism so ingeniously natural, which was in its rather vapory form only the personification of the very spirit of things. Nothing can be less Dutch.

As to Rousseau, a complex artist, much reviled and much renowned, very difficult to be defined with propriety, the most truthful thing that can be said is that he represents, in his beautiful and exemplary career, the efforts of the French mind to create in France a new Dutch art; I mean an art as perfect while being national, as precise while more various, and as dogmatic while more modern.

From his date and his rank in the history of our school, Rousseau is an intermediary man, a transition between Holland and the painters to come. He derives something from the Dutch painters, and separates from them. He admires them, and forgets them. In the past he gives them one hand, but with the other he excites and calls to himself a whole current of ardor and good-will. In nature he discovers a thousand unwritten things. The repertory of his sensations is immense. Every season, every hour of the day, the evening and the dawn; all the varieties of weather, from the winter frosts to the dog-day heats; every altitude, from the beaches to the hills, from the plains to Mont Blanc; villages, fields, copses, forests, the naked land and all its cover of foliage, — there is nothing which has not tempted him, arrested him, convinced him of its interest, persuaded him to paint it. It might be said that the Dutch painters had only revolved around themselves, when they are compared to the ardent explorations of this seeker of new impressions. All of them could have had their careers, with an abridgment of the drawings of Rousseau. In this point of view he is absolutely original, and in that very thing he belongs to his own time. Once plunged into the study of the relative, the accidental, and the true, one must go to the very end. Not wholly, but almost entirely alone, he contributed to create a school that might be called the School of Sensations.

If I were studying intimately our school of contemporary landscape, instead of sketching some of its wholly characteristic traits, I should have other names to join to the preceding. In this, as in all schools, would be seen contradictions, countercurrents, academic traditions, which continue to filter through the vast movement which is leading us to the truly natural; the memories of Poussin, the influences of Claude, the Spirit of Synthesis pursuing its work among the multitude of analytical works and artless observations. There might be noticed, also, salient individualities, which, although held in subjection, repeat the great men without resembling them too closely, and make side discoveries without appearing to discover. Finally, I could cite names which are an infinite honor to us; and I should take care not to except an ingenious, brilliant, multiform painter,* who has treated a thousand things, fancy, mythology, landscape, — who has loved the country and old paintings, Rembrandt and Watteau, — who has particularly loved Correggio, and passionately the coppices of Fontainebleau, and above all, perhaps, the combinations of a slightly chimerical palette, — the one who, among all contemporary painters (and this is indeed an honor), first divined Rousseau, understood him, caused him to be understood, proclaimed him a master and his master, and placed at the service of this inflexible originality his more supple talent, his better understood originality, his accepted influence, and his well-won renown.

What I desire to show, and that will suffice here, is that from the first day the impulse given by the Dutch School and Ruysdael, the direct impulse, stopped short, or was turned aside; and that two men especially contributed to substitute the exclusive study of nature for the study of the masters of the North, — Corot, who had no union

* Diaz. — Tr.

with them, and Rousseau, who had a livelier affection for their works, a more exact remembrance of their methods, but had also an imperious desire to see more, to see differently, and to express everything which had escaped them. The result was two consequent and parallel facts, — studies subtler if not better made, and methods more complicated if not more learned.

What Jean Jacques Rousseau, Bernardin de Saint Pierre, Chateaubriand, and Sénancour, our first landscape masters in literature, observed at a glance, expressed in brief formulas, will be only a very incomplete abridgment, and a very limited survey on the day when literature shall become purely descriptive. In the same way the needs of travelling, analytical, and imitative painting found themselves greatly straitened in foreign styles and methods. The eye became more curious and precise; sensitiveness, without being more lively, became more nervous; drawing penetrated farther; observations were multiplied; nature, more closely studied, swarmed with details, incidents, effects, and shades; a thousand secrets were demanded of her, that she had kept to herself either because no one had known how or because no one had wished to interrogate her profoundly on all these points. A language was necessary to express this multitude of new sensations; and it was Rousseau almost alone who invented the vocabulary we employ to-day. In his sketches and rough draughts and in his finished works you will perceive trials, efforts, inventions, successful or unsuccessful, excellent neologisms, or phrases hazarded, with which this profound seeker of formulas sought to enrich the ancient language and the ancient grammar of the painters. If you take one of his pictures, the best, and place it beside a picture by Ruysdael, Hobbema, or Wynants, of the same order and the same acceptation, you will be struck by the differences, almost as much as if you read, one after the other, a page of a modern descriptive writer, after having read a page of the *Confessions* or of *Obermann.* There is the same effort, the same increase of studies, and the same result in the work. The terms are more characteristic, the observation more uncommon, the palette infinitely more rich, the color more expressive, even the construction more scrupulous. All seems to be more felt, everything is more thoughtful, more scientifically reasoned and calculated. A Hollander would gape with wonder at such scrupulousness, and be stupefied by such analytical faculties. And yet are these works better, more powerfully inspired? Are they more living? When Rousseau represents a White Frost on the Plain, is he nearer the truth than are Ostade and Van de Velde with their Skaters? When Rousseau paints a Trout-Fishing, is he graver, moister, more shady, than is Ruysdael with his sleeping waters and his sombre cascades?

A thousand times there have been described, in voyages, romances, or in poems, the waters of a lake beating upon a deserted beach, at night when the moon is rising, while a nightingale is singing afar off. Did not Sénancour sketch this picture once for all in a few grave, brief, and ardent lines? A new art was born then on the same day under the double form of book and picture, with the same tendencies, with artists endowed with the same spirit, and with the same audience to enjoy them. Was it a progress, or the contrary? Posterity will decide upon it better than we can.

What is positive is, that in twenty or twenty-five years, from 1830 to 1855, the French School had made great attempts, had produced enormously, and had greatly advanced matters, since, starting from Ruysdael with his Windmills, Flood Gates, and Bushes, — that is to say, from a very Dutch sentiment expressed in wholly Dutch formulas, — it had reached the point on one side of creating an exclusively French style with Corot, and on the other side of preparing through Rousseau the future of an art still more universal. Did it stop there? Not entirely.

Love of home has never been, even in Holland, anything but an exceptional sentiment and a slightly singular habit. In all epochs have been found people whose feet burned to go to some new place. The tradition of journeys to Italy is perhaps the sole one common to all the schools, whether Flemish, Dutch, English, French, German, or Spanish. From Both, Berghem, Claude, and Poussin to the painters of our day, there have been no landscape painters who have not longed to see the Apennines and the Roman Campagna, and there never has been a school local enough to prevent Italian landscape from introducing into it that foreign flower which has never borne anything but hybrid fruit. In the last thirty years people have gone much farther. Distant journeys have tempted the painters, and changed many things in painting. The motive for these adventurous excursions was at first that need of new ground proper to all populations grown to excess in one spot, a curiosity for discoveries, and a sort of necessity of changing place in order to invent. It was also the consequence of certain scientific studies whose progress was obtained only by travels around the globe, among climates and races. The result was the style you are familiar with, — a cosmopolitan painting, rather novel than original, very slightly French, which will represent in our history (if history remarks upon it at all) but a moment of curiosity, uncertainty, and unrest, which is really only a change of air tried by people in not very good health.

However, without leaving France, we continue to seek for landscape a more decided form. It would be a curious work to record this latent elaboration, so slow and confused, of a new fashion which has not been discovered, which is even very far from being found; and I am astonished that criticism has not more closely studied this fact at the very time when it was being accomplished under our eyes.

A certain unclassing seems to be operating to-day among painters. There are fewer categories, I would willingly say castes, than there were formerly. History borders on genre, which itself borders on landscape and even on still life. Many boundaries have disappeared. How many new relations the picturesque has brought about! Less stiffness on one side, more boldness on the other, less huge canvases, the need of pleasing, and pleasing one's self, country life which opens so many eyes, — all this has mingled styles and transformed methods. It would be impossible to say up to what point the broad daylight of the fields, entering the most austere studios, has there produced conversions and confusions.

Landscape makes every day more proselytes than progress. Those who practise it exclusively are not more skilful on that account, but there are more painters who try it. *Open air*, diffused light, *the real sunlight*, take to-day in painting, and in all paintings, an importance which has never before been recognized, and which, let us say it frankly, they do not deserve.

All the fancies of the imagination, and what were called the mysteries of the palette at a time when mystery was one of the attractions of painting, give place to the love of the absolute textual truth. Photographic studies as to the effects of light have changed the greater proportion of ways of seeing, feeling, and painting. At this present time painting is never sufficiently clear, sharp, formal, and crude. It seems as if the mechanical reproduction of what is, becomes to-day the highest expression of experience and knowledge, and that talent consists in struggling for exactitude, precision, and imitative force with an instrument. All personal interference of sensibility is out of place. What the mind has imagined, is considered an artifice; and all artifice, that is, all conventionality, is proscribed by an art which can be nothing but conventional. Hence the controversies in which the pupils of nature have numbers on their side. There are even scornful appellations to designate contrary practices. They are called *the old game*, as much as to say, an antiquated, doting, and superannuated fashion of comprehending nature by introducing one's own into it. Choice of subject, drawing, palette, everything participates in this impersonal manner of seeing and treating things. We are far from the ancient customs; I mean, the customs of forty years ago, when bitumen rippled in streams upon the palettes of the Romantic painters, and passed for the auxiliary color of the ideal.

Every year there is a time and a place where these new fashions proclaim themselves with boldness, — that is, at our spring exhibition. If you keep yourself at all familiar with the novelties there produced, you will remark that the most recent painting aims at striking the eye by salient, textual pictures, easily recognizable by their truth and absence of artifice, and also giving us exactly the sensations produced by what we could see in the street, while the public is quite disposed to applaud an art which represents with so much fidelity its habits, its face, its clothes, its taste, its inclination, and its mind. But, you will say, the historical painter? In the first place, in the way things are going, is it quite certain that an historical school still exists? Finally, if this appellation of old fashion is applied still to traditions brilliantly defended, but very little followed, do not imagine that the historical painters escape the fusion of styles and resist the temptation of entering themselves into the current. They hesitate, they have some scruples, but finally they launch themselves in it. Look from year to year at the conversions that occur, and without examining profoundly, consider the color of the pictures alone; if from dark they become light, if from black they become white, if from deep they become superficial, if from supple they become stiff, if oily matter turns to thick impasto, and chiaroscuro into Japanese paper, you have seen enough to learn that there is a spirit which has changed its surroundings, and a studio which is open to light from the street. If I did not conduct this analysis with extreme caution, I would be more explicit and would make you touch with your finger undeniable truths.

The conclusion I wish to draw is that in the latent state, as in the state of professional studies, landscape has invaded everything, and, what is singular, while waiting for its own formula, it has overthrown all formulas, troubled many clear minds, and compromised some talents. It is none the less true that it is labored for; that the attempts undertaken are for its profit; and that to excuse the harm that it has done to painting in general, it would be desirable at least that it should gain something itself.

In the midst of changing fashions there is, however, a sort of continuous thread of art. You can, in passing through the rooms at our exhibitions, perceive here and there pictures which impress by a breadth, a gravity, a powerful gamut, an interpretation of effects and things, where are felt almost the palette of a master. There are in them neither figures nor ornaments of any sort. Grace is wholly absent from them, but the rendering is strong, the color deep and grave, the material thick and rich, and sometimes a great subtlety of eye and hand is concealed under the wilful negligences or the slightly displeasing brutalities of the art. The painter* of whom I speak, whom I would be glad to name, joins to true love of the country a not less evident love of old painting and the old masters. His pictures prove it; his etchings and drawings are also of a nature to testify to it. Is not this the hyphen which attaches us still to the schools of the Netherlands? In any case it is the sole corner

* Jules Dupré.—Tr.

of French painting of the present day where their influence is still suspected.

I know not which of the Dutch painters is most valued in the laborious studio that I indicate. And I am not very certain that at present Van der Meer, of Delft, is not more heeded there than Ruysdael. One would think so from a certain disdain for drawing, for delicate and difficult constructions, and for care in rendering, that the Amsterdam master would neither have counselled nor approved. But it is certain that there is present the living and present remembrance of an art everywhere else forgotten.

This ardent and powerful touch is of good augury. There is no well-informed mind that does not feel that it comes in a quite direct line from the country where above all others they knew how to paint, and that, by following it with some persistency, modern painting will have a chance of finding its lost way. I should not be surprised if Holland rendered us still another service, and after having restored to us the literature of nature, some day or other, after long circuits, she should bring back nature to our painting. To this we must come sooner or later. Our school knows a great deal; it is exhausted with wandering; its store of studies is considerable; it is even so rich that it is satisfied with them, forgets itself in them, and spends in collecting documents the forces that it would better employ by making use of them in production.

There is a time for everything, and the day when painters and men of taste shall be persuaded that the best studies in the world are not worth one good picture, the public mind will have made one more revolution, which is the surest way of making progress.

X.

THE ANATOMICAL LECTURE.

I AM very much tempted to be silent about the Anatomical Lecture. It is a picture that one ought to find very fine, absolutely original, almost perfect, under penalty of committing in the eyes of many sincere admirers an error in propriety and good sense. I regret to make the avowal that it has left me unmoved. And having said that, it is necessary that I should explain myself, or, if you will, that I should justify myself.

Historically, the Anatomical Lecture is of great interest, for it is known that it is derived from analogous pictures, lost or preserved, and thus bears witness of the way in which a man with a great destiny appropriates the attempts of his predecessors. In this regard it is an example, not less celebrated than many others, of the law that a man has a right to take his own wherever he may find it, when that man is Shakespeare, Rotrou, Corneille, Calderon, Molière, or Rembrandt. Note that in this list of inventors for whom the past labors, I cite but one painter, and I might cite them all. Finally, by its date in the work of Rembrandt, by its spirit, and by its merits, it shows the road that he had passed over since the uncertain gropings that are revealed by the two overestimated canvases at the Hague Museum. I speak of the St. Simeon and a Portrait of a Young Man, which appears to me to be evidently his, and which in any case is the portrait of a child made with some timidity by a child.

When it is remembered that Rembrandt was a pupil of Pinas and of Lastman, if one has seen a work or two of the latter, it seems to me that the novelties that Rembrandt showed in the beginning become less surprising. To tell the truth, and to speak wisely, neither in inventions, nor subjects, nor in the picturesque marriage of small figures with grand architecture, nor even in the Israelitish type and rags of his figures, nor in the rather greenish mist, and the slightly sulphurous light which bathes his canvases, is there anything very unexpected, or consequently entirely his own. We must come to 1632, that is, to the Anatomical Lecture, to finally perceive something like the revelation of an original career. Finally, it is right to be just not only to Rembrandt, but to every one. We must remember that in 1632 Ravesteyn was fifty or sixty years old, Frans Hals forty-eight, and that from 1627 to 1633 this marvellous workman had produced the most important and also the most perfect of his fine works.

It is true that both of them, Hals especially, were what is called painters of the outside; I mean by this, that the exterior of things struck them more than the interior, that they used their eyes more than their imagination, and that the sole transfiguration that Nature was made to undergo was that they saw her elegantly colored and posed, true in all her features, and reproduced her with the best of palettes and ablest of hands. It is also true that the mystery of form, light, and tone had not exclusively preoccupied them ; that in painting without much analysis, and according to prompt sensations, they painted only what they saw, added neither much shade to the shadows nor much light to the light ; and that in this way the grand invention of Rembrandt in chiaroscuro remained with them in the condition of a current medium, but not in the condition of a medium rare and even poetical. It is none the less true that if Rembrandt be placed in this year 1632, between the professors who had greatly enlightened him and the masters who were extremely superior to him in practical ability and in experience, the Lesson of Anatomy cannot fail to lose a good part of its absolute value.

The real merit of the work is, then, to mark a stage in the career of the painter ; it indicates a great step, reveals with distinctness what it undertakes, and if it does not yet permit us to measure all that he would become in a few years, it gives the first warning of it. It is the germ of Rembrandt ; there would be reason for regret if it were already himself, and it would be to misunderstand him to judge him from this first witness. The subject having been already treated in the same manner, with a dissecting table, a foreshortened corpse, and the light acting in the same way upon the central object which it is important to show, it should have been Rembrandt's business to have treated the subject better perhaps, and certainly to have felt it more delicately. I will not go so far as to seek the metaphysical meaning of a scene where the picturesque effect and the cordial sensi-

bility of the painter suffice to explain everything; for I have never well understood all the philosophy supposed to be contained in these grave and simple heads, and in these personages without gesture, posing (which is a mistake) quite symmetrically for their portraits. The most living figure in the picture, the most real, the one that most *stands out*, as one might say in thinking of the limbos that a painted figure must successively traverse to enter into the realities of art, and also the best likeness, is that of Dr. Sulp. Among the others there are some rather dead ones that Rembrandt left on the way, which are neither well seen nor well felt nor well painted. Two, on the other hand, — I might count three by including the accessory figure in the middle distance, — are, if carefully examined, those in which this distant point of view is most clearly revealed. In them there is that inexpressible something, alive and floating, undecided and ardent, which is the whole genius of Rembrandt. They are gray, executed with the stump; perfectly constructed without visible outlines, modelled from within, wholly alive with a life of their own, infinitely rare, that Rembrandt alone discovers under the surfaces of real life. This is a great deal, since in this relation the art of Rembrandt already could be spoken of, and his methods considered as a finished fact, but it is too little when one thinks of what a complete work of Rembrandt contains, and the extraordinary celebrity of this one is considered.

The general tone is neither cold nor warm; it is yellowish. The execution is thin and has but little warmth. The effect is salient without being powerful, and in no part of the stuffs, the background, or the atmosphere where the scene is placed, is the work or the tone very rich.

As to the corpse, it is pretty generally agreed that it is bloated, slightly constructed, and lacks study. I might add to these reproaches two others of a graver nature, — first, that apart from the soft and so to speak liquid whiteness of the tissues, it is not a dead body; it has neither the beauty, the hideousness, the characteristic accidents, nor the terrible accents of a corpse; it has been viewed with an indifferent eye, beheld by an absent soul. In the second place, — and this fault results from the first, — this corpse is (let us not be deceived) simply an effect of pale light in a dark picture; and as I shall say to you later, this preoccupation with the light on its own account, independent of the object illuminated, I might say without pity for the illuminated object, during Rembrandt's whole life was to serve him or injure him according to circumstances. This is the first memorable circumstance when his fixed idea manifestly deceived him by making him say a different thing from what he had to say. He had a man to paint, but he did not take enough care about this human form; he had death to paint, and he forgot it in seeking upon his palette a whitish tone that should be his light. I wish to believe that a genius like Rembrandt has frequently been more attentive, more deeply moved, and more nobly inspired by the subject he wished to render.

As to the chiaroscuro, of which the Anatomical Lecture offers almost the first formal example, as we shall see it elsewhere applied in a masterly way to those diverse expressions either of intimate poetry or of novel modelling, I shall have other and better occasions to speak of it.

To sum up my conclusions, I think I can say that fortunately for his glory, Rembrandt has given, even in this same style, decisive notes which singularly diminish the interest of this first picture. I will add that if the picture were of small dimensions, it would be judged a feeble work, and that if the size of this canvas gives it a particular value, it cannot be called a masterpiece, as too often has been repeated.

XI.

FRANS HALS AT HAARLEM.

As I have told you, it is at Haarlem that a painter in search of fine, strong lessons ought to give himself the pleasure of seeing Frans Hals. Everywhere else, in our French cabinets or museums, in the Dutch galleries or collections, the idea that one forms of this brilliant master, so very unequal in his manner, is seductive, agreeable, clever, rather frivolous; but it is neither true nor equitable. The man loses in it as much as the artist is belittled. He astonishes and amuses. With his unexampled celerity, the prodigious good-humor and the eccentricities of his method, he seems to stand out in relief, by the jocoseness of his mind and hand, from the severe background of the paintings of his time. Sometimes he is striking; he makes you think that he is as learned as he is gifted, and that his irresistible fire is only the happy grace of a profound talent; but almost immediately he compromises himself, does himself discredit, and discourages you. His portrait, which figures at the Amsterdam Museum, in which he is reproduced life size, standing upon a sylvan slope beside his wife, represents him to us quite well, as we should imagine him in his moments of impertinence, when he is jesting and lightly mocking us. Painting and gesture, execution and countenance, everything in this portrait, which is altogether too unceremonious, is in keeping. Hals laughs in our faces, the wife of this gay jester does the same, and, skilful as the painting is, it is not much more serious than they.

Such, to judge him only by his light side, is the famous painter whose renown was great in Holland during the first half of the seventeenth century. To-day the name of Hals reappears in our school at the moment when the love of the natural re-enters it with some clamor and no little excess. His method serves as a programme to certain doctrines by virtue of which the most word-for-word exactness is wrongly taken for truth, and the most perfectly indifferent execution taken for the last word of knowledge and taste. By invoking his testimony for the support of a thesis to which he never gave anything but contradictions in his fine works, a mistake is made, and in so doing, an injury is done to him. Among so many high qualities, are only his faults to be seen and extravagantly extolled? I fear so, and I will tell you what makes me dread it. It would be, I assure you, a new error and an injustice.

In the great hall of the Academy at Haarlem, which contains many pages analogous to his, but where he compels you to look only at him, Frans Hals has eight great canvases, whose dimensions vary from two and a half metres to over four metres. They are, first, Repasts or Reunions of officers of the Corps of Archers of St. George, of the Corps of Archers of St. Adrian; finally, and later, the Regents or Hospital Regents. The figures in them are of life size, and very numerous. These paintings are very imposing. The pictures appertain to all the periods of his life, and the series embraces his long career. The first, of 1616, shows him to us at thirty-two years of age. The last, painted in 1664, shows him to us only two years before his death, at the extreme age of eighty years. He is taken, so to speak, at the outset, and is seen to grow and grope. His blossoming came late, about the middle of his life, even a little beyond it; he fortifies himself, and develops himself in the midst of old age; finally, we are present at his decline, and are greatly surprised to see what self-possession this indefatigable master still maintained when his hand first failed, and then life.

There are few, if any, painters concerning whom we possess such complete information, so well graded and precise. The spectacle is rarely given to us to embrace at a glance fifty years of an artist's labor, to be present at his researches, behold him in his successes, and judge him from himself, in his most important and best work. Moreover, all his canvases are placed at a convenient height, they can be examined without effort; they yield to you all their secrets, even supposing Hals was a mysterious painter, which he was not. If you saw him paint, you would know no more. Consequently the mind is not slow in deciding, nor the judgment in forming.

Hals was only a workman. I warn you of that at once; but as a workman he is certainly one of the most clever and expert masters who has ever existed anywhere, even in Flanders in spite of Rubens and Vandyck, even in Spain in spite of Velasquez. Permit me to copy my notes; they have the merit of brevity, of being taken on the spot, and of measuring and analyzing things according to their interest. With such an artist one is easily tempted to say too much or too little. With the thinker we could soon finish, but with the painter we could go far; we must restrain ourselves and give him his due proportion.

"No. 54, 1616.— His first great picture. He is thirty-two; he is seeking his way; he has before him Ravesteyn, Pieter de Grebber, Cornelis van Haarlem, who enlighten him, but do not tempt him. Is his master, Karel van Mander, more capable of guiding him? The painting is strong in tone, red in principle; the modelling is rough and difficult; the hands are heavy; the darks ill observed. With all that the work is very characteristic. There are three charming heads to notice.

"No. 56, 1627.— Eleven years later. He is already himself; here he is in full flower. The painting is gray, fresh, natural, a dark harmony. Scarfs tawny, orange, or blue; ruffs white. He has found his register, and fixed his elements of coloring. He employs pure white, colors the lights with a few glazings, and adds a little green. The brown and dull backgrounds seem to have inspired Pieter de Hoogh, and remind one of the father of Cuyp. The features are more studied, the types perfect.

"No. 55, 1627.— Same year; better still. More execution; the hand more skilful and free. The execution has shades, he varies it. Same tone; the whites are more delicate, the detail of the ruffs indicated with more caprice. In all, the ease and grace of a man sure of himself; there is a scarf of tender blue which is all Hals. Heads unequally fine as to rendering, but all expressive and astonishingly individual. The face of the standard bearer, standing in the centre, is in a warm, frank value upon the silk of the banner, and he, with his head a little on one side, his eye twinkling, his small mouth delicate, and made thinner by a smile, is from head to foot a delicious piece of work. The darks are stronger; he separates them from the red, composes them, amalgamates them in a fashion more ample and healthy. The modelling is flat, the atmosphere becomes rare, the tones are placed in juxtaposition without prepared transitions. No use of chiaroscuro; it is the open air of a room well and equally lighted. Hence there are spaces between the tones that nothing unites, a suppleness when the values and the natural colors support each other closely, and hardness when the relation is more distant. A little system. I see very clearly what conclusion our present school draws from it. It is right in thinking that Hals remains excellent, in spite of this accidental intention; it would be wrong if it thought that his great learning and his merits depend upon this. And what would assure us of it is No. 57, 1633.

"Hals is forty-seven. This is in his brilliant style, with a rich keyboard, — his masterwork, absolutely fine, not the most piquant, but the most elevated, the most abundant, the most substantial, and the most learned. Here there is no intention, no affectation of placing his figures outside of, rather than in the air, and of creating a void around them. None of the difficulties of an art which, if it is well understood, accepts and solves them all, are eluded.

"Perhaps, taken individually, the heads are less perfect than in the preceding number, less spiritually expressive. With this exception, which is an accident that might be the fault of the models as well as the painter, as a whole the picture is superior. The background is dark (*noir*), and consequently the values are reversed. The black of the velvets, silks, and satins plays with more fancifulness on it; the colors separate themselves from it with a breadth, certainty, and a harmony that Hals has never exceeded. As beautiful, as faithfully observed in shadow as in light, in strength as in softness, it is charming to see in them such richness and simplicity, to examine their choiceness, their number, their infinite shades, and to admire their perfect union. The right side in full brilliancy is surprising. The material in itself is of the rarest kind; thick and flowing paint, that is firm and full, thick or thin, according to need; handling free, intelligent, supple, bold, never foolish, never insignificant; everything is treated according to its interest, its own nature, and its value. In one detail application is felt, another is hardly touched. The guipures are flat, the laces light, the satins shining, the silks lustreless, the velvets absorb more light, all without minuteness or petty observation. A sentiment prevails of the substance of things; a moderation without the least error; the art of being precise without too much explanation, of making everything understood with half a word, of omitting nothing but suppressing the useless; the touch expeditious, prompt, and sharp; the true phrase, and nothing but the true phrase, found at once, and never oppressed by overloading; no turbulence and no superfluity; as much taste as in Vandyck, as much skilful execution as in Velasquez, with the hundredfold difficulties of a palette infinitely richer,—for instead of being reduced to three tones, it is the entire repertory of all the tones known,—such are, in the full brilliancy of his experience and fire, the almost unique qualities of this fine painter. The central personage, with his blue satins and his greenish yellow jacket, is a masterpiece. Never was there better painting, never will there be any better painting. It is with these two masterworks, Nos. 55 and 57, that Frans Hals defends himself against the mistaken use they seek to make of his name. Certainly he has more naturalness than any one, but his cannot be called ultra-simplicity. He certainly colors with fulness, he models flatly, he avoids vulgar roundness; but although he has his own special modelling, he nevertheless observes the reliefs of nature; his figures have backs, even when you see them in front, and they are not boards. It is also true that his colors are simple, with a cold foundation, and they are broken; they show the use of as little oil as possible, their substance is homogeneous, the pigment solid; their deep radiance comes from their first quality as well as from their shading, but of these colors, of such delicate choiceness, such sure and sober taste, he is neither miserly nor even economical. He lavishes them, on the contrary, with a generosity which is hardly imitated by those who take him for an example, and they do not sufficiently observe with what infallible tact he knows how to multiply them without their injuring each other. Finally, he assuredly permits himself great liberties of hand, but till then not one moment of negligence can be observed in him. He executes as every one else did, only he shows his art better. His address is incomparable; he knows it, and is not displeased that it should be observed: in this respect, especially, his imitators scarcely resemble him. Agree also that he draws marvellously, first a head, then the hands, then everything which relates to the body, clothes it, aids it in its gesture, contributes to its attitude, completes its physiognomy. Finally, this painter of fine groups is none the less a consummate portrait painter, much subtler, much more living, much more elegant, than Van der Helst; neither is this quality one of the habitual merits of the school which attributes to itself the exclusive privilege of understanding him properly."

Here finishes at Haarlem the flowery manner of this excellent master. I pass over the No. 58, 1639, executed about his fiftieth year, and which, by an unfortunate mischance, rather heavily closes the series.

With the No. 59, which dates from 1641, two years after, we enter upon a new fashion, the grave method, with a gamut entirely black, gray, and brown, conformed to the subject. This is the picture of the Regents of St. Elizabeth's Hospital. In its strong and simple way of execution, with its heads in light, its costumes of black cloth, the quality of the flesh, the quality of the stuffs, its relief and its seriousness, its richness in these sober tones, this magnificent picture represents Hals differently, but no better. The heads, as fine as possible, have so much the more value that nothing around them struggles with the master interest of the living portions. Is it to this example of rare sobriety, to this absence of coloring, joined to the accomplished science of the colorist, that the neocolorists of whom I speak attach themselves most particularly? I do not yet see a very evident proof of it; but if such were, as people like to say, the very noble object of their researches, what torments must be inflicted upon these men of studies by the profound scrupulousness, the accomplished drawing, and the edifying conscientiousness which make the strength and beauty of this picture?

Far from recalling vain attempts, this masterly picture reminds us, on the contrary, of masterpieces. The first memory it awakens is of the Syndics. The scene is the same, the rendering similar; the conditions to be filled are exactly the same. A central figure, as fine as any that Hals has painted, suggests striking comparisons. The relations of the two works are most evident; with them appear the differences between the two painters, not contrary views, but an opposition of two natures; equal force in execution, superiority of hand in Hals and of mind in Rembrandt, with a different result. If, in the hall of the Amsterdam Museum, where the Clothiers figure, Van der Helst were replaced by Frans Hals, and the Arquebusiers by the Regents, what a decisive lesson it would be, and what miscomprehensions would be avoided! There would be a special study to make of these two Regent pictures. It would be necessary to remember that in them are not seen all the manifold merits of Hals, nor all the still more manifold faculties of Rembrandt, but upon a common theme, almost as if they were in competition, we are present at a trial of these two workmen. It can be seen at once where each excels and is weak, and the wherefore can be understood. There can be learned unhesitatingly that there are still a thousand things to discover under the exterior execution of Rembrandt, and that there is not much to divine behind the fine exterior execution of the Haarlem painter. I am very much surprised that no one has used this text for the purpose of telling the truth for once upon this point.

Finally Hals grows old, very old; he is eighty. It is 1664. This same year, he signs the last two canvases of the series, the last to which he ever put his hand, — the Regents' Portraits, and the portraits of the Regents of the Old Men's Hospital. The subject coincided with his age. His hand is no longer here. He displays instead of paints; he does not execute, he daubs; the perceptions of his eye are still vivid and just, the colors entirely pure. Perhaps in their first composition they have a simple and masculine quality, which betrays the last effort of an admirable eye, and says the last word of a consummate education. It is impossible to imagine finer blacks or finer grayish whites. The regent on the right with his red stocking, that is seen above the garter, is for a painter a priceless morsel, but you find no longer either consistency in design or execution. The heads are an abridgment, the hands of no importance, if the forms and articulations are sought for. The touch, if touch there be, is given without method, rather by chance, and no longer says what it would say. This absence of all rendering, this failing of his brush, he supplies by tone, which gives a semblance of being to what no longer exists. Everything is wanting, — clearness of sight, surety in the fingers, — and he is therefore all the more eager to make things live as powerful abstractions. The painter is three quarters dead; there remain to him, I cannot say thoughts, I can no longer say a tongue, but sensations that are golden.

You saw Hals at his beginning, I have tried to represent him to you as he was when in full force, this is the way he ends; and if, taking him at the two extremities of his career alone, I were to choose between the hour when his talent was born and the far more solemn hour in which his extraordinary talent abandoned him, between the picture of 1616 and the picture of 1664, I should not hesitate, and it would certainly be the last that I should choose. At this final moment Hals is a man who knows everything because he has successively learned everything in difficult enterprises. There are no practical problems that he has not attempted, disentangled, and solved, and no perilous exercise that he has not made a habit. His rare experience is such that it survives almost intact in this organization which is a wreck. It reveals itself still, and even more strongly because the great virtuoso has disappeared. However, as he is no longer anything but the shadow of himself, do you not think that it is very late to consult him?

The error of our young comrades is then really only a mistake of *à propos.* Whatever may be the surprising presence of mind and the vivacious vigor of this expiring genius, however worthy of respect may be the last efforts of his old age, they must agree that the example of a master eighty years old is not the best that there is to follow.

XII.

AMSTERDAM.

A ZIGZAG of narrow streets and canals led me to the Doelenstraat. Day was done. The evening was soft, gray, and hazy. Fine summer fogs bathed the ends of the canals. Here, still more than in Rotterdam, the air is impregnated with that fine odor of Holland, which tells you where you are, and makes you recognize the turf-pits by a sudden and original sensation. An odor conveys everything, — the latitude, the distance that one is from the pole and the equator, from oil or aloes, the climate, seasons, places, and things. Every one who has travelled at all knows that there are no favored countries but those whose smoke is aromatic, and whose firesides speak to the memory. As to those which only recall to mind sensations of the confused exhalations of animal life and of crowds, they have other charms, and I will not say that one forgets them, but they are differently remembered. Thus, drowned in odorous baths, seen at such an hour, while traversing the heart of the town, not muddy but moistened by the falling night, with workmen in the streets, its multitude of children on the steps, its shopmen before their doors, its little houses riddled with windows, its boats of merchandise, its distant port, its luxury quite apart in the new quarters, Amsterdam is just what one imagines when one dreams of a Northern Venice, whose Amstel is the Giudecca, the Dam another Piazza San Marco; and when beforehand one refers to Van der Heyden and forgets Canaletto.

It is antiquated, burgher-like, stifled, busy, and swarming, with Jewish airs even outside the Jewish quarter; less grandly picturesque than Rotterdam seen from the Meuse, less nobly picturesque than the Hague, but more picturesque when intimately known than in its exterior. One must know the profound artlessness, the passion for children, the love of little nooks, that distinguishes the Dutch painters, to understand the lovable and lively portraits that they have left us of their native town. The colors there are strong and gloomy, the forms symmetrical, the house fronts kept renewed; it is destitute of architecture and without art; the little trees on the quay are puny and ugly, the canals muddy. The feeling prevails that this is a people hurrying to plant itself upon the conquered mud, solely occupied with finding a lodging for its business, its commerce, its industries, and its labor, rather than for its comfort, and which never, even in its greatest days, thought of building there a palace for itself.

Ten minutes passed upon the Grand Canal at Venice, and ten other minutes passed in the Kalverstraat, will tell all that history can teach us about these two cities, the genius of the two peoples, the moral condition of the two republics, and consequently the spirit of the two schools. Only from seeing the lantern-like habitations where glass takes as much room and is as indispensable as stone, the little balconies carefully and poorly supplied with flowers, and the mirrors fixed in the windows, it can be understood that in this climate the winter is long, the sun unfaithful, the light sparing, the life sedentary and of necessity curious; that contemplation out of doors is rare; that enjoyment with closed shutters is very keen; and that the eye, the mind, and the soul there contract that form of patient, attentive, minute observation, a little strained, and, so to speak, blinking, common to all the Dutch thinkers from the metaphysicians to the painters.

I am here in the country of Spinoza and Rembrandt. Of these two great names, which represent the most intense effort of the Dutch brain in the order of abstract speculation or purely ideal invention, one only occupies me, — the last. Rembrandt has his statue here, the house he inhabited in his fortunate years, and two of his most celebrated works, — which is more than is necessary to eclipse many glories. Where is the statue of the national poet Joost van den Vondel, his contemporary, and at his time his equal at least in importance? They tell me it is in the New Park. Shall I see it? Who goes to see it? Where did Spinoza live? What has become of the house where Descartes sojourned, the one where Voltaire dwelt, and those in which died Admiral Tromp and the great Ruyter? What Rubens is at Antwerp, Rembrandt is here. The type is less heroic, the prestige is the same, the sovereignty equal. Only, instead of being resplendent in the high transepts of basilicas, over sumptuous altars, in votive chapels, upon the radiant walls of a princely museum, Rembrandt is shown here in the little dusty rooms of an almost private house. The destiny of his works continues in conformity with his life. From the lodging that I inhabit at the angle of the Kolveniers Burgwal, I perceive on the right, at the edge of the canal, the red and smoky façade of the Trippenhuis Museum ; that is to say, through closed windows, and in the pallor of this soft twilight of Holland, I already see shining, like a sort of cabalistic glory, the sparkling fame of the Night Watch.

I need not conceal that this work, the most famous in Holland, one of the most celebrated in the world, is the object of my journey. It inspires in me a great attraction and great doubts. I know no picture that has been more discussed, more argued about, and consequently has had more nonsense talked about it. Not that it charms equally all those who are excited by it ; but certainly there is no one, at least among the writers on art, whose clear good sense has not been more or less disturbed by the merits and eccentricity of the Night Watch.

From its title, which is a mistake, to its lighting, whose key can hardly be found, people have pleased themselves, I do not know why, with mingling all sorts of enigmas with technical questions which do not seem to me so very mysterious, though they are rather more complicated than elsewhere. Never, with the exception of the Sistine Chapel, have less simplicity, kindness, and precision been brought to the examination of a painted work ; it has been praised beyond measure, admired without saying very clearly why, a little discussed, but very little, and always with trembling. The boldest, treating it like a piece of unintelligible mechanism, have taken it to pieces, examined all the parts, and have not much better revealed the secret of its strength and its evident weaknesses. On a single point are found in accord those whom the work offends and those whom it transports, — which point is, that, perfect or not, the Night Watch belongs to that sidereal group in which universal admiration has collected, like stars, a few almost celestial works of art! They have gone so far as to say that the Night Watch is one of the wonders of the world, and that Rembrandt is the most perfect colorist that ever existed, — which are so many exaggerations or ironies for which Rembrandt is not responsible, and which certainly would have seemed obscure to this great, reflective, and sincere mind; for he knew better than any one that he had nothing in common with the colorists of blue blood, to whom he is opposed, and nothing to do with perfection as they understand it.

In two words, taken as a whole, — and even an exceptional picture would not disturb the rigorous economy of this powerful genius, — Rembrandt is a master unique in his own country, in all the countries of his time, in all time; a colorist, if you will, but in his own way; a draughtsman also, if you will, but like no one else; better than that, perhaps, but it would be necessary to prove it; very imperfect if one thinks of perfection in the art of expressing beautiful forms, and painting them well with simple means; admirable, on the contrary, by his hidden sides, independently of his form and his color, in essence; incomparable, then, in the literal sense that he resembles no one, and thus escapes the mistaken comparisons he is made to undergo, and in this sense also, that in the delicate points where he excels, he has no one analogous to him, and I believe no rival.

A work which represents him as he was in the midst of his career at thirty-four years of age, just ten years after the Anatomical Lecture, could not fail to reproduce in all their brilliancy some of his original faculties. Does it follow that it expressed them all? And is there not in this rather forced attempt something which was opposed to the natural use of what was most profound and rare in him?

The enterprise was new. The page was vast and complicated. It contained — what is unique in his work — movement, gesticulation, and commotion. The subject was not his own choice, it was a theme with portraits.

Twenty-three well-known persons expected that he would paint them all in sight, in some sort of action, and yet in their military clothes. The theme was too common for him not to make some sort of a story out of it, and on the other hand too definite for him to use much invention. It was necessary, whether they pleased him or not, to accept the types and paint the faces. In the first place there was required of him the likeness; and, great portrait painter as he is called, and as he is in certain respects, formal exactitude in features is not his strong point. Nothing in this studied composition exactly suited his visionary eye, his soul tending to something beyond truth; nothing but the fancy he intended to put into it, which the least misstep might change into a phantasmagoria. What Ravesteyn, Van der Helst, and Frans Hals did so freely and so excellently, could he do with the same ease, with equal success,— he the opposite in everything of those perfect physiognomists, and those fine workmen of impulse?

The effort was great. And Rembrandt was not one of those whom tension fortifies, and to whom it gives balance. He inhabited a sort of dark chamber where the true light of things was transformed into strange contrasts, and he lived in the midst of eccentric reveries among which this company of men-at-arms would introduce a good deal of confusion. During the execution of these twenty-three portraits we behold him constrained to occupy himself for a long time with others, and very little with himself, neither belonging to the others nor to himself, tormented by a demon who scarcely ever left him, restrained by people who were posing, and did not expect to be treated as fictions. For those who know the suspicious and fantastic habits of such a mind, it was not in such a work that the inspired Rembrandt of his finest moments could appear. Everywhere that Rembrandt forgets himself, I mean in his compositions, whenever he does not put himself into them wholly, the work is incomplete, and if it be extraordinary, *a priori* we can affirm that it is defective. This complicated nature has two very distinct faces, — one interior, the other exterior; and the latter is seldom the most beautiful. The error one is tempted to commit in judging him depends on this, that often one is deceived in the aspect, and is looking at the wrong side.

Is the Night Watch then, could it be, the last word of Rembrandt? Is it even the most perfect expression of his manner? Are there not in it obstacles that belong to the subject, difficulties of stage arrangement, circumstances new for him, which have never since been reproduced in his career? This is the point to be examined. Perhaps some light may be thrown upon it. I think Rembrandt will lose nothing by it. There will be only one legend the less in the history of his work, one less prejudice in current opinion, and one superstition the less in criticism.

With all its rebellious airs, the human mind at bottom is really idolatrous. Sceptical certainly, but credulous, its most imperious need is to believe, and its native habit to be submissive. It changes masters, it changes idols, but its subject nature exists through all these variations. It does not like to be enchained, but it chains itself. It doubts and denies, but it admires, which is one of the forms of faith; and as soon as it admires there is obtained from it the most complete abandonment of that faculty of free judgment of which it pretends to be so jealous. With regard to political, religious, philosophical beliefs, does one remain which it has respected? And remark that at the same time, by subtle turns, in which are discovered under its revolts the vague need of adoring and the proud consciousness of its greatness, it creates for itself alongside, in the world of art, another ideal and other religions, not suspecting to what contradictions it exposes itself in denying the true, to fall on its knees before the beautiful. It seems as if it did not really see their perfect identity with each other. The things of art appear to it as its own domain, where its reason need fear no surprises, where its adhesion can be given without constraint. It chooses celebrated works, makes for them titles of nobility, attaches itself to them, and permits no one henceforward to dispute their claim. There is always some foundation for its choice, — not everything, but something. It would be possible, in looking over the work of the great artists for three centuries, to prepare a list of these persistent credulities. Without examining too closely whether its preferences are always rigorously exact, one will see that at least the modern spirit has no great aversion for the conventional, and its secret leaning towards dogmas can be discovered by perceiving all those with which it has sown its history for good or ill. There are, it would seem, dogmas and dogmas. There are those that imitate, there are others which please and flatter. It costs nobody anything to believe in the sovereignty of a work of art that is known to be the product of a human brain. Every man of the smallest information believes, simply because he judges it and says he understands it, that he holds the secret of this visible and tangible thing that came from the hands of his fellow-man. What is the origin of this thing of human appearance, written in every one's language, painted equally for the mind of learned men and for the eyes of the simple, which so resembles life? Whence comes it? What is its inspiration? Is it a phenomenon of natural order, or a real miracle? All these questions, which give much occasion for thought, have been sifted to the bottom by no one; people admire, they cry, "A great man! a masterpiece!" and everything is said. No one troubles himself about the inexplicable formation of a work fallen from heaven; and thanks to this inadvertence, which will reign over the world so long as the world shall live, the very man who mocks at the supernatural will bow before the supernatural without seeming to suspect that he does so.

Such are, I believe, the causes, the empire, and the effect of superstitions in the matter of art. More than one example could be cited, and the picture of which I wish to speak with you is perhaps the most notable and the most brilliant. I needed some boldness to awaken your doubts, and what I am going to add will probably show still more temerity.

XIII.

THE NIGHT WATCH.

You know how the Night Watch is placed. It is opposite the Banquet of Arquebusiers by Van der Helst, and whatever may have been said about it, the two pictures do each other no harm. They are as opposed as day and night, as the transfiguration of things and their literal imitations, slightly vulgar and yet learned. Admit that they are as perfect as they are celebrated, and you will have before your eyes a unique antithesis, which La Bruyère calls "an opposition of two truths which throw light upon each other." I shall not speak to you of Van der Helst to-day, nor probably at any other time. He is a fine painter, that we might envy Holland, for in certain periods of penury he has rendered great service to France as a portrait painter, especially as a painter of great compositions, but in the matter of imitative and purely sociable art, Holland has something much better. And when Frans Hals of Haarlem has been seen, one can without difficulty turn his back upon Van der Helst to simply occupy himself with Rembrandt.

I shall astonish no one by saying that the Night Watch has no charm, and the fact is without example among the fine works of picturesque art. It astonishes, it disconcerts, it is imposing, but it is wanting absolutely in that first insinuating attraction which persuades, and it almost always begins by displeasing. In the first place it wounds that logic and habitual rectitude of the eye which loves clear forms, lucid ideas, daring flights distinctly formulated; something warns you that the imagination, like the reason, will be only half satisfied, and that the mind that is most easy to be persuaded will submit only after a time, and will not yield without dispute. This depends upon divers causes which are not entirely the fault of the picture, — upon the light, which is detestable; upon the frame of dark wood, in which the painting is lost, which determines neither its medium values nor its bronze gamut nor its power, and which makes it appear still more smoky than it is; finally, and above all, it depends upon the contracted nature of the room, which does not permit the canvas to be placed at the proper height, and, contrary to all the most elementary laws of perspective, obliges you to see it on a level, or, so to speak, at swords' point.

I know that people are generously of opinion that the place is, on the contrary, in perfect keeping with the requirements of the work, and that the force of illusion obtained by thus exhibiting it comes to the help of the painter's efforts. In this there are many mistakes in a few words. I know but one way of well placing a picture, which is to determine what is its spirit, to consult consequently its needs, and to place it according to its needs.

In speaking of a work of art, especially a picture by Rembrandt, one speaks of a work not untruthful, but imaginative, which is never the exact truth, nor is it the contrary, but which in any case is separated from the realities of the exterior life by its profoundly calculated approaches to truth. The personages who move in this special atmosphere, largely fictitious, whom the painter has placed in the distant perspective appropriate to the inventions of the mind, can issue from it, if by some indiscreet arrangement the point of view is misplaced, only at the risk of being no longer either what the painter made them, or what one would wrongly wish they should become. There exists between them and us an inclined plane, to use the expression used in optics and in theatrical arrangements. Here this inclined plane is very contracted. If you examine the Night Watch, you will perceive that, by a rather daring arrangement upon the canvas, the two foremost figures in the picture, placed close to the frame, have hardly the remoteness required by the necessities of the light and shade and the obligations of a well-calculated effect. It shows then a poor understanding of the spirit of Rembrandt, of the character of his work, his aims, his uncertainties, their instability in a certain balance, to make him undergo a proof which Van der Helst resists, it is true, but we know on what conditions. I may add that a painted canvas is a discreet thing, which says only what it wants to say, and says it from afar when it does not suit it to say it near by, and that every painting which attaches importance to its secrets is badly placed when it is forced to acknowledge them.

You are not ignorant of the fact that the Night Watch passes, rightly or wrongly, for an almost incomprehensible work, and that is one of its great attractions. Perhaps it would have made much less noise in the world if for two centuries people had not kept up the habit of seeking its meaning instead of examining its merits, and persisted in the mania of considering it as a picture above all things enigmatic.

To take it literally, what we know of the subject seems to me to suffice. First we know the names and the quality of the personages, thanks to the care the painter has taken to inscribe them on a cartouche in the background of the picture; and this proves that if the fancy of the painter has transfigured many things, the first rendering belongs at least to the habits of the local life. We do not know, it is true, with what purpose these men go forth in arms, whether they are going to a shooting-match, to a parade, or elsewhere; but, as this is not a very mysterious matter, I persuade myself that if Rembrandt has neglected to be more explicit, it was that he did not desire or did not know how to be so, and there are a whole series of hypotheses that could be very simply explained by something like either powerlessness or a voluntary reticence. As to the question of the hour, which is the most discussed of all, and also the only one which could be decided the first day, there was no need to fix it to discover that the extended hand of the captain casts a shadow upon the tail of a coat. It sufficed to remember that Rembrandt never treated light otherwise; that nocturnal obscurity is his habit; that shadow is his ordinary poetical form, his usual means of dramatic expression; and that in his portraits, his interiors, his legends, his anecdotes, his landscapes, and in his etchings as well as his paintings, it is usually with darkness that he makes his light. Perhaps reasoning thus by analogy, and at least from certain inductions of pure good sense, we may succeed in removing certain other doubts, and in the end there will remain, as irremediable obscurities, only the embarrassment of a mind struggling with the impossible, and the *almosts* of a subject mingled, as this must have been, with insufficient realities and scarcely justifiable fancies.

I will then try — what I wish had been done long ago — a little more criticism and a little less exegesis. I will abandon the enigmas of the subject to examine, with the care that it requires, a work painted by a man who has rarely been mistaken. Since this work has been given to us as the highest expression of his genius, and the most perfect expression of his manner, there is reason for examining very closely, and in all senses, an opinion so universally accredited. So I warn you that I shall not escape the technical controversies that the discussion necessitates. I ask your pardon in advance for the rather pedantic terms that I feel already coming from my pen. I shall try to be clear, I shall not promise to be as brief as I ought to be, nor shall I engage not to scandalize at first some of the fanatical spirits.

It is agreed that the composition does not constitute the principal merit of the picture. The subject was not chosen by the painter, and the way in which he undertook to treat it did not permit the first draught to be either very spontaneous or very lucid. Also the scene is undecided, the action nearly wanting, the interest consequently divided. A vice inherent to the first idea, a sort of irresolution in the fashion of conceiving, distributing, and posing, is revealed from the beginning. Some of the people are marching, some stopping, one priming a musket, another loading his gun, another firing; there is a drummer who sits for his head while he is beating his drum, a standard-bearer who is a little theatrical; finally, a crowd of figures fixed in the immobility proper to portraits, and these are, if I am not mistaken, the sole picturesque features of the picture.

Is this enough to give it that characteristic, anecdotic, and local meaning that is expected from Rembrandt painting the places, things, and men of his time? If Van der Helst, instead of seating his arquebusiers, had represented them moving in any action whatever, there is no doubt that he would have given us about their ways more just if not more subtle indications. And as to Frans Hals, imagine with what clearness, what order, and what naturalness he would have arranged the scene, how keen he would have been, how living, ingenious, abundant, and magnificent. The rendering conceived by Rembrandt is then more ordinary, and I dare say the most of his contemporaries would have judged him poor in resources; some because his abstract line is uncertain, too narrow, thin, symmetrical, and singularly disconnected; others, the colorists, because this composition, full of gaps and of spaces poorly occupied, did not lend itself to the large and generous use of colors which is the ordinary practice of learned palettes. Rembrandt was alone in knowing how with his individual intentions to escape from this dangerous position; and the composition, good or ill, was to properly suffice for its design, for its design was to resemble in nothing either Frans Hals, Grebber, Ravesteyn, Van der Helst, or any one else.

Thus there is no merit, and very little picturesque invention, in the general arrangement. Have the individual figures more? I do not see a single one that can be indicated as a choice piece of work. What is very striking, is that there exist between them disproportions for which there is no reason, and in each of them insufficiencies and, so to speak, an embarrassment in characterizing them, that nothing justifies. The captain is too large, and the lieutenant too small, not only beside Captain Kock, whose stature crushes him, but beside the accessory figures, whose length and breadth give to this rather poorly finished young man the appearance of a child who wears mustaches too early. Considering each as a portrait, they are unsuccessful portraits, of doubtful resemblance, of unpleasant countenance, which is surprising in a portrait painter who in 1642 had given proofs of his capacity; and this rather excuses Captain Kock for having addressed himself afterward to the infallible Van der Helst. Is the guard who is loading his musket better observed? And what do you think of the musket-bearer at the right, and the drummer? It may be said that the hands are failures in all these portraits, so vaguely are they sketched, and so little significant in action. The result is, that what they hold is badly held, — muskets, halberds, drumsticks, staves, lances, the banner staff, — and that the gesture of an arm is abortive when the hand which should act does not work clearly, and as if alive with either energy, precision, or spirit. I will not speak of the feet, which are mostly hidden by the shadow. Such are effectively the necessities of the system of obscurity adopted by Rembrandt, and such is the imperious intention of his method, that the same dark cloud envelops the base of the picture, in which the forms float to the great detriment of their point of support.

Must I add that the costumes are, like the resemblances, *almost* seen, sometimes odd and unnatural, and again stiff and rebellious to the shape of the body? They may be said to be badly worn. The casques are put on awkwardly, the felt hats are queer and cover the head ungracefully. The scarfs are in their place, but they are knotted awkwardly. There is nothing of the natural elegance, the unique array, the carelessness taken by surprise and rendered from life, of the costumes with which Frans Hals knows how to clothe all ages, all statures, all corpulences, and certainly also all ranks. We feel no more satisfied upon this point than on many others. We ask ourselves if this is not like a laborious fancy, like an effort to be strange, which is neither agreeable nor striking.

Some of the heads are very fine; I have indicated those which are not. The best, the only ones in which the hand and sentiment of a master are recognized, are those which from the depths of the canvas dart at you, with vague eyes, the delicate spark of their mobile glance. Do not examine severely either their construction, their planes, or their bony structure; accustom yourself to the grayish pallor of their complexion, interrogate them from afar, as if they were looking at you from a great distance, and if you want to know how they live, look at them as Rembrandt desires his human effigies to be looked at, attentively, for a long time, in the eyes and mouth.

There remains an episodical figure, which, until now, has foiled all conjectures, because it seems to personify, in its features, its array,

its singular brilliancy, and its want of appropriateness, the magic, the romantic feeling, or, if you will, the other side of the picture; I mean that little witch-like woman, childish and antiquated, with her comet of a cap and her pearl-wreathed hair, who slips, no one knows why, in among the feet of the guards, and, which is a not less inexplicable detail, who wears hanging at her girdle a white cock, that might be taken on a pinch for a large purse.

Whatever may be her reason for mingling with the procession, this little figure does not pretend to be human at all. She is colorless, almost formless; her age is doubtful because her features are indefinable. Her figure is the figure of a doll, and her movements are automatic. She has the gait of a beggar, and something like diamonds all over her body. She has the airs of a little queen, with an array that looks like rags. She looks as if she came from the Jewish quarter, from the region of old clothes, from the theatre or from Bohemia, and she seems the product of a dream, and to have arrayed herself in the most extraordinary of worlds. She has the gleams, waverings, and uncertainties of a pale fire. The more she is examined, the less can be seized the subtle lineaments which serve as an envelope for her incorporeal existence. In the end you see in her only a sort of extraordinarily curious phosphorescence, which is not the natural light of things, nor is it the ordinary brilliancy of a well-regulated palette, and this adds a new sorcery to the intimate strangeness of her physiognomy. Note that in the place she occupies, in one of the dark corners of the canvas, rather low down in the middle distance, between a dark red man and the captain dressed in black, this eccentric light has the more activity, because the contrast with what is near it is so sudden; and without extreme precautions, this explosion of accidental light would have been enough to disorganize the whole picture.

What is the meaning of this little imaginary or real being, who is only a supernumerary, and who has, as it were, taken possession of the first rôle? I cannot undertake to say; cleverer men than I have not failed to ask who she was, what she was doing there, and they have imagined nothing that satisfied them.

One thing only astonishes me, which is that people argue with Rembrandt as if he were himself a reasoner. They go into ecstasies over the novelty, the originality, the absence of all rule, the free range of an entirely personal individuality, which make, as has been very well said, the great attraction of this adventurous work; and it is precisely the fine flower of these rather unruly imaginations that is submitted to the examination of logic and pure reason. But if, to all these rather idle questions upon the why and wherefore of so many things, which probably have none at all, Rembrandt should answer thus, — "This child is only a caprice not less singular and quite as plausible as many others in my engraved or painted work. I placed it as a narrow light between great masses of shade, because its minuteness rendered it more vibrating, and it suited me to reveal by a flash one of the obscure corners of my picture. Her array is, moreover, the quite usual costume of my figures of women, large or small, young or old, and you will find a nearly similar type frequently in my works. I like what shines, and so I have clothed her with shining stuffs. As to these phosphorescent gleams that astonish you here, while elsewhere they pass unperceived, it is, in its colorless brilliancy and in its supernatural quality, the light I habitually give to my figures when I light them rather vividly," — do you not think that such a response would be enough to satisfy the most difficult, and that, finally, the rights of the arranger of the scene being reserved, he will only be obliged to explain to us one point, — the way in which he treated the picture?

We know what to think about the effect produced by the Night Watch when it appeared in 1642. This memorable effort was neither understood nor liked. It added fame to the glory of Rembrandt, aggrandized him in the eyes of his faithful admirers, and compromised him in the eyes of those who had only followed him with effort, and did not expect this decided step. It made of him a more singular painter, but a less sure master. It proved exciting, and divided people of taste according to the warmth of their blood and the unbending character of their reason. In short, it was considered as an absolutely new adventure, but doubtful, which brought him applause, some blame, and which at bottom satisfied no one. If you know the judgments on this subject, expressed by the contemporaries of Rembrandt, his friends, and his pupils, you must see that opinions have not much altered in two centuries, and that we repeat very nearly what this audacious great man must have heard said during his life.

The sole points upon which opinion is unanimous, especially in our day, are the color of the picture, which is called *dazzling*, *blind-*

ing, unheard of, (and you must admit that such words are rather made to spoil an eulogium,) and the execution, which people agree in finding sovereign. Here the question becomes very delicate. Cost what it may, we must abandon convenient ways, enter into the briers, and talk shop.

If Rembrandt was a colorist in no sense, no one would have made the mistake of taking him for a colorist, and in any case, nothing would be easier than to indicate why he is not one; but it is evident that his palette is his most ordinary and powerful means of expression, and that in his etchings as in his painting, he expresses himself still better by color and effect than by drawing. Rembrandt is then, with great reason, classed among the most powerful colorists that have ever existed. So that the sole way of separating and putting on one side the gift which is his own, is to distinguish him from the great colorists known as such, and to establish what is the profound and exclusive originality of his notions about color.

It is said of Veronese, Correggio, Titian, Giorgione, Rubens, Velasquez, Frans Hals, and Vandyck, that they are colorists, because in nature they perceive color still more delicately than form, and because they color more perfectly than they draw. To color well is, according to their example, to seize shades delicately or richly, choose them well on the palette, and bring them into proper juxtaposition in the picture. A part of this complicated art is ruled into a principle by certain sufficiently precise laws of physics, but the greater part is made by the aptitudes, the habits, instincts, caprices, and sudden sensitiveness of each artist. There is a great deal to say upon this topic, for color is a thing about which people who are strangers to our art speak very readily without understanding it well, and upon which, so far as I know, the men of the craft have never spoken their mind.

Reduced to its most simple terms, the question can thus be formulated, — to choose colors beautiful in themselves; and, secondly, to combine them in beautiful, learned, and just relations. I will add that colors may be deep or light, rich in tint or neutral, that is, more dull; *frank*, that is to say, nearer the *mother color*, or shaded and *broken*, as is said in technical language; finally, they may be of different values (I have told you elsewhere what is meant by that), and all this is a matter of temperament, of preference, and also of convenience. Thus Rubens, whose palette is very limited as to the number of the colors, whose mother colors are very rich, and who runs through the most extended scale, from pure white to absolute black, knows how to reduce himself when it is necessary, and break his color whenever it suits him to introduce a dull tone. Veronese, who proceeds in a very different way, bends no less than Rubens to the necessities of circumstances; nothing can be more flowery than some of the ceilings in the ducal palace; nothing can be more sober in its general bearing than the Supper at the House of Simon, at the Louvre. It must also be said that it is not necessary to color highly in order to do the work of a great colorist.

There are men, witness Velasquez, who color marvellously with the saddest colors, — black, gray, brown, white tinged with bitumen; what masterpieces have been executed with these few rather undertoned notes! It suffices for this that color should be rare, tender, or powerful, but resolutely composed by a man skilful in feeling shades and in proportioning them. The same man, when it suits him, can extend or reduce his resources. The day when Rubens painted, with all the varieties of bistre, the Communion of St. Francis of Assisi, was, even speaking only of the adventures of his palette, one of the most inspired days of his life.

Finally, — and this is a fact to be retained particularly in this most brief definition, — a colorist properly so called is a painter who knows how to preserve in the colors of his gamut, whatever it may be, rich or not, broken or not, complicated or reduced, their principle, their fitness, their resonance, and their truth; and that everywhere and always, in the shade, in the half-tint, and even in the most vivid light. It is in this especially that schools and men are distinguished. Take an anonymous painting, examine the quality of its local tone, — what that tone becomes in light, whether it exists in the half-tint, if it exists in the most intense shadow, — and you can say with certainty whether or not this painting is the work of a colorist, and to what epoch, what country, and what school it belongs.

There exists on this subject, in technical language, a regular formula which is excellent to quote. Every time that color undergoes all the modifications of light and shade without losing anything of its constituent qualities, it is said that the shadow and the light are of the same family, — which means that both should preserve, whatever may happen, the relationship most easy to seize with the local tone. Ways of understanding color are very different. There are, from Rubens to Giorgione and from Velasquez to Veronese, varieties which prove the immense elasticity of the art of painting, and the astonishing liberties of method that genius can take without changing its aim ; but one law is common to them all, and is observed only by them, whether at Venice, Parma, Madrid, Antwerp, or Haarlem ; it is precisely the relationship of shade and light, and the identity of the local tone through all the changes of the light.

Is it thus that Rembrandt proceeds ? A glance at the Night Watch is sufficient to perceive exactly the contrary. With the exception of one or two frank colors, two reds, and a dark purple, except one or two sparks of blue, you perceive nothing in this colorless and violent canvas which recalls the palette, and the ordinary method of any of the known colorists. The heads have rather the appearance than the coloring of life. They are red, winy, or pale, without having on that account the true pallor that Velasquez gives to his faces ; or those ruddy, yellow, grayish, or purple shades that Frans Hals opposes with so much dexterity when he wishes to specify the temperaments of his figures. In the clothes and head-gear, in the very differing parts of the adjustments, the color is neither more exact nor more expressive than is the form itself. When a red appears, it is a red not very delicate in its nature, which expresses indistinctly silk, cloth, or satin. The guard who is loading his musket is dressed in red from head to foot, from his felt hat to his shoes. Do you perceive that the characteristic peculiarities of this red, its nature, and its substance, which a real colorist would not have failed to seize, have occupied Rembrandt for a single moment? It is said that this red is admirably consistent in its light and in its shadow; in truth, I do not believe that any man who is at all used to handling a tone can be of this opinion, and I do not suppose that either Velasquez, Veronese, Titian, or Giorgione, setting aside Rubens, would have admitted its first composition and its use. I defy any one to say how the lieutenant is dressed, and what color is his coat. Is it white tinged with yellow? Is it yellow faded to white? The truth is, that, this person having to express the central light of the picture, Rembrandt clothed him with light, very intelligently as to his brilliancy, but very negligently as to his color.

Now here Rembrandt begins to betray himself, since for a colorist there is no abstract light. Light in itself is nothing; it is the result of colors differently lighted, and diversely radiant according to the nature of the ray they reflect or absorb. One very dark tint may be extraordinarily luminous; another very light one may not be so at all. There is not a pupil of the school who does not know this. Among the colorists the light then depends exclusively upon the choice of the colors employed to render it, and is so united to the tone that it can be said in very truth that with them light and color are one. In the Night Watch there is nothing of the kind. The tone disappears in the light, as it disappears in the shadow. The shadow is blackish, the light whitish. Everything is lightened or darkened; everything radiates or is obscured by an alternate effacing of the coloring principle. There are in it variations of values rather than contrasts of tone. And that is so true that a fine engraving, a well-rendered drawing, a Mouilleron lithograph, or a photograph, give an exact idea of the picture in its great intentional effects, and a representation only altered from light to dark does not at all destroy its lines. If I am well understood, this is what shows evidently that to make combinations of color as they are habitually understood is not Rembrandt's way of working, and that we must continue to seek elsewhere the secret of his real power and the familiar expression of his genius. Rembrandt is in everything a dealer in the abstract, who can be defined only by elimination. When I shall have said with certainty all that he is not, perhaps I shall succeed in determining exactly what he is.

Is he a great workman? Assuredly. Is the Night Watch in its workmanship, and in relation to himself, when it is compared to the masterworks of the great virtuosos, a fine piece of execution? I do not think it is; this is another miscomprehension that it is a good thing to cause to disappear.

The handiwork, as I said concerning Rubens, is only the consequent and adequate expression of the sensations of the eye and the operations of the mind. What is in itself a well-turned phrase, a well-chosen word, but the instantaneous witness of what the writer wished to say, and of the intention that he had to say it thus rather than otherwise? Consequently, to paint well generally means to draw well or color well; and the manner in which the hand acts is only the definite announcement of the painter's intentions. If the execution of men sure of themselves is examined, it can be seen how obedient is the hand, how prompt in well expressing the dictation of the mind, and what shades of sensitiveness, of ardor, of delicacy, of wit, of depth, pass from the ends of their fingers, whether these fingers are armed with the chisel, the brush, or the burin. Every artist, then, has his manner of painting, as he has his size and his *way of working with the thumb,* and Rembrandt escapes this common law no more than the rest of them.

How does he execute in the picture which occupies us? Does he treat any of the stuffs well? No. Does he ingeniously and vividly express their folds, their breaks, their suppleness, or their tissue? Certainly not. When he puts a feather in a hat, does he give to this feather the lightness, the floating grace, that are seen in Vandyck or Hals or Velasquez? Does he indicate with some shining touches on a dull ground, in their form and the feeling of the body, the human aspect of a well-adjusted garment, rustling with a gesture or crumpled by use? Does he know how, in a few brief touches, and proportioning his trouble to the value of things, to indicate a lace, induce belief in jewelry and rich embroideries?

There are, in the Night Watch, swords, muskets, partisans,* polished helmets, damasked gorgets, funnel-shaped boots, shoes with ribbons, a halberd with its pennon of blue silk, a drum, and lances. Imagine with what ease, with what lack of ceremony, and what a wonderful way of making things probable without emphasizing, Rubens, Veronese, Vandyck, Titian himself, finally Frans Hals, that workman of unparalleled cleverness, would have briefly indicated,

* A kind of pike or halberd.

and superbly carried off all these accessories. Do you find honestly that Rembrandt, in the Night Watch, excels in treating them thus? Look, I entreat you, — for in this punctilious discussion proofs are necessary, — at the halberd which the little Lieutenant Ruÿtenberg holds at the end of his stiff arm; see the foreshortened pike; see especially the floating silk, and tell me if a workman of such power could possibly express more painfully an object which ought to be born under his brush without his knowing it. Look at the laced sleeves that are spoken of with such praise, the cuffs, the gloves; examine the hands. Consider well how in their negligence, affected or unaffected, the form is accentuated, the foreshortening expressed. The touch is thick, embarrassed, almost awkward and groping. It might really be said that it is falsely applied, and that, put across when it ought to be put up and down, laid on flat when anybody else would have applied it in a circular fashion, it confuses form rather than determines it. Everywhere there are bright spots (*réhauts*), that is, decided accents that are not necessary and are neither true nor appropriate. There are thicknesses that are overloaded, roughnesses that nothing justifies, except the need of giving consistency to the lights, and the obligation in his new method to work over rugged tissues rather than a smooth basis; salient points, which mean to be real and are not so, distract the eye and have the reputation of being original art; there are ellipses that are omissions, forgetfulnesses that would make one believe in the artist's impotence. In all the salient parts we see a convulsive hand, an embarrassment in finding the proper phrase, a violence of terms, and a turbulence of execution that are at variance with the small degree of reality obtained, and the rather dead immobility of the result. Do not take my word for it. Go elsewhere and see good and beautiful examples among the most serious as well as the most lively; address yourself in succession to the rapid hands and to the patient ones, see their finished works, their sketches, and then return to the Night Watch, and compare. I will say more: address yourself to Rembrandt himself when he is at his ease, free in his ideas, free in his art; when he is imagining, when he is moved, and nervous without too much exasperation, and when master of his subject, his sentiment, and his language, he becomes perfect, that is, admirably skilful and profound, which is better than being adroit. There are circumstances in which the method of Rembrandt equals that of the best masters, and maintains itself at the height of his finest gifts. But it is when it is subject to perfectly natural obligations, or when it is animated by the interest of an imaginary subject. Beyond that, as in the case of the Night Watch, you have only Rembrandt mixed, that is to say, the ambiguities of his mind, and false pretences of skill of hand.

Finally, I come to the incontestable interest of the picture, to the grand effort of Rembrandt in a new direction. I speak of the application on a great scale of that manner of seeing which is his own, that has been called *chiaroscuro*.

Here there is no mistake possible. What one bestows on Rembrandt is entirely his own. Chiaroscuro is, there is no doubt, the native and necessary form of his impressions and of his ideas. Others than he used it; none used it so continually, so ingeniously as he. It is the mysterious form above all, the most veiled, the most elliptical, the most rich in suppressions and surprises, that exists in the picturesque language of painters. In this regard it is, more than any other, the form of intimate sensations or of ideas. It is light, misty, veiled, discreet; it lends its charm to things which conceal themselves, invites curiosity, adds an attraction to moral beauty, gives a grace to the speculations of conscience. Finally, it partakes of sentiment, of emotion, of the uncertain, the indefinite and the intimate, of the dream and the ideal. And this is why it is, as it should be, the poetical and natural atmosphere that the genius of Rembrandt has not ceased to inhabit. It would be possible, then, by means of this habitual form of his thought, to study Rembrandt in his most intimate and true nature. And if, instead of touching it lightly, I were to profoundly penetrate so vast a subject, you would see his whole psychologic nature issue of itself from the mists of chiaroscuro; but I shall not say what is necessary to say, and yet I trust Rembrandt will none the less stand forth.

In very ordinary language, and in its action common to all schools, chiaroscuro is the art of rendering the atmosphere visible, and of painting an object enveloped in air. Its aim is to create all the picturesque accidents of shadow, of half tint and light, of relief and distances, and consequently to give more variety, unity of effect, caprice, and relative truth, whether to forms or to colors. The contrary is an acceptation more ingenuous and more abstract, by virtue of which objects are shown such as they are, seen as if near, the air being suppressed, and consequently without other perspective than linear perspective, which results from the diminution of objects in relation to the horizon. Aerial perspective presupposes already a little chiaroscuro.

Chinese painting ignores it. Gothic and mystical painting did without it. Witness Van Eyck and all the early painters, whether Flemings or Italians. Must I add that if it is not contrary to the spirit of fresco, chiaroscuro is not indispensable to its needs. At Florence it begins late, as it does everywhere that line takes precedence of color. At Venice it does not appear till the time of the Bellini. As it corresponds to quite personal ways of feeling, it does not always pursue in the schools, and parallel with their progress, a very regular chronological advance. Thus in Flanders, after having had a presentiment of it in Memling, it is seen to disappear for half a century. Among the Flemings returned from Italy, very few adopted it among those who nevertheless had lived with Michael Angelo and Raphael. At the same time that Perugino and Mantegna judged it useless for the abstract expression of their ideas, and continued, so to speak, to paint with the burin of an engraver or jeweller, and to color with the methods of a glass painter, a great man, a great spirit, a great soul, found in it, for the height or the depth of his sentiment, the rarest elements of expression, and the means of rendering the mystery of things by a mystery. Leonardo, to whom, not without reason, Rembrandt has been compared, on account of the torment that it caused them both to formulate their ideal sense of things, — Leonardo is in fact, in the midst of the archaic period, one of the most unexpected representatives of chiaroscuro.

In the course of time, in Flanders, from Otho Vœnius we come to Rubens. And if Rubens is a very great painter of chiaroscuro, although he more habitually uses light than dark, Rembrandt is not the less the definite and absolute expression for many reasons, and not only because he uses more willingly dark than light. After him the whole Dutch School, from the beginning of the seventeenth century till the height of the eighteenth, the fine and fruitful school of half tints and narrow lights, moves only in that element common to all, and offers so rich and various a whole only because, having once admitted this fashion, it knew how to vary it by the most delicate metamorphoses.

Any other than Rembrandt in the Dutch School would sometimes make one forget that he obeyed the fixed laws of chiaroscuro; with him this oblivion is impossible; he has digested, established, and, so to speak, promulgated its code; and if one could believe in his doctrines at this period of his career, when he was acting much more from impulse than reflection, the Night Watch would have redoubled interest, for it would take the character and the authority of a manifesto.

To veil everything, to immerse everything in a bath of shadow, to plunge the light itself into it, to extract it afterwards in order to make it appear more distant and radiant; to make the dark waves revolve around bright centres, to shade them, deepen them, thicken them; to render nevertheless the darkness transparent, the half-darkness easy to pierce; to give, finally, to the strongest colors a sort of penetrability, which prevents their being black, — such is the first condition, such are also the difficulties of this very special art. It is unnecessary to say that if any one excelled in it, it was Rembrandt. He did not invent, he perfected everything, and the method he employed oftener and better than any one else bears his name.

The consequences of this way of seeing, feeling, and rendering the things of real life can be divined. Life has no longer the same appearance. The edges become faint or disappear, the colors are volatilized. The modelling, no longer imprisoned by a rigid outline, becomes more uncertain in its touch, more undulating in its surfaces, and when it is treated by a learned and feeling hand, it is the most living and the most real of all, because it contains a thousand artifices, thanks to which it lives, so to speak, a double life, — the life it has by nature, and that which comes to it from a communicated emotion. To sum up, there is a way of hollowing the canvas, of making it distant or near, of dissimulating, of showing and of drawing the true in the imaginary, which is *art,* and nominally the *art of chiaroscuro.*

Because such a method authorizes many licenses, does it result that it permits every liberty? Neither a certain relative exactitude, nor truth of form, nor its beauty when it is sought for, nor the permanence of color, would suffer, if many principles were changed in the way of perceiving and translating objects; on the contrary, it must be said that among the great Italians (let us take Leonardo and Titian), if the habit of introducing much shadow and very little light expressed better than another the sentiment they had to render, this way of working would not do the least harm to the beauty of the coloring, the outline, or the work. It was one more lightness in the material, like a more exquisite transparency of language. The language lost nothing by it, either in purity or clearness; it became in a certain sort rarer, more limpid, more expressive, and more powerful.

Rubens did nothing but embellish and transform by numberless artifices what seemed to him to be the preferable acceptation of life. And if his form is not more correct, it is certainly not the fault of the chiaroscuro. Heaven knows, on the contrary, what service this incomparable veil has rendered to his drawing. What would he be without it, and when he is well inspired, what does he not become, thanks to it? The man who draws, draws still better with its help; and he who colors, colors so much the better when he makes it enter his palette. A hand does not lose its form because it is bathed with obscure fluidities, nor a face its character, a resemblance its exactness, a stuff, if not its texture, at least its appearance, a metal the polish of its surface and the density appropriate to its material; finally, a color does not lose its local tone, that is, the very principle of its existence. It might be quite another thing and yet remain as true. The learned works of the Amsterdam School are a proof of it. Among all the Dutch painters, among all the excellent masters of whom chiaroscuro was the common and current language, it enters into the art of painting as an auxiliary, and among them all it concurs in producing a whole more homogeneous, more perfect, and more true. From the works so picturesquely true of Pieter de Hoogh, Van Ostade, Metzu, and Jan Steen, to the loftier inspirations of Titian, Giorgione, Correggio, and Rubens, everywhere is seen the use of half tints, and the large shadows are born of the need of expressing with more salience things perceptible, or of the necessity of embellishing them. Nowhere can they be separated from the architectural line or the line of the human form, from the true light or the true color of objects.

Rembrandt alone, upon this point as upon all the others, sees, thinks, and acts differently; and I am not wrong then in denying this eccentric genius the greater part of the exterior gifts which are the ordinary possession of the masters, for I am doing nothing but visibly setting apart the dominant faculty which he shares with no one.

If you are told that his palette has the virtue proper to the opulent Flemish, Spanish, and Italian palettes, I have made you recognize the motives by which you are permitted to doubt it. If you are told that he has a swift, adroit hand, prompt in saying things clearly, that it is natural in its play, brilliant and free in its dexterity, I ask you not to believe it at all, at least in presence of the Night Watch. Finally, if his chiaroscuro is spoken of as a discreet and light atmosphere, solely destined to veil very simple ideas, or very positive colors, or very clear forms, examine to see if there is not in that a new error, and if upon this point, as upon others, Rembrandt has not altered the whole system of ways of painting. If, on the contrary, you hear it said that, despairing of classing him, for want of names in the vocabulary, he is called a *luminarist*, ask what this barbarous word signifies, and you will perceive that this exceptional term expresses something very strange and very just. A luminarist would be, if I am not deceived, a man who would conceive light outside of recognized laws, would attach to it an extraordinary meaning, and would make great sacrifices to it. If such is the meaning of the new word, Rembrandt is at once defined and judged; for under its unpleasing form the word expresses an idea difficult to render, a true idea, a rare eulogium, and a criticism.

I told you, apposite to the Anatomical Lecture, — a picture which means to be dramatic, and is not so, — how Rembrandt used the light when he used it inappropriately; this is to judge the luminarist when he goes astray. I will tell you, further on, how Rembrandt uses light when he makes it express what no painter in the world has expressed by known means; you can judge by that what the luminarist becomes when he accosts with his dark lantern the world of the marvellous, of conscience and the ideal, and there he has no master in the art of painting, because he has no equal in the art of showing the invisible. The whole career of Rembrandt turns then around this troublesome objective point, to paint only by the help of light, to draw only with light; and all the differing judgments that have been pronounced upon his works, whether beautiful or defective, doubtful or incontestable, can be brought back to this simple question, Was this or was it not an occasion for making light an exclusive condition? Did the subject require it, did it allow it, or exclude it? In the first case the work results from the spirit of the work; infallibly it must be admirable. In the second the result is uncertain, and almost invariably the work is disputable or a poor success. It is idle to say that light in the hand of Rembrandt is like a marvellously submissive and docile instrument of which he is sure. Examine his work well; take it from his earliest years to his latter days,—from the St. Simeon at the Hague to the Jewish Bride at the Hoop Museum, and the St. Matthew at the Louvre,—and you will see that this dispenser of light has not always disposed it as he should, not even as he would have wished; that it has possessed him, governed him, inspired him to the point of sublimity, conducted him to the impossible, and sometimes betrayed him.

Explained by this desire of the painter to express a subject only by the brilliancy and darkness of objects, the Night Watch has, so to speak, no secrets. Everything which might make us hesitate is deducted from it. The merits have their reason for being, the errors one succeeds at last in understanding. The embarrassment of the workman when he executes, of the draughtsman when he constructs, of the painter when he colors, of the costumer when he dresses, the inconsistency of the tone, the ambiguity of the effect, the uncertainty of the hour, the strangeness of the figures, their lightning-like apparition in the midst of darkness, all result by chance from an effect conceived contrary to probability, pursued in spite of all logic; an effect of small necessity, whose theme was this,—to illumine a true scene by a light which was not true, that is to say, to give to a fact the ideal character of a vision. Seek nothing beyond this very audacious project, which agreed with the aims of the painter, conflicted with received renderings, opposed a system to habit, boldness of spirit to skill of hand, and whose temerity certainly did not fail to prick him on till the day when, I believe, insurmountable difficulties were revealed; for if Rembrandt solved some of them, there were many he could not solve.

I appeal to those who cannot believe without reserve in the infallibility of even the best minds. Rembrandt had to represent a company of men at arms: it was simple enough to tell us what they were going to do; he has done this so negligently that up to this time no one understands it even at Amsterdam. He had likenesses to paint, and they are doubtful; costumes in character, and they are for the most part apocryphal; a picturesque effect, and that effect is such that the picture becomes from it indecipherable;—the country, the place, the moment, the subject, the men, the objects, have disappeared in the stormy phantasmagoria of his palette. Generally he excels in rendering life, he is marvellous in the art of painting fictions, his habit is to think, his master faculty to express light; here fiction is out of place, life is wanting, and the thought redeems nothing. As to the light, it adds still another inconsistency. It is supernatural, disquieting, artificial; it radiates from within out; it dissolves the objects that it illuminates. I see many brilliant focuses, but I do not see one object lighted; it is neither beautiful nor true, nor has it a purpose. In the Anatomical Lecture the corpse is forgotten for a trick of the palette. Here two of the principal figures lose their body, their individuality, and their human signification in the gleam of an *ignis fatuus*.

How then does it happen that such a mind was so mistaken that he did not say what he had to say, and did say precisely what he was not required to say? Why is he who, when it is necessary, can be so clear, when there is occasion, so profound, — why is he here neither profound nor clear? Has he not, I ask you, drawn better and colored better even in his own manner? As a portrait painter has he not made portraits a hundred times better? Does the picture which occupies us give even an approximate idea of the forces of this inventive genius when he is peaceably working from his inmost recesses? Finally, his ideas, which always are drawn, at bottom, from the marvellous, as his Vision of Dr. Faustus, which appears in a dazzling circle of rays, — those rare ideas, where are they in this? And if the ideas are not here, why so many rays? I think that the reply to all these doubts is contained in the preceding pages, if those pages have any clearness.

Perhaps you at length perceive, in this genius made up of exclusiveness and contrasts, two natures which up to this time have not been very well distinguished from each other, which moreover contradict each other, and scarcely ever meet together at the same time and in the same work, — one a thinker who bends himself uneasily to the requirements of the truth, while he becomes inimitable when the obligation of veracity is not there to hamper his hand; and the other a workman who can be magnificent when the visionary does not trouble him. The Night Watch, which represents him in a day of great ambiguity, cannot be then the work of his thought when it is free, nor the work of his hand when it is healthy. In a word, the true Rembrandt is not here; but very happily for the honor of the human mind, he is elsewhere, and I think I shall have diminished nothing of his lofty glory, if, thanks to less celebrated works, which yet are superior, I can show you, one after the other, in all their brilliancy, the two sides of this great mind.

XIV.

REMBRANDT AT THE SIX AND VAN LOON GALLERIES.—REMBRANDT AT THE LOUVRE.

Rembrandt would indeed be inexplicable, if one did not see in him two men of adverse nature, who are very much embarrassed by each other. Their force is almost equal, their power has no comparison; as to their object it is absolutely opposite. They tried to be in harmony, and only succeeded after a long time on occasions which have become very celebrated, but are very rare. It was their habit "to act and think separately, which always succeeded." The long efforts, the audacities, the occasional failures, the last masterpiece of this doubly great man,—the Syndics,—are nothing but the struggle and the final reconciliation of his two natures. The Night Watch will have given you an idea of the want of understanding which existed between them when too soon, without doubt, Rembrandt undertook to make them labor together in the same work. It remains for me to show you each in its domain. In seeing up to what point they are contrary and complete, you will better understand why Rembrandt had such difficulty in finding a work of mixed character in which they could be manifested together without injuring each other.

In the first place there is the painter whom I shall call the exterior man; with a clear mind, a vigorous hand, and infallible logic, the opposite in everything of the romantic genius to whom the admiration of the world has been given almost entirely, and sometimes, as I have just told you, rather too promptly. In his way, at certain times, the Rembrandt of whom I am speaking is a superior master. His manner of seeing is thoroughly healthy, his way of painting edifying by the simplicity of the means employed; his manner attests that he wishes to be above all things comprehensible and veracious. His palette is wise, limpid, tinged with the true colors of the daylight, and without cloudiness. His drawing makes you forget it; but it forgets nothing. He is admirably lifelike. He expresses and characterizes, in their individuality, features, glances, attitudes, and gestures, that is to say, the normal habits and the furtive accidents of life. His execution has the propriety, breadth, the high bearing, the firm tissue, the force and conciseness proper to practitioners who are passed masters in the art of fine language. His painting is gray and black, unshining (*mate*), solid, and exceedingly thick and agreeable. It has for the eyes the charm of an opulence which hides instead of proclaiming itself, and of a skill which is betrayed only by outbursts of the greatest learning.

If you compare it to the paintings of the same fashion and the same gamut which make the renown of the Dutch painters, Hals excepted, you will perceive, by something more sustained in the tone, by a certain interior warmth in the shades, in the flowing of the color, in the ardor of the execution, that a fiery temperament is hidden under the apparent tranquillity of the method. Something warns you that the artist who paints thus is doing his very best not to paint differently; that this palette affects sobriety for the occasion; finally, that this unctuous and grave material is much richer at bottom than it appears, and that if it were analyzed there would be discovered in it, like a magnificent alloy, remains of melted gold.

Under this unexpected form Rembrandt is revealed, every time that he comes out of himself to yield to quite accidental obligations; and such is the power of such a mind, when it is borne in sincerity from one world to another, that this performer of miracles is one of the witnesses most capable of giving us a faithful and a hitherto unexpressed idea of the exterior world as it is. His works thus conceived are few. I do not believe—and the reason is easy to grasp—that any of his pictures, I mean any of his imaginary or imagined works, ever were clothed in this relatively impersonal form and color. Thus you do not meet in him with this manner of feeling and painting except in those cases when, whether from fancy or necessity, he subordinates himself to his subject. In this may be classed certain exceptional portraits disseminated in European collections, which deserve to be made a separate study. It is also to those moments of rare abandonment in the life of a man who seldom forgot himself, and only yielded himself from complacence, that we owe the portraits in the Six and Van Loon galleries; and it is to these perfectly beautiful works that I should recommend one to recur, who wishes to know how Rembrandt treated the human being, when, for the reasons that have been suggested, he consented to occupy himself only with his model.

The most celebrated is that of the Burgomaster Six. It dates from 1656, the fatal year, that in which Rembrandt grew old, became bankrupt, and retired to the Roosgracht (Rose Canal), saving from his prosperity only one thing, which was worth it all, his genius intact. It is astonishing that the burgomaster who had lived in intimate familiarity with Rembrandt for fifteen years, and whose portrait he had already engraved in 1647, should have waited till so late to be painted by his illustrious friend. Was it that, while greatly admiring his portraits, Six had some reason to doubt their likeness? Did he not know how the painter had formerly used Saskia,* with what little scruple he had painted himself already thirty or forty times; and did he fear in his own representation one of those infidelities which he had witnessed oftener than any one else?

What is certain is, that at this time, of all others, and undoubtedly out of regard for a man whose friendship and patronage had followed him in his ill fortune, Rembrandt suddenly mastered himself, as if his mind and his hand had never practised the least deviation. He is free but scrupulous, agreeable and sincere. From this unchimerical person he made an unchimerical picture, and with the same hand that signed two years before, in 1654, the Bathsheba in the Lacase Museum, a rather eccentric study from the life, he signed one of the best portraits he ever painted, and one of the finest bits of execution that he ever produced. He abandons himself more than he watches himself; nature here directs him. The transformation he makes things undergo is imperceptible, and a real object must be placed near the

* Saskia Nilenburg, Rembrandt's first wife.—Tr.

canvas to perceive the artifice in this picture, which is so delicate and so masculine, so learned and so natural. The work is rapid, the material rather thick and smooth; it is painted at once without useless relief; it is flowing, abundant, a little faint, and lightly blended at the edges. There is no too sudden digression, no abruptness, not a detail which has not its primary or secondary interest.

A colorless atmosphere circulates around this personage, viewed at home, in his habits of body, and his every-day clothes. He is not entirely a nobleman, nor is he exactly a burgher; he is a distinguished man, well dressed, perfectly at ease in his mien; his eye is steady without being too fixed, his face is calm, his bearing a little absent. He is going out, his head is covered, he is putting on gloves of a grayish color. His left hand is already gloved, the right is bare; neither of them is finished, and could not be more so, for the rough draught is left with a definite purpose. Here the truth of tone, the veracity of gesture, the perfect rigor of form, are such that everything is expressed as it should be. The rest was a matter of time and care, and I can reproach neither painter nor model for remaining satisfied with so clever an *almost*. The hair is red, the felt hat is black; the face is as true a likeness in complexion as in expression, as individual as it is living. The doublet is pale gray, the short mantle thrown over the shoulder is red, with trimmings of gold braid. Both have their appropriate color, and the choice of these two colors is as subtle as the relation of the two colors is just. As moral expression, it is charming; as truth, it is absolutely sincere; as art, it is of the highest quality.

What painter would have been capable of making a portrait like this? You can test it by the most redoubtable comparisons, and it resists them. Would Rembrandt himself have brought to it so much experience and freedom, that is, such a harmony of ripe qualities, before having passed through his profound researches, and the great audacities which had occupied the most laborious years of his life? I think not. No effort of a man is lost, and everything serves him, even his mistakes. There are in this picture the good nature of a mind which unbends itself, the want of ceremony of a hand which is resting, and, above all, that way of interpreting life which belongs only to thinkers trained to the loftiest problems. In this relation, and remembering the attempts in the Night Watch, the perfect success of the portrait of Six is, if I am not mistaken, an unanswerable argument.

I do not know whether the portraits of Martin Daey and his wife, the two important panels which adorn the grand drawing-room of the Van Loon mansion, are worth more or less than the Burgomaster. In any event they are more unexpected, and much less well known, the name of the personages having, in the first place, been less of a recommendation. Moreover, they belong visibly neither to Rembrandt's first nor to his second manner.

Much more than the portrait of Six are they an exception to the work of his years of middle life; and the need of classing the works of a master according to such and such an ultra-celebrated picture has made them, I think, considered as canvases without a type, and on this account they have been a little neglected. One of them, that of the husband, is dated 1634, two years after the Anatomical Lecture; the other, that of the wife, was executed in 1643, a year after the Night Watch. Nine years separate them, and yet they seem to have been conceived at the same time ; and if nothing in the first recalls the timid, patient, thin, and yellow period of which the Anatomical Lecture remains as the most important specimen, nothing, absolutely nothing, in the second bears the trace of the audacious undertakings, upon which Rembrandt had just entered. Here, very briefly, indicated by notes, is recorded the peculiar value of these two admirable pages.

The husband is standing facing us, in a black doublet and black breeches, with a hat of black felt, a guipure lace collar and cuffs, a knot of guipure at his garters, and large rosettes of the same on his black shoes. He has his left arm folded, and the hand hidden under his black mantle, which is braided with black satin ; with the right hand extended forward, he holds a doeskin glove. The background is blackish, the floor gray. It is a fine head, sweet and grave, rather round, with handsome eyes looking honestly at you ; charming drawing, grand, easy, and familiar, of the most perfect naturalness. The painting is even, firm at the edges, of a consistency and breadth so great that it could be thinner or thicker without our expecting more or less ; imagine a Dutch Velasquez, more intimate and more thoughtful. As to the rank of the person, it is indicated in the most delicate manner ; he is not a prince, hardly a great lord, but he is a nobleman of high birth, fine education, and elegant habits. In this work of pure good faith you find the race, age, temperament, — life, in a word, in its most characteristic expression, — everything that had been lacking in the Anatomical Lecture, and which would be wanting later in the Night Watch.

The woman, of the same full-length size, is placed against a blackish background, upon a gray floor, and she also is dressed all in black with a necklace and bracelet of pearls; there are knots of silver lace at her girdle, and rosettes of silver lace upon her delicate slippers of white satin. She is thin, white, and tall. Her pretty head, a little inclined, gazes at you with quiet eyes, and her complexion, of uncertain color, lends a more lively brilliancy to the warmth of her reddish hair. A slight enlargement of the waist, very decently expressed under the amplitude of her robe, gives her an infinitely respectable appearance as a young matron. Her right hand holds a fan of black feathers with a little golden chain; the other, which hangs by her side, is white, slender, and long, of exquisite lineage.

Black, gray, white, — nothing more, nothing less; and the whole tone is unequalled. An invisible atmosphere, and yet air; slight modelling, and yet all possible relief; an inimitable manner of being precise without littleness, of opposing the most delicate work to the largeness of the whole, of expressing by tone the luxury and value of objects, — in a word, a security of eye, a sensitiveness of palette, a certainty in the hand which would suffice for the glory of any master, — these are, if I am not mistaken, astonishing qualities obtained by the same man who a few months before had signed the Night Watch.

Was I not right in appealing from Rembrandt to Rembrandt? If one were to suppose in effect that the Anatomical Lecture and the Night Watch were treated thus, with respect for necessary things, for faces, costumes, typical features, would they not be in this style of portrait composition an extraordinary example to meditate upon and follow? Did not Rembrandt risk much in being complicated? Was he less original when he confined himself to the simplicity of his fine method? What healthy and powerful language, a little traditional, but entirely his own! Why change it at all? Had he then such pressing need to create for himself an idiom, strange, expressive, but incorrect, which no one since has been able to speak without falling into barbarisms? Such are the questions that would suggest themselves if Rembrandt had consecrated his life to painting the personages of his time, such as Dr. Tulp, Captain Kock, the Burgomaster Six, and M. Martin Daey; but what Rembrandt cared for was not that. If the painter of the *outside* had so spontaneously found his formula, and at the first blow, as it were, attained his aim, it was not the same with the inspired creator that we are going to see at work. The latter was very difficult to satisfy in a different way, because he had things to say which could not be treated like fine eyes, pretty hands, rich laces upon black satin, and for which would not suffice a categorical estimate, a bright palette, a few frank, clear, and concise expressions.

Do you remember the Good Samaritan that we have at the Louvre? Do you remember that half-dead man, bent double, supported by the shoulders, borne by the legs, shattered, his whole body out of shape, panting with the movements of the walkers, his legs bare, his feet close together, his knees touching, one arm awkwardly contracted over his hollow chest, and his brow enveloped in a bandage on which blood is seen? Do you remember that small suffering face with its half-closed eye, its dim glance, its dying expression of agony, one eyebrow raised, the groaning mouth, the two lips separated by an imperceptible distortion in which the wail expires? It is late; everything is in shadow, except one or two floating gleams, which seem to change places upon the canvas, so capriciously are they arranged, so mobile and light; nothing disturbs the tranquil uniformity of the twilight. Hardly in this mystery of the dying day do you remark, on the left of the picture, the horse so beautiful in style, and the miserable-looking child standing on tiptoe, peering over the shoulders of the animal, without much compassion following with his eyes to the inn this wounded man picked up on the road, who is being carefully carried, weighing heavily in the hands of his bearers, and groaning.

The canvas is smoky, all impregnated with sombre gold, very rich in the undertones, and particularly grave. The material is muddy and yet transparent; the execution is heavy and yet subtle, hesitating and resolute, painful and free, very unequal, uncertain, vague in some places, of astonishing precision in others. Something invites you to reflection, and would warn you, if wanderings of mind were permissible before so imperious a work, that the author was himself singularly attentive and thoughtful when he painted it. Stop and look at it from a distance, then near by; examine it for a long time. There is no apparent outline, not one accent given from routine; an extreme timidity which is not ignorance, and which comes, one would say, from the fear of being commonplace, or from the value the thinker attached to the immediate and direct expression of life; a construction of objects which seems to exist of itself, almost without the aid of the known formulas, and renders without any perceptible medium the uncertainties and precision of nature. Naked legs and feet, of irreproachable form and style, cannot be overlooked in their small dimensions, any more than the legs and feet of the Christ can be forgotten in Titian's Entombment. In this pale, thin, and groaning countenance there is nothing which is not an expression, something coming from the soul, from within out; the weakness, the suffering, and something of the sad joy with which a man finds that he is self-possessed when he feels that he is about to die. There is not a contortion, not a feature, which exceeds moderation, not a touch in this manner of rendering the inexpressible which is not pathetic and restrained, and the whole is dictated by a profound emotion, and translated by means that are entirely extraordinary.

Look around this picture, without any grand exterior, which is imposing to those who know how to see, solely from the power of its general scale of color; search the great gallery, return even to the Salon Carré, consult the most powerful and most skilful painters, from the Italians to the cunning Dutchmen, from Giorgione in his Concert to Metzu in his Visit, from Holbein in his Erasmus to

Terburg and Ostade; examine the painters of sentiment, of physiognomy, of attitudes, the men of scrupulous observation or of impulse; discover what they propose to themselves, study their researches, measure their domain, weigh well their language, and ask yourself if you perceive anywhere such inwardness in the expression of a face, emotion of such a nature, such simplicity in the way of feeling, — anything, in a word, so delicate in conception and expression, or which has been said in terms either more original, more exquisite, or more perfect.

Up to a certain point that which makes the perfection or even the strange beauty of Holbein can be defined. We can almost say to what attentive and powerful examination of human features the former owes the excellence of his likenesses, the precision of his form, the clearness and rigor of his language. Perhaps it might be suspected in what ideal world of high formulas or dreamed-of types, Leonardo divined what *La Joconde* must be in herself, and how from this first conception he drew the semblance of his St. John and of his Virgins. With still less difficulty can be explained the laws of drawing among the Dutch imitators. Everywhere Nature is present to teach them, sustain them, restrain them, and assist their hand as well as their eye. But Rembrandt? If his ideal is sought for in the upper world of forms, it is perceived that in it he has seen only moral beauty and physical ugliness. If his hold upon the real world is sought, it is discovered that he excludes from it everything which serves other people, that he also knows it well, but only half looks at it, and that if he adapts it to his needs, he almost never conforms himself to it. Moreover, he is more natural than any one else, at the same time that he is less near to nature, more familiar while less literal, more trivial and quite as noble, ugly in his types, extraordinarily fine in his feeling for countenances, less adroit of hand, that is, less smoothly and equally sure of his work, and yet of a skill so rare, so fruitful, and so full, that he can go from the Samaritan to the Syndics, from the Tobias to the Night Watch, from the Joiner's Family to the portrait of Six, and the portraits of Martin Daey and his wife, — that is, from pure sentiment to almost pure display, and from what is most intimate to what is most superb.

What I say to you concerning the Samaritan I could say about the Tobias, and with still more reason I can say it about the Disciples at Emmaus, — a marvel undeservedly lost in a corner of the Louvre, which can be counted among the masterpieces of the painter. This little picture, of poor appearance, of insignificant arrangement, of tarnished color, of reserved and almost awkward execution, would alone suffice to establish the greatness of a man. Without speaking of the disciple who understands and folds his hands, or of him who is astounded, and, placing his napkin on the table, looks straight at the head of Christ, and says clearly what in ordinary language could be translated by the exclamation of a man in amazement; without speaking of the young servant with black eyes, who is bringing a dish and sees but one thing, a man who was going to eat but does not eat, and crosses himself with contrition; — one might retain in this unique work only the Christ, and that would be enough. What painter has not made a Christ, at Rome, Florence, Sienna, Milan, Venice, Basle, Bruges, or Antwerp? From Leonardo, Raphael, and Titian to Van Eyck, Holbein, Rubens, and Vandyck, how has he not been deified, humanized, transfigured, shown in his history, his passion, and his death? How have been recited the adventures of his terrestrial life, how have been conceived the glories of his apotheosis! Has he ever been imagined thus? Pale, emaciated, sitting facing us, breaking the bread as on the evening of the Last Supper, in his pilgrim's robe, with his blackened lips on which the torture has left its traces, his great brown eyes, soft, widely opened, and raised towards heaven, with his cold nimbus, a sort of phosphorescence around him which envelops him in an indefinable glory, and that inexplicable look of a living, breathing human being who certainly has passed through death. The attitude of this divine shade, that gesture impossible to describe, surely impossible to copy, the intense ardor of his countenance, whose type is expressed without features, and whose physiognomy depends upon the movement of his lips and glance, — these things, inspired no one knows where, and produced no one knows how, are all priceless. No art recalls them; no one before Rembrandt, no one after him, has expressed them.

Three of the portraits signed by his hand, that our gallery possesses, are of the same essence and of the same value, — his Portrait (No. 413 of the Catalogue), the fine bust of the Young Man with the small mustaches and long hair (No. 417), and the Portrait of a Woman (No. 419), perhaps that of Saskia at the end of her short life. To multiply examples, that is to say, witnesses of his suppleness and his force, of his presence of mind when he is dreaming, of his prodigious lucidity when he discerns the invisible, we must cite the Joiner's Family, in which Rembrandt throws himself fully into the marvellousness of light, this time with great success, because the light is in the truth of his subject; and especially the Two Philosophers, two miracles of chiaroscuro, which he alone was capable of accomplishing upon this abstract theme, Meditation.

Thus, I think, in a few and not the most celebrated of his works, we have an exhibition of the unique faculties and of the fine manner of this great spirit. Note that these pictures are of every date, and consequently it is hardly possible to establish at what moment of his career he was most completely master of his thought and of his craft as well as a poet. It is positive that from the time of the Night Watch there was a change in his material way of working, sometimes a progress, sometimes merely a positive intention, a new habit; but the true and profound merit of his productions has almost nothing to do with the novelties of his labor. He returns elsewhere to his incisive and light language when the need of saying profound things with expression conquers in his mind the temptation to say them more energetically than before.

The Night Watch is dated 1642; the Tobias, 1637; the Joiner's Family, 1640; the Samaritan, 1648; the Two Philosophers, 1633; the Disciples at Emmaus, the most limpid and trembling of all, 1648; and if his portrait was made in 1634, that of the Young Man, one of the most finished that ever came from his hand, dates from 1658. What I should conclude, solely from this enumeration of dates, is that six years after the Night Watch, he signed the Disciples at Emmaus and the Samaritan. Now when, after such a renown, in the midst of his glory, — and what a far-famed glory, applauded by some, contradicted by others, — a man can calm himself and remain so humble, can possess himself sufficiently to turn from so much turbulence to so much wisdom, it is because beside the innovator who seeks and the painter who exerts himself to perfect his resources, there exists the thinker who pursues his work as best he can, as he feels it, almost always with the force of clairvoyance which belongs to brains illuminated by intuitions.

XV.

THE SYNDICS.

FROM the Syndics we learn what was the character of the final Rembrandt. In 1661 he had only eight more years to live. During these last years, sorrowful, difficult, forsaken, always laborious, his handling was to grow heavier, but his manner was to undergo no further change. Had it indeed changed much? Taking Rembrandt from 1632 to the Syndics, from his starting-point to his goal, what are the variations produced in this obstinate genius who mingled so little with others? His method has become more rapid, his brush larger, the paint heavier and more substantial, the material (*le tuf*) of a more resisting character. The strength of the first construction is all the greater because the hand must move so impetuously over the surfaces. This is what is called treating a canvas in a masterly way, because really such elements are so difficult to handle that often, instead of easily governing them, a man becomes their slave, and a long past, full of successful experiments, is necessary to enable one to use such expedients without too great risk.

Rembrandt had attained this confidence gradually, or rather by shocks, — a sudden rush forward followed by a recoil. Sometimes pictures of great wisdom were succeeded, as I have told you, by works wholly lacking in it; but finally, after this long journeying for thirty years, he became satisfied on all points, and the Syndics may be considered as the summing up of his acquisitions, or rather as the brilliant result of his certainty.

They are portraits grouped in one frame, not his best, but to be compared with the best that he produced in his last years. Unquestionably they do not at all recall those of Martin Daey and his wife, nor have they the fresh accent and the clear color of that of Six. They are conceived in the shadowy, tawny, and powerful style of the Young Man at the Louvre, and are much better than the St. Matthew which dates from the same year, in which old age is already betrayed. The clothes and felt hats are black, but through the black a depth of red is felt; the linens are white, but strongly glazed with bistre; the faces, which are wonderfully living, are animated by fine luminous and direct eyes, which do not exactly look at the spectator, but yet their glance follows, interrogates, and listens to him. They are individual, and are likenesses. They are certainly burghers and merchants, but notables, assembled in their own house before a table with a red cover, with an open register upon it, surprised in full counsel. They are occupied without acting, they speak without moving their lips. Not one of them is posing; they are living. The blacks are sharp or indistinct; a warm atmosphere, increased tenfold in value, envelops the whole with rich, grave half-tints. The relief of the linens, the faces, and the hands is extraordinary, and the extreme vivacity of the light is as delicately observed as if

Nature herself had given its quality and measure. It might almost be said of this picture that it is one exhibiting the greatest restraint and moderation, there is such exactitude in its balance, were it not that beneath all this maturity full of cool self-possession can be felt nervous force, impatience, and fire.

It is superb. Take several of the fine portraits conceived in the same spirit, — and they are numerous, — and you will have an idea of what may be an ingeniously arranged assemblage of four or five portraits of the first order. The *ensemble* is grand, the work a decisive one. It cannot be said that it reveals an abler or even a bolder Rembrandt, but it bears witness that the seeker has revolved the same problem often in his mind, and has at last found the solution.

This page, moreover, is too celebrated and too deservedly consecrated for me to emphasize it. What I hold to establishing is this : it is at once very real and very imaginative, both copied and conceived, prudently managed, and magnificently painted. All Rembrandt's efforts have there borne fruit ; not one of his researches has been in vain. What then did he propose to himself ? He meant to treat living nature about as he treated fictions, that is, by mingling the ideal with the true. By means of a few paradoxes he succeeded. He thus binds together all the links of his beautiful career.

The two men who had long divided the forces of his mind joined hands in this hour of perfect success. He closed his life by an understanding with himself, and by a masterpiece. Was he permitted to know what is peace of mind ? The Syndics once signed, might at least have believed that the day for it had come.

One last word, to finish with the Night Watch.

I have told you that the rendering in this picture seemed to me too real to admit of so much magic, and consequently the fantastic part which disturbs it appeared to me to be out of place, — that, considered as the representation of an actual scene, the picture does not explain itself, and, viewed as art, it lacks the ideal resources which are the natural element in which Rembrandt asserts himself with all his merits. I have, moreover, told you that an incontestable quality already had manifested itself in this picture, — the art of introducing in a large frame and in a widely expanded scene a picturesque novelty, a transformation of objects, a force of chiaroscuro, the secrets of which have been known so profoundly to no one before or after him. I have dared to say that this picture did not show that Rembrandt was a great draughtsman in the sense in which drawing is ordinarily understood, and that it manifested all the differences which separate him from the great and true colorists; I did not say the distance, because between Rembrandt and the great masters of the palette there are only dissimilarities, and not degrees. Finally, I have tried to explain why, in this particular work, he is not what might be called a good workman, and I have used his pictures in the Louvre and his portraits of the Six family to show that, when he consents to see nature as it is, his method is admirable, and when he expresses a sentiment, even if that sentiment appears inexpressible, his workmanship is then unrivalled. Have I not almost therein traced the outlines and the limits of this great spirit, and is it not easy for you to form a conclusion?

The Night Watch is an intermediary picture in his life, which divides it nearly in half, at least in the domain of his faculties. It reveals and manifests all that could be expected from so supple a genius. It does not contain him, nor does it mark his perfection in any of the styles he has treated, but it makes one foresee that in many of them he can be perfect. The heads in the background, and one or two faces in the foreground, show what the portrait painter must be, and what is his new manner of treating a resemblance by abstract life, by life itself. Once for all, the master of chiaroscuro has given a distinct expression of that element, confounded until then with many others. He has proved that it exists in itself independent of exterior form and of coloring, and that it can, by force and variety in its usage, by the power of its effects, the number, the depth, or the subtlety of the ideas which it expresses, become the principle of a new art. He has proved that an overwhelming comparison can be sustained without coloring, by the sole action of the lights upon the shadows. He has formulated by that, more decidedly than any one else, the law of values, and rendered incalculable service to our modern art. His fancy has been led astray in this work, into commonplace expression by his rendering. And yet the Girl with the Cock, apposite or not, exists to testify that this great portrait painter is, before all, a visionary; that this very exceptional colorist is, above all things, a painter of light; that his strange atmosphere is the air appropriate to his conceptions; and that there are, outside of Nature, or rather in her depths, things that this pearl-fisher alone has discovered.

To me the most positive thing contained in this picture is the interesting testimony it bears of a mighty effort. It is incoherent simply because it attempts many contrary results. It is obscure only because the rendering was uncertain and the conception vague. It is violent solely because the painter's mind was on a strain to compass it, and excessive only because the hand which executed it was less resolute than it was bold. We seek in it a mystery which does not exist. The sole mystery I discover in it is the eternal and secret struggle between the reality, which asserts itself, and the truth as it is conceived in a brain enamored with chimeras. Its historical importance comes from the grandeur of the work, and the importance of the attempts of which it is the substance; its celebrity arises from its strangeness; and, finally, its least doubtful title comes, not from what it is, but, as I have told you, from what it affirms and promises.

A masterpiece has never, so far as I know, been a faultless work, but generally it is at least the explicit and complete exhibition of the faculties of a master. Thus considered, is the Amsterdam picture a masterpiece? I think not. Could one, having seen this page alone, write a truly judicious study of this far-reaching genius? Could his measure be taken from it? If the Night Watch should disappear, what would happen? Would there be a void or an hiatus? And what would happen, on the other hand, if certain pictures or certain choice portraits should disappear? Which loss would most diminish the glory of Rembrandt, and from which would posterity really suffer the most? Finally, is Rembrandt perfectly known when he has been seen at Paris, London, and Dresden? and would he be perfectly understood if he had been seen only at Amsterdam in the picture which passes for his master-work?

I think that the Night Watch is, like Titian's Assumption, an important and very significant page, but not one of his very best pictures. I think also, without any comparison between the merits of the works, that Veronese would remain unknown if he had to represent him only the Rape of Europa, which is one of his most celebrated pages, and certainly one of the most degenerate, — a work which, far from exhibiting an advance, announces the decadence of the man and the decline of a whole school. Thus, it may be seen, that the Night Watch is not the only misconception in the history of art.

XVI.

REMBRANDT.

The life of Rembrandt is, like his painting, full of half-tints and dark corners. Often as he shows himself as he was in the full light of his works, of his public and private life, clear, luminous, and sparkling with wit, good humor, and haughty grace and grandeur, — equally often he secretes himself, and seems always to be hiding something, whether he painted or whether he lived. He had no palace with the conditions of a great lord's house, no train and galleries in the Italian fashion, but a modest abode, the blackened house of a petty merchant, the interior confusion of a collector, a book-hunter, a lover of prints and curiosities. He had no public business to draw him from his studio, and make him enter into the politics of his time; no great favor ever attached him to any prince. He had no official honors, nor orders, nor decorations, — nothing which connects him closely or distantly with such a fact or with such personages as would have kept him from being forgotten; for history in mentioning them might incidentally have spoken of him. Rembrandt belonged to the third estate, and hardly to that, as would have been said in France in 1789. He belonged to those crowds in which individuals are lost, whose manners are on a dead level, their habits without any character to elevate them; and even in Holland, that country of so-called equality in classes, Protestant, republican, without prejudices of nobility, the singularity of his genius did not prevent the social mediocrity of the man from keeping him down in the obscure layers, and drowning him in them.

For a long time nothing was known of him but from the testimony of Sandrart or his pupils, — those at least who have written, Hoogstraaten and Houbraken; and these reports were reduced to a few legends of the studios, to doubtful authorities, to too hasty judgments, and to gossip. What was perceived of himself were his eccentricities, his manias, a few trivialities, and certain faults that were almost vices. He was called interested, grasping, even miserly, rather disposed to bargain; and on the other hand he has been called dissipated, and disorderly in his expenses, witness his bankruptcy. He had many pupils, whom he put into cells in his rooms which were divided into compartments, watched them to see that between them was no contact, no influence, and drew a great revenue from this mistrustful teaching. Some fragments of oral lessons are collected by tradition, which are truths of simple good sense, but they brought about no particular result. He had not seen Italy, did not recommend that journey; which was for his ex-disciples, become doctors in æsthetics, a grievance and an occasion for regretting that their master had not added this necessary culture to his healthy doctrines and his original talent. He was known to have singular tastes, a love for old monkish robes, for Oriental frippery, for helmets, swords, and Asiatic carpets. Before knowing more exactly the detail of his artistic furniture, and all the instructive and useful curiosities with which he had encumbered his house, it seemed to be but a disorder of fantastic things, belonging to natural history and bric-a-brac, savage panoplies, stuffed animals, and dried grasses. It savored of the *capharnäum* and the laboratory, a little of occult science and the cabala; and this oddity, joined to the passion he was supposed to have for money, gave to the meditative and crabbed face of this furious worker the indescribable and suspicious air of an alchemist.

He had a passion for sitting in front of a mirror and painting himself, not as Rubens did in his heroic pictures, under a chivalrous exterior, as a warrior amid a confusion of epic figures, but all alone, in a little frame, looking right into his own eyes, for himself alone, and solely for the value of a shimmering light, or a more rare half-tint, playing over the rounded planes of his fat face with its flushed pulp. He turned up his mustache, put air and movement into his curly hair, smiled with a strong and ruddy lip; and his little eye, lost under thick jutting brows, darted a singular glance, in which were ardor, fixity, insolence, and contentment. It was not everybody's eye. The face had strong planes, the mouth was expressive, the chin wilful. Between his two eyebrows labor had traced two vertical furrows, two swellings, and that fold contracted by the habit of frowning, which belongs to concentrated brains which refract received sensations, and make an effort from without in. He adorned himself besides, and travestied himself after the fashion of theatrical people. He borrowed from his store the wherewithal to clothe himself, cover his head, or adorn himself; he put on turbans, velvet caps, felt hats, doublets, mantles, sometimes a cuirass; he hooked jewelry into his headgear, fastened round his neck chains of gold with precious stones: and when you get a little into the secret of his researches, you begin to ask if all this complacency of the painter for the model was not the weakness of the man, to which the artist lent himself. Later, after his mature years, in his days of difficulty, he is seen to appear in graver, more modest, and more truthful garments, without gold or velvet, in sombre raiment, with a handkerchief tied round his head, his countenance saddened, wrinkled, emaciated, the palette in his rough hands. This costume of a man disenchanted was a new form which prevailed with him when he had passed fifty years, but it only complicates the more the true idea that one would like to form of him.

All this together did not make a very harmonious whole, did not sustain itself, accorded ill with the meaning of his works, the high aim of his conceptions, the profound seriousness of his habitual purposes. The outbursts of this character difficult to define, the revealed points of his almost unprecedented habits, were relieved with a certain sharpness upon the background of a dull, neutral existence, smoky with uncertainties and biographically sufficiently confused.

Since then, light has been shed upon almost all of the doubtful parts of this shadowy picture. Rembrandt's history has been written and very well written in Holland, and even in France after the

Dutch writers. Thanks to the labors of one of his most fervent admirers, M. Vosmaert, we know now of Rembrandt, if not all that is necessary to know, at least all that will probably ever be known; and this suffices to make us love, pity, esteem, and I believe comprehend him well. Considering him by the exterior, he was an excellent man, loving his home, his domestic life, his fireside; a family man, with the nature of a husband rather than a libertine; a man of one wife, who could never bear either celibacy or widowhood, whom circumstances not wholly explained forced to marry three times; a retired man of course, — not very economical, for he did not know how to balance his accounts; not avaricious, for he became bankrupt; and if he spent little money for his comfort, he lavished it apparently for the curiosities of his mind; difficult to live with, perhaps suspicious, solitary; — in everything and in his modest sphere a singular being. He lived in no luxury, but he had a kind of concealed opulence, — treasures buried in valuable objects of art, which caused him much joy, but which he lost in the final disaster, and which under his eyes, before the door of an inn, on a truly sinister day, were sold at a low rate. All this personal property was not bric-a-brac, as has been seen from the inventory published at the time of the sale, though posterity occupied itself a long time with it without understanding it. There were marbles, Italian pictures, Dutch pictures, a great number of his own works, and especially engravings of the rarest kind, which he exchanged for his own, or paid dearly for. He cared for all these things, which were beautiful, curiously collected, and choice, as the companions of his solitude, the witnesses of his work, the confidants of his thought, the inspirers of his mind. Perhaps he treasured them as would a dilettante, a man of erudition, a person delicate in his intellectual enjoyments; and such was probably the unaccustomed form of an avarice whose intimate meaning was not understood. As to his debts which crushed him, he already had them at the epoch when, in a correspondence which has been preserved, he called himself rich. He was proud enough, and signed his bills of exchange with the carelessness of a man who does not know the value of money, and does not count with sufficient exactness either what he possesses or what he owes.

He had one charming wife, Saskia, who, like a ray of sunshine in this perpetual chiaroscuro, during those two brief years, in spite of a lack of elegance and very real charm, put into them something of a more lively brilliancy. What is wanting to this gloomy interior, as to this labor, morose with all its profundity, is expansion, a little loving youth, feminine grace, and tenderness. Did Saskia bring him all that? It cannot be seen distinctly. He was in love with her, it is said; painted her often, muffled her, as he did himself, in eccentric or magnificent disguises; covered her, as he did himself, with I know not what luxury of the moment; represented her as a Jewess, an Odalisque, a Judith, perhaps as a Susanna, and a Bathsheba, never painted her as she really was, and never left of her one portrait, dressed or not, which was faithful, — that is, we prefer to believe so. This is all that we know of his too soon extinguished domestic joys. Saskia died young, in 1642, the very year when he produced the Night Watch. The pleasant and laughing faces of his children — for he had several in his three marriages — are not once met with in his pictures. His son Titus died some months before him. The others disappeared in the obscurity which covered his last years and followed his death.

It is known that Rubens, in his grand life which was so exciting and always happy, had, on his return from Italy, when he felt himself out of place in his own country, and again after the death of Isabel Brandt, when he found himself a widower and alone in his house, a moment of great weakness, and something like a sudden failing of power. The proof of it is in his letters. With Rembrandt it is impossible to know what his heart suffered. Saskia died, and his labor continued without stopping a day; this is proved by the date of his pictures, and better still by his etchings. His fortune crumbled, he was dragged into the Insolvent room, everything he loved was taken from him; he took his easel, installed himself elsewhere, and neither his contemporaries nor posterity have heard a cry or a complaint from this strange nature, that might have been believed to be wholly overwhelmed. His productiveness neither weakens nor declines. Favor abandons him with fortune, happiness, and comfort; he replies to the injustice of Fate and the unfaithfulness of opinion by the portrait of Six, and the Syndics, not to speak of the Young Man at the Louvre, and ever so many others classed among his most composed, most satisfying and vigorous works. During his mourning, in the midst of humiliating misfortunes, he preserved a strange impassibility, which would be wholly inexplicable if it were not known what is the capability, as a moving spring to produce indifference or prompt forgetfulness, of a soul occupied with profound views.

Had he many friends? It is not thought that he had. It is certain that he did not have all those he deserved to have, — not Vondel, who himself was a familiar friend of the house of Six; nor Rubens, whom he knew well, who came to Holland in 1636, visited all the celebrated painters, Rembrandt alone excepted, and died in the year preceding the Night Watch, without the name of Rembrandt figuring either in his letters or his collections. Was he honored, much surrounded, very well known? Not at all. When he is spoken of in the *Apologies*, in the writings, in the little fugitive poems, made for an occasion in his time, it is under orders, rather from a spirit of justice, as if by chance, and without great warmth. The literary men had other preferences, after whom came Rembrandt, the only one of all who was illustrious. In official ceremonies, in the great days of pomp of all kinds, he was forgotten, or, so to speak, he was never seen anywhere in the front ranks or on the platforms.

In spite of his genius, his glory, the prodigious infatuation which attracted painters to him in the beginning, what was called society was, even at Amsterdam, a social circle which perhaps half opened its doors to him, but to which he never belonged. His portraits recommended him no better than his person. Although he had made magnificent ones of people of distinction, they were not those pleasant, natural, lucid works which could give him a position in a certain kind of society, would be appreciated there, and give him admittance to it. I have told you that Captain Kock, who figures in the Night Watch, consoled himself later with Van der Helst; as to Six, — a young man in relation to Rembrandt, and who, I insist upon believing, only let himself be painted because he could not help it, — when Rembrandt went to the house of this official personage, he went rather to see the Burgomaster and Mecænas than a friend. From habit and preference, he consorted with people of low rank, shopmen, and petty citizens. His associations have been even too much vilified; they were very humble, but not degrading, as has been said. He has even been occasionally reproached with having drunken habits (though he hardly ever frequented drinking-houses, which was rare at that time), because, ten years after the loss of his wife, people thought they perceived that this lonely man had some suspicious relations with his serving-maid.

The servant was reprimanded, and Rembrandt passably condemned. Moreover, at that moment everything went ill, fortune as well as honor; and when he left the Breestraat, homeless, penniless, but at quits with his creditors, neither his talent nor his acquired glory sustained him. His trace was lost, he was forgotten, and for the time he disappeared in the lowly, needy, and obscure life from which, to tell the truth, he had never issued.

In everything, as can be seen, he was a man apart, a dreamer; perhaps a silent man, although his face says the contrary; possibly an angular character, rather rough, unbending, cutting, not pleasant to contradict, still less to convince; vacillating at bottom, stiff in his manner, undoubtedly peculiar. If he was celebrated and cherished and praised at first, in spite of the jealous and short-sighted, the pedants and the fools, they well revenged themselves when he was no longer there.

In his execution he neither painted, drew, nor engraved like any one else. His works were, even in their methods, enigmas. He was admired not without disquietude, he was followed without being very well understood. It was especially at his work that he seemed like an alchemist. Seeing him at his easel, with a palette that must certainly have been daubed, from which came so much heavy paint, and whence escaped so many subtle essences; or leaning over his copperplates, and using his burin contrary to all rules, — one would seek, at the tip of his burin or his brush, secrets which came from much farther off. His manner was so novel that it confounded the strong minds, and filled with enthusiasm the simple spirits. All the young, enterprising, insubordinate, and giddy scholars in painting ran after him. His immediate pupils were mediocre, their followers were detestable. A striking thing resulted from the teaching in cells of which I have spoken; not one kept his independence. They imitated him as no master was ever imitated by servile copyists, and it is evident took from him only the worst of his methods.

Was he learned and cultivated? Was he even a man of any reading? Because he had a taste for theatrical effects, and touched upon history, mythology, and Christian dogmas, people say he was. It is said that he was not, because the examination of his furniture revealed innumerable engravings and almost no books. Was he, in fine, a philosopher, as the word philosopher is understood? What did he gain from the movement of reform? Did he, as has been maintained in our day, contribute his part as an artist towards destroying dogmas, and revealing the purely human sides of the Gospel? Did he pronounce his opinion intentionally upon the political, religious, and social questions which had turned his country upside down for so long, and which very fortunately were finally solved? He painted mendicants, the disinherited and beggars, even more than rich men, Jews oftener than Christians; does it follow that he had for the wretched classes anything but purely picturesque predilections? All this is more than conjectural, and I do not see the necessity of sifting farther a subject already so profound, and adding another to so many hypotheses.

The fact is, that it is difficult to isolate him from the intellectual and moral movement of his country and his time, which he breathed in the seventeenth century in Holland as he did the native air on which he lived. Had he come earlier, he would have been inexplicable; had he been born anywhere else, he would play still more strangely this rôle of a comet outside of the axis of modern art, which has been attributed to him; had he come later, he would have no longer the immense merit of closing a past, and opening one of the great gates of the future. In every relation he has deceived many people. As a man he was lacking in exterior, whence it has been concluded that he was coarse. As a student he has disturbed more than one system, whence it has been concluded that he was wanting in taste. As an artist loving the beautiful, he has given of the things of the earth some very ugly ideas. It has not been remarked that he was looking elsewhere. In short, greatly as he was praised, wickedly as he was vilified, unjustly as he was esteemed, for good or for evil, or contrary to his nature, no one exactly suspected his true grandeur.

Observe that he is the least Dutch of the Dutch painters, and that if he belongs to his time, he does not wholly belong to it. What his compatriots observed he did not see; to that from which they turned aside, he returned. They had bidden farewell to the fable, and he came back to it; to the Bible, and he illustrated it; to the Gospels, and he delighted in them. He clothes them in his own way, but he extracts from them a meaning unique, new, and universally intelligible. He dreams of St. Simeon, of Jacob and Laban, of the Prodigal Son, of Tobias, the Apostles, the Holy Family, King David, Calvary, the Samaritan, Lazarus, and the Evangelists. He wanders around Jerusalem and Emmaus, ever, as one feels, attracted by the synagogue. These consecrated themes he sees appear in nameless surroundings, in meaningless costumes. He conceives them, formulates them, with as little care for tradition as slight regard for local truth. And still, such is his creative force, that this mind, so individual and personal, gives to the subjects it treats a general expression, an intimate and typical meaning, which the grand epic thinkers and draughtsmen do not always attain.

Somewhere in this study I have said that his principle was to extract from things one element among all others, or rather to abstract them all to seize one expressly. He has thus, in all his works, performed the labor of an analyzer, a distiller, or, to speak more nobly, of a metaphysician, rather than a poet. Never did reality seize him as a whole. To see the way in which he treated bodies, one might doubt the interest he took in their envelope. He loved women, and has seen them only deformed; he loved the tissues, and did not imitate them; but in return, in spite of lack of grace, beauty, pure lines, and delicacy of flesh, he expressed the naked body by suppleness, roundness, elasticity, with a love for substances, a feeling for the living being, which are the delight of artist workmen. He decomposed and reduced everything, color as well as light, so that, while eliminating from appearances everything that is manifold, condensing what is scattered, he succeeded in drawing without outlines, in painting a portrait almost without apparent features, in coloring without color, in concentrating the light of the solar system into a ray. It is not possible in a plastic art to push farther the curiosity of a being about itself. For physical beauty he substitutes moral expression; for the imitation of things, their almost entire metamorphosis; for examination, psychological speculations; for clear, learned, or simple observation, the perceptions of a visionary, and apparitions so real that he is the dupe of them himself. By this faculty of second sight, thanks to his somnambulistic intuition, in the supernatural he sees farther than any one soever. Life he perceives in a dream, as an accent of the other world which renders real life almost cold, and makes it seem pale. See at the Louvre his Portrait of a Woman, two paces from Titian's Mistress. Compare the two beings, interrogate well the two paintings, and you will understand the difference of the two brains. His ideal, as in a dream pursued with closed eyes, is light; the nimbus around objects, phosphorescence on a black ground. It is fugitive, uncertain, formed of imperceptible lineaments, all ready to disappear before they are fixed, ephemeral and dazzling. To arrest the vision, place it upon canvas, give it its form and relief, preserve its fragile texture, give it its brilliancy, and let the result be a strong, masculine, and substantial painting, as real as any other, which would resist contact with Rubens, Titian, Veronese, Giorgione, Vandyck, — this is what Rembrandt attempted. Did he accomplish it? Universal testimony is there to say.

One last word. Proceeding as he proceeded himself, by extracting from this work, so vast and of such manifold character, what represents him in his principle, reducing it to its natural elements, eliminating his palette, his brushes, his coloring oils, his glazings, his thick paints, all the mechanism of the painter, one might finally come to where he could seize the primal essence of the artist in the engraver. Rembrandt is wholly to be found in his etchings. His spirit, tendency, imaginations, reveries, good sense, chimeras, difficulties in rendering the impossible, realities in the nothings, are revealed by twenty of his etchings; they give one a presentiment of the painter, and, better still, explain him. There is the same workmanship, the same purpose, the same neglect, the same persistency, the same singularity in execution, the same tormenting and sudden success by expression. Confronting them closely, I see no difference between the Tobias at the Louvre and an engraved plate. There is no one who does not set this engraver above all others. Without going so far, when it is a question of his painting, it would be well to think often of the Hundred Florin Piece, when one fails to understand him in his pictures. It would then be seen that all the dross of this art, one of the most difficult in the world to purify, alters nothing of the incomparably beautiful flame which burns within; and I think that finally every name that has been given to Rembrandt would be altered to give him opposite names.

In truth, his was a brain served by an eye that could see at night, and by an able hand with no great dexterity. This painful labor came from an agile and free mind. This man of no account; this ferreter, this costumer, this erudite being nourished on extravagances; this man of the lower levels, of so lofty a flight; this moth nature, which flies to whatever shines; this soul, so sensitive to certain forms of life, so indifferent to others; this ardor without tenderness, this lover without visible flame; this nature of contrasts, contradictions, and double meanings, moved and eloquent, loving and not very lovable; this disgraced man so well endowed; this pretended materialist; this *trivial*, *hideous* person, — was a pure spiritualist, or, to express it in a single word, an *idealist;* I mean, a spirit whose domain is that of ideas, and whose language is the language of ideas. The key of the mystery is there.

Taken thus, Rembrandt is wholly explained; his life, his work, his leanings, his conceptions, his poetry, his methods, his way of working, even to the color of his painting, which is only a bold and studied spiritualization of the material elements of his art.

PART III.

BELGIUM.

BELGIUM.

THE VAN EYCKS AND MEMLING.

BRUGES.

I AM returning by way of Ghent and Bruges. It is here that logically I should have started if I had thought of writing an accurate history of the schools of the Low Countries; but the chronological order is not of much account in these studies, which have, you perceive, neither plan nor method. I am ascending the stream instead of descending it. I have followed its course irregularly, with some negligence and many omissions. I have even quitted it far from its mouth, and have not shown you how it finishes; for after a certain point it ends, and is lost in insignificance. Now I like to think that I am at the source, and that I am about to see the gushing of that first flood of crystalline and pure inspiration, whence issued the vast movement of art in the North.

For other countries, other times, other ideas, I leave Amsterdam and the seventeenth century in Holland. I leave the school after its great renown; let us suppose that it is about 1670, two years before the assassination of the brothers De Witt, and the hereditary stadtholdership of the future King of England, William III. At this date, of all the fine painters whose birth we have seen in the first thirty years of the century, who remain? The great ones preceding Rembrandt or closely following him are dead, or about to die. Those who remain are old men at the end of their career. In 1683, except Van der Heyden* and Van der Neer,† who represent alone an extinct school, not one survives. It is the reign of such as Tempesta,‡ Mignon,§ Netscher,|| Lairesse,¶ and Van der Werff.** All is over. I pass through Antwerp. I see once more Rubens imperturbable and replete, like a great mind which contains in itself good and evil progress and decline, who terminates in his own life two epochs, the preceding and his own. After him I see, as after Rembrandt, those who poorly understand him, have not strength enough to follow him, and who question him. Rubens helps me to pass from the seventeenth to the sixteenth century. We no longer have Louis XIII. nor Henri IV., nor the Infanta Isabella, nor the Archduke Albert; nor even have we the Duke of Parma, nor the Duke of Alva, nor Philip II., nor Charles V. We ascend still through politics, manners, and painting. Charles V. is not born, nor near birth; nor is his

* Jan van der Heyden, an architectural painter who finished pictures with exquisite care. — Tr.

† Aart van der Neer, a Dutch landscape painter who excelled in moonlights and conflagrations. — Tr.

‡ Peter Molyn, called Tempesta from his pictures of sea storms. He was also a good painter of wild animals. Haarlem, 1637–1701. — Tr.

§ Abraham Mignon, Frankfort, 1639–1697; an inferior painter of flowers, insects, fruits, etc. — Tr.

|| Caspar Netscher, Heidelberg, 1639–1684; an imitator of Terburg and Metzu; a figure and genre painter who excelled in portraits. — Tr.

¶ Gérard Lairesse, called the Poussin of Belgium, born at Liege, 1640–1711. — Tr.

** Adrian van der Werff, Rotterdam, 1659–1722; an ideal painter, smooth and careful in execution. — Tr.

father. His grandmother, Marie de Burgundy, is a young girl, twenty years old, and his great-grandfather, Charles the Bold, has just died at Nancy, when at Bruges, by a series of unparalleled masterpieces, comes to an end this astonishing period comprised between the beginning of the Van Eycks and the disappearance of Memling, or at least his presumed departure from Flanders. Placed as I am between the two towns, Ghent and Bruges, between the two names that make them most illustrious by the novelty of their attempts, and the pacific bearing of their genius, I am between the modern world and the Middle Ages ; and I am in the midst of memories of the little Court of France, and the great Court of Burgundy, — with Louis XI., who wishes to make a France ; with Charles the Bold, who dreams of unmaking it ; with Commines, the diplomate-historian, who passes from one house to the other. I am not to speak to you of these times of violence and stratagem, of cunning in policy, of savageness in action, of perfidies, treasons, oaths sworn and violated, revolts in towns, massacres upon the battle-field, democratic efforts, and crushing feudalism, of intellectual semi-culture, of unheard-of ostentation. Recall this high Burgundian and Flemish society, — that Court of Ghent, so luxurious in its habits, so refined in its elegance, so careless, so brutal, so unclean at bottom, so superstitious and dissolute, pagan in its festivals, and bigoted through it all. See the ecclesiastical pomps, the princely pageants, the holidays, the carousals, their feasts and their drinkings, their scenic representations, and their license ; the gold of chasubles, the gold of armor, the gold of tunics, jewels, pearls, and diamonds ;

imagine below this the condition of souls; and of this picture which is no longer to be painted, retain but one feature, which is, that the greater part of the primordial virtues were wanting at that time to the human conscience, — straightforwardness, sincere respect for sacred things, the sentiments of duty and of country, and among women as among men, modesty. This especially must be remembered when in the midst of this brilliant and frightful society is seen to blossom the unexpected art which it seems was to represent its moral foundation and its surface.

In 1420 the Van Eycks established themselves at Ghent. Hubert, the elder, put his hand to the grand triptych of St. Bavon; he conceived the idea of it, arranged the plan, executed a part of it, and died at his task about 1426. Jan, his younger brother and his pupil, pursued the labor, finished it in 1432, founded at Bruges the school which bears his name, and died there in 1440, on the 9th of July. In twenty years the human mind, represented by these two men, found in painting the most ideal expression of its beliefs, the most characteristic expression of countenances, not the most noble, but the first correct manifestation of bodies in their exact forms, the first image of the sky, the air, the country, clothes, and exterior richness made by true colors; it created a living art, invented or perfected its mechanism, fixed its language, and produced imperishable works. Everything there was to do was done. Van der Weyden * has no other historical importance but that he attempted at

* Roger van der Weyden, pupil of Jan van Eyck, who flourished in the fifteenth century; official painter to the city of Brussels. He represented the symbolic subjects of the Middle Ages. — Tr.

Brussels what was marvellously accomplished at Ghent and Bruges, and then passed later into Italy, to popularize there the Flemish way of working, and the Flemish spirit ; but his especial renown is that he left among his works a masterpiece which is unique, — I mean a pupil, who is called Memling.

Whence came the Van Eycks, when they were seen to establish themselves at Ghent, in the midst of a corporation of painters which already existed ? What did they bring there ? What did they find there ? What is the importance of their discoveries in the use of oil colors ? What was finally the part of each of the brothers in that imposing page, the Adoration of the Paschal Lamb ? All these questions have been propounded, learnedly discussed, poorly answered. What is probable as to their collaboration is that Hubert was the inventor of the work ; that he painted the upper parts of it, the great figures, — God the Father, the Virgin, and St. John, certainly also the Adam and Eve in their minute and hardly decent nudity. He conceived the feminine, and especially the masculine type which afterwards served his brother. He put heroic beards upon countenances which in the society of his day wore none ; he designed these full ovals, with their protruding eyes, their fixed look, both gentle and untamed, their curled hair, their haughty and sullen mien, their violent lips, — in fine, all those characters, half Byzantine, half Flemish, which are so strongly marked with the spirit of the time and place. God the Father, with his sparkling tiara, with falling ribbons, his hierarchical attitude, his sacerdotal robes, is still the double representation of the divine idea as it was presented upon earth in its two redoubtable personifications, the Empire and the Pontificate.

Already the Virgin has the hooked mantle, the adjusted garments, the round forehead, the very human character, and the physiognomy, wholly without grace, that Jan some years later will give to all his Madonnas. The St. John has neither rank nor type in the social scale whence this painter-observer took his forms. He is a man of no particular class, thin, long, even sickly; a man who has suffered, languished, fasted, something like a vagabond. As to our first parents, they must be seen in the original panels, which appeared too slightly clothed for a chapel, and not in the copy at St. Bavon, which is still more curious on account of the black leather aprons in which they are dressed. It must be well understood that you will find nothing in them which recalls the Sistine Chapel or the Loggie. They are two savages, horribly hairy, both going forth without being intimidated by any feeling of their own ugliness, from I know not what primitive forests, hideous, swollen in body, thin in the legs; Eve bearing about her the too evident marks of the first maternity. All this in its simple eccentricity is strong, rough, and very imposing. The touch is rigid; the painting firm, smooth, and full; the color clear, grave, and already harmonious, from its energy, its restrained radiance, and the brilliancy and consistency of the bold coloring of the future school of Bruges.

If, as everything leads us to believe, Jan van Eyck is the author of the central panel and the lower wings, of which unfortunately St. Bavon only possesses copies made an hundred years after by

Coxcien, he had nothing more to do but to develop his mind conformably to his brother's manner. He joined to it on his own account more truth in the faces, more luxury and minute reality in the architecture, the fabrics, and the gilding. He introduced especially open air, the sight of fertile country, and bluish distances. Finally, what his brother had maintained in the splendors of the myth, and upon a Byzantine foundation, he made descend to the level of terrestrial horizons.

Times have changed. The Christ is born and dead. The work of redemption is accomplished. Do you wish to know how, plastically, not as a missal illuminator, but as a painter, Jan van Eyck understood the exhibition of this great mystery? It was thus: A vast lawn all spangled with spring flowers; in front the Fountain of Life, a pretty fountain falling in sheaves into a marble basin; in the centre, an altar draped with purple, and upon this altar a white Lamb; immediately around, a garland of little winged angels, almost all in white, with shades of pale blue and rosy gray. A great open space isolates the august symbol, and upon this untrodden turf there is nothing but the dark green of the thick growth, and hundreds of the white stars of the field daisy. The foreground on the left is occupied by kneeling prophets, and by a large group of men standing. These are those who, believing before the time, predicted Christ, and also the pagans, the doctors, the philosophers, the unbelievers, from the ancient bards to the burghers of Ghent; thick beards, rather flat faces, pouting lips, countenances full of life, little gesture or attitude, — a small abstract in twenty figures of the moral world, before and after Christ, taken from outside the confessors of the new faith. Those who still doubt, hesitate and reflect; those who had denied, are confounded; the prophets are in ecstasy. The foreground on the right, opposite,—and with that intentional symmetry without which there would be neither majesty in the idea nor rhythm in the arrangement,—the right foreground is occupied by the group of the twelve apostles kneeling, and by the imposing assembly of the true servants of the Gospel, priests, abbots, bishops and popes, all beardless, plump, pale and calm, scarcely looking,—sure of the fact, adoring in a state of beatitude, magnificent in their red robes, with their golden chasubles, their mitres of gold, their crosses of gold, their stoles woven with gold, all loaded with pearls, rubies, and emeralds, the sparkling jewels playing upon this glowing purple, which is Van Eyck's red. In the background, far behind the Lamb, and upon an elevated ground which leads to the horizon, is a green wood, a grove of orange-trees, rose-bushes, and myrtles all in flower and fruit, whence issue on the right the long procession of Martyrs, on the left that of the Holy Women, crowned with roses and bearing palms. These latter, clothed in tender colors, are all in pale blue, blue, rose color, or lilac. The Martyrs, almost all bishops, are in blue mantles, and nothing is more exquisite than the effect of these two distant theories, fine, precise, always vivid, detaching themselves, by these notes of delicate or dark blue, from the austere background of the sacred wood. Finally, there is a line of darker hills; then Jerusalem figured by the outline of a city, or rather by spires, high towers, and belfries, and for the extreme distance, blue mountains. The sky has the immaculate serenity appropriate to such a moment; it is of palest blue, feebly tinged with ultramarine at the top; it has the pearly whiteness, the morning clearness, and the poetical signification of a beautiful dawn.

Such is, translated, that is to say, traduced by a cold abstract, the central panel, and the master portion of this colossal triptych. Have I given you an idea of it? Not at all. The mind can dwell upon it forever, dream of it forever, without finding all that it expresses or evokes. Even the eye can delight in it without exhausting the extraordinary wealth of the enjoyment that it causes, or the instruction that it gives us. The little picture of the Magi, at Brussels, is only the delicate amusement of a goldsmith beside this powerful concentration of the soul and the manual gifts of a truly great man.

There remains, to be considered attentively when this has been seen, the Virgin and St. Donatus, at the Museum of Bruges. This picture, of which a reproduction is found at the Antwerp Museum, is the most important that Van Eyck has signed, at least as to the dimensions of the figures. It belongs to 1436, and consequently is four years later than the Adoration of the Lamb. By the arrangement, the style, the character of the form, the color, and the work, it recalls the Virgin of the Donor, that we have at the Louvre. It is not more precise in finish, nor more delicately observed in detail. The ingenuous chiaroscuro that bathes the little composition at the Louvre, the perfect truth, and the idealization of all things obtained by care of hand, beauty of workmanship, and the inimitable transparency of the material; this mingling of minute observation and of reveries pursued through half-tints, — show superior qualities that the picture of Bruges attains and does not exceed. But here everything is broader, more mature, more grandly conceived, constructed, and painted; and the work thence becomes more masterly, because it enters fully into the aims of modern art, and comes near satisfying them all.

The Virgin is ugly. The child, a rickety nursling, with thin hair, copied, without alteration, from some poor little half-starved model, bears a bunch of flowers and is caressing a perroquet. On the right of the Virgin is St. Donatus, with a golden mitre and blue cape; on the left, forming a side scene, St. George, a handsome young man, a sort of androgynous being in chased armor, raises his helmet, salutes the child-God with a strange look, and smiles upon him. Mantegna, when he conceived his Minerva banishing the Vices, with her chiselled cuirass, her golden helmet, and her fair angry face, could not have engraved the St. George I speak of with a firmer burin, or made its border with a more incisive touch, and never could have painted or colored like this. Between the Virgin and the St. George, upon his knees figures the Canon George de Pala (Van der Paele), the donor. It is incontestably the strongest part of the picture. He is in a white surplice; he holds in his clasped hands — his short, square, wrinkled hands — an open book, gloves and horn spectacles; over his left arm hangs a band of gray fur. He is an old man. He is bald; little scattered hairs play around his temples, of which the bones are visible and hard under the thin skin. His face is thick, his eyes half closed, the muscles contracted, hardened, seamed, and furrowed by old age. This great, lank, wrinkled visage is a marvel of characteristic drawing and painting. All the art of Holland is there. Add to the scene its frame, and its ordinary furniture, — the throne, the dais with a black background with red figures, a complicated architecture, a few dark marbles, a bit of painted glass, through whose lens-shaped panes sifts the greenish light of the pictures of Van Eyck ; a marble floor, and under the feet of the Virgin, that fine Oriental carpet, that old Persian rug, perhaps well enough copied to deceive the eye, but in any case kept like the rest in perfect subordination to the picture. The whole tone is grave, deep, and rich, extraordinarily harmonious and powerful. The color flows in a broad stream. It is unbroken, but very learnedly composed, and still more learnedly united by subtle values. In truth, when attention is concentrated upon it, it is a picture that makes one forget everything that is not it, and gives reason to think that the art of painting has found its highest expression, and found it at its very first hour. And yet, without changing either theme or manner, Memling was to say something more.

The history of Memling, transmitted by tradition, is singular and touching. He was a young painter attached, after the death of Van Eyck, to the house of Charles the Bold, perhaps a young soldier of the wars of Switzerland and Lorraine, a fighter at Granson and Morat, who returned to Flanders much disabled; and one day in January, 1477, on one of the icy days which followed the defeat at Nancy and the death of the Duke, he came and knocked at the door of St. John's Hospital, and asked a lodging, rest, food, and care.

They gave him all. He recovered from his fatigues and his wounds, and on the following year, in the solitude of this hospitable home, in the quiet of the cloister, he undertook the Shrine of St. Ursula, and then executed the Marriage of St. Catherine, and the other little diptychs or triptychs that are seen there to-day. Unfortunately, as it appears, — and what a pity it is! — this pretty story is only a legend that must be renounced. According to the true history, Memling was simply a burgher of Bruges, and painted like many another, having learned the art at Brussels, practised it in 1472, lived, not at the Hospital of St. John, but in the Rue St. George as a comfortable proprietor, and died in 1492. Of his journeys to Italy, of his sojourn in Spain, of his death and burial at the Convent of Mirafiori, what is there true or false? From the moment when the flower of the legend disappears, all the rest must follow. Nevertheless there exists something more than a strangeness in the education, the habits, and the career of this man, — a quite marvellous thing, the very quality of his genius, so surprising at such a time and amid such surroundings.

Moreover, in spite of the contradictions of historians, it is still at the Hospital of St. John, which has preserved his works, that one likes to picture Memling when he was painting them. And when they are found in the depths of this unchanged hospice, between these walls like those of a stronghold, in this damp, narrow, grassy square, only two paces from Notre Dame, it is still there, and not elsewhere, that, in spite of all, their birth was seen. I will say nothing of the Hunting of St. Ursula, which is quite the most celebrated of Memling's works, and passes wrongly for the best. It is a miniature in oil, ingenious, artless, exquisite in certain details, infantile in many others, a charming inspiration, — to tell the truth, quite too minute in detail; and painting, far from making a step forward, must have retrograded after Van Eyck, and even after Van der Weyden (see at Brussels his two triptychs, and especially the Weeping Woman), if Memling had stopped there.

The Marriage of St. Catherine, on the contrary, is a decisive page. I do not know whether it marks a material advance upon Van Eyck; that is to be examined: but at least it marks, in the manner of feeling and in the ideal, a quite personal impulse, which did not exist in Van Eyck, and that no art whatever manifests so deliciously. The Virgin is in the centre of the composition, on a platform, seated and enthroned; on her right she has St. John the Forerunner, and St. Catherine with her emblematic wheel; on her left, St. Barbara; and above, the donor, Jan Floreins, in the usual costume of a brother of the Hospital of St. John. In the middle distance figure St. John the Evangelist and two angels in priestly robes. I neglect the Virgin, who is very superior as a choice of types to the Virgins of Van Eyck, but very inferior to the portraits of the two saints.

The St. Catherine is in a long, training, clinging petticoat with a black ground flowered with gold; the sleeves of crimson velvet, and the bodice closely fitting and clinging; a little diadem of gold and jewels circles her rounded brow. A veil, transparent as water, adds to the whiteness of her complexion the paleness of an impalpable fabric. Nothing can be more exquisite than this infantile and feminine face, so delicately framed in her head-dress of jewels and gauze; and never did painter, in love with a woman's hands, paint anything more perfect in gesture, in design, in contour, than the long, well-shaped hand, so slender and pearly, which extends a finger for the betrothal ring.

The St. Barbara is sitting. With her pretty erect head, her straight neck, with the nape high and smooth, with firm ligaments, her tightly closed and mystical lips, her beautiful pure eyelids downcast over a glance that can be divined, she reads attentively in a mass-book at the back of which is seen a bit of the blue silk cover. Her bosom is outlined under the closely fitting corsage of a green robe. A dark red mantle clothes her rather more amply with its large folds, which are very picturesque and very learned.

Had Memling made but these two figures, — and the Donor and the St. John are also works of the first rank of merit, and of the same interest as to their spirit, — it might almost be said that he had done enough for his glory at first, and especially for the astonishment of those who study certain problems, and for the delight that is experienced in seeing them solved. Observing only the form, the perfect drawing, the natural, unaffected gesture, the clearness of the tints, the satin softness of the skin, its unity and suppleness; considering the draperies in their rich colors, so true and characteristic in their cut, — it might be called Nature herself observed by an eye admirably sensitive and sincere. The backgrounds, the architecture, and the accessories have all the sumptuousness of the arrangements of Van Eyck. There is a throne with black columns, a marble portico, and a marble floor; under the feet of the Virgin a Persian carpet; finally, for a perspective, a fair country, and the Gothic outline of a town with belfries bathed in the tranquil gleam of an Elysian light; the same chiaroscuro as in Van Eyck, with new suppleness; better indicated distances between the half-lights and the lights; in all, a work less energetic and more tender,— such is, summing it up at a glance, the first aspect of the Mystical Marriage of St. Catherine.

I shall speak neither of the other little pictures so respectfully preserved in this same old hall in the Hospital of St. John, nor of the St. Christopher of the museum at Bruges, any more than I have spoken of the portrait of the Wife of Van Eyck, and his famous Head of Christ exhibited at the same museum. These are fine or curious works, which confirm the idea that one should form of Van Eyck's way of seeing, and Memling's way of feeling; but the two painters, the two characters, the two geniuses, are more powerfully revealed than elsewhere in their pictures of St. Donatus and St. Catherine. It is upon the same ground and in the same acceptation that they can be compared, opposed, and made clearly evident each by the other.

How were their talents formed? What superior education could have given them so much experience? Who bade them see with this strong simplicity, this moved attention, this energetic patience, this always equable sentiment, in a labor so studied and so slow? Both formed so early, so quickly, and so perfectly! The first Italian Renascence has nothing like it; and in this particular order of expression of sentiment, and of subjects introduced, it is agreed that no school of Lombardy, Tuscany, or Venice ever produced anything that resembles this first bursting forth of the school of Bruges. The handiwork itself is perfect. The language has since been enriched, has become more supple, and has been better developed, that is, before it was corrupted; but it has never recovered either this expressive conciseness, or this appropriateness of method, or this splendor.

Consider Van Eyck and Memling by the externals of their art, and it is the same art which, applied to august objects, renders them by what is most precious. Rich fabrics, pearls and gold, velvets and silks, marbles and wrought metals, — the hand occupies itself only with making the luxury and beauty of these materials felt by the luxury and beauty of labor. In that painting is still very near its origin, for it seems to understand that it struggles with the resources of the art of jewellers, engravers, and enamellers. On the other hand, we see how far it is from that. With regard to methods, there is no very apparent difference between Memling and Jan Van Eyck, who preceded him by forty years. One might ask which advanced the more rapidly, and the farther. And if the dates did not show us who was the inventor and who the disciple, one would imagine, by this still greater security of result, that Van Eyck had rather profited by the lessons of Memling. At first one would think them contemporaries, so identical are their compositions, so identical their method, their archaisms being of the same period.

The main differences which appear in their execution are differences of blood, and depend upon the shades of temperament in the two natures.

In Van Eyck there is more body, muscle, and flow of blood, hence the striking virility of his faces, and the style of his pictures. He is in everything a portrait painter of the family of Holbein, precise, sharp, penetrating even to violence. He sees more truly, and also sees men stouter and shorter. The sensations he receives from the aspect of things are more robust; those which come from their tint, more intense. His palette has a plenitude, an abundance, and severity that Memling's lacks. His gamut is more equably strong, and better maintained as a whole, and is composed of more learned values. His whites are more unctuous, his red is richer, and the indigo blue — the fine blue of the old Japanese enamel, which is his own — is more sustained by coloring principles, and of thicker substance. He is more strongly impressed by the luxury and the high price of the rare objects which abound in the luxurious habits of his time. Never did Indian Rajah adorn his clothes with more gold and jewels than Van Eyck puts into his pictures. When a picture by Van Eyck is fine, — and that of Bruges is the best example of this, — it might be called jewel work enamelled on gold, or one of those fabrics of varied colors whose warp is gold. Gold is felt everywhere, above and below. When it does not play over the surface, it appears under the tissue. It is the bond, the base, the visible or latent element, of this the most opulent painting in the world. Van Eyck is also more adroit, because his copyist hand obeys his marked preferences. He is more precise, he asseverates more; he imitates admirably. When he paints a carpet, he weaves it with a choice of the best tints. When he paints marbles, he is very near the polish of marble, and when in the shadow of his chapels he makes the opaline lenses of his colored glass gleam, he absolutely deceives the eye.

In Memling there is the same power of tone and the same brilliancy, with less ardor and real truth. I would not dare to say that in the marvellous triptych of the St. Catherine, in spite of the extreme resonance of the coloring, its gamut is as sustained as that of his great predecessor. On the other hand, he already has misty and melting passages, and half-tints that Van Eyck never knew. The figure of the St. John and that of the Donor indicate, in the way of sacrificing, in the relations of the principal light to the secondary ones, and in the connection of things with the plane they occupy, an advance since the St. Donatus, and, above all, a decided step beyond the triptych of St. Bavon. The very color of the vestments, one of dark maroon, the other a rather dull red, reveals a new art in the composition of a tone seen in shadow, and combinations of the palette, already more subtle. The handiwork is not very different. Still it differs in this: everywhere that he is sustained, animated, and moved by sentiment, Memling is as firm as Van Eyck. Everywhere, where the interest of the object is less, and particularly where the value affectionately attached to it is less, relatively to Van Eyck, he may be said to be more feeble. Gold is in his eyes only an accessory, and living nature is more studied than still life. To the heads, hands, necks, the pearly pulp of a rosy skin, he applies himself, and in them he excels, because, in fact, as soon as they are compared from the point of view of sentiment there is no longer anything in common beween him and Van Eyck. A world separates them. In forty years, which is very little, there has taken place, in the way of seeing and feeling, believing and inspiring belief, a strange phenomenon, which here bursts forth like light.

Van Eyck saw with his eye, Memling begins to see with his mind. One thought well and truly; the other has not so much the air of a thinker, but his heart beats quite differently. One copied and imitated; the other also copies, imitates, and transfigures. The former reproduced, without any care for the ideal, human types, especially the masculine types which passed under his eyes in all ranks of the society of this time. The latter dreams while he looks at Nature, imagines while he translates her, chooses what is most lovely and delicate in human forms, and creates, especially as a feminine type, an elect being, unknown till then, and who has since disappeared. They are women, but women seen as he loved them, and according to the tender predilection of a mind turned towards grace, nobility, and beauty. Of this unknown image of woman, he made a real person and also an emblem. He did not embellish her, but he perceived in her what no one else had seen. It might be said that he paints her thus only because he discovers in her a charm, an attraction, and a conscience that no one else had suspected. He adorns her physically and morally. In painting the fair face of a woman, he paints a lovely soul. His application, his talent, the carefulness of his hand, are only forms of his regard, and of the tender respect he has for her.

There is no uncertainty about the epoch, the race, or the rank to which belong these fragile blond creatures, pure and yet of this world. They are princesses of the best blood; they have the delicate ligaments, the indolent white hands, and the pallor contracted in a sequestered life. They have a natural way of wearing their clothes and diadems, of holding their missals and reading them, that is neither borrowed nor invented by a man who is a stranger to the world and to this society.

But if nature was thus, whence comes it that Van Eyck did not see it thus, — he who knew the same world, was placed in it probably in still higher station, and lived in it as a painter and gentleman of the bedchamber of John of Bavaria and later of Philip the Good, in the heart of this more than royal society? If such were the little princesses of the Court, how is it that Jan van Eyck has not given us any idea of them that is delicate, attractive, and beautiful? Why did he only see the men truly? Why was there always something strong, squat, rough, or at least ugly, when he undertook to pass from masculine attributes to feminine? Why has he not visibly embellished his brother Hubert's Eve? Why is there so little decency above the Mystic Lamb, while we find in Memling all the adorable delicacy of chastity and modesty, — pretty women with the air of saints, fine honest brows, pure temples, lips without a fold; all innocence in flower, every charm enveloping the purity of angels; a beatitude, a tranquil softness, an inward ecstasy, which is found nowhere else? What grace of heaven had descended upon this young soldier or rich burgher to fill his soul with tenderness, purify his eye, cultivate his taste, and open to him, at the same time in the physical and moral worlds, such new perspectives?

Less celestially inspired than the women, the men painted by Memling resemble, no more than they, those of Van Eyck. They are gentle and sorrowful persons, rather long of body, of bronzed complexion, with straight noses, thin light beards, and pensive looks. They have fewer passions, but the same ardor. They have a less prompt and masculine muscular action, but there is found in them I know not what that is grave and tried, which gives them the look of having passed through life suffering and reflective. The St. John, whose fine Evangelical head, lost in the half-tint, is of such velvety execution, personifies once for all the type of masculine figures as Memling conceives them. It is the same with the Donor, with his Christlike face and pointed beard. Note, I beg, that his saints, both men and women, are manifestly portraits.

They live a deep, serene, and recollected life. In this art, which is so human, there is not a trace of the villanies and atrocities of the time. Consult the work of this painter, who, however he may have lived, must have known his age; you will find in it not one of those tragic scenes which it has pleased men to represent since. No quarterings, nor boiling pitch, except incidentally, as an anecdote, or medallion; no wrists hewed off, no skinning of naked bodies, no ferocious arrests, no assassin judges, and no executioners. The Martyrdom of St. Hippolytus, that is to be seen at the Cathedral of Bruges, and is attributed to him, is by Bouts, or Gérard David. Old and touching legends, like St. Ursula or St. Christopher, the Virgins, the Saints wedded to Christ, believing priests, and saints who make one believe in them, a passing pilgrim under whose features the artist is recognized, — these are Memling's figures. In all there is a good faith, a simple goodness, an ingenuousness, which are something like a prodigy; a mysticism of sentiment betrayed rather than shown, whose perfume is felt without any affectation breathed into the form; a Christian art, if you will, exempt from all mingling of pagan ideas. If Memling escapes his own age, he forgets the others. His ideal is his own; perhaps he announces the Bellini, Botticelli, and Perugino, but not Leonardo, nor Luini, nor the Tuscans, nor the Romans of the true Renascence. Here is no St. John that might be mistaken for a Bacchus; no Virgin nor St. Elizabeth, with the strangely pagan smile of a *La Joconda;* no prophets resembling antique gods and philosophically confounded with the sibyls; no myths nor hidden symbols. There is no need of a very learned exegesis to explain this sincere art, full of good faith, ignorance, and belief. He says what he wishes to say with the candor of the simple in heart and mind, with the naturalness of a child. He paints what was venerated and believed, as it was believed. He retires to his interior world, shuts himself in, there his soul is lifted up and there he expands. Nothing of the exterior world penetrates into this sanctuary of souls in deep repose, — neither what is done, nor thought, nor said there, and not in the least what is there seen.

Imagine, amid the horrors of that age, a sanctuary, a sort of angelic retreat, ideally silent and sequestered, where passions are silent, where troubles cease, where men pray or worship, where everything is transfigured, physical ugliness and moral hideousness, where new sentiments are born, where, like lilies, grow ingenuousness, gentleness, a supernatural mildness, and you will have an idea of the unique soul of Memling, and of the miracle he performed in his works.

It is a singular thing; but to speak worthily of such a soul, out of regard to him and to one's self, peculiar terms must be used, and in our language a sort of virginity must be reconstructed for the occasion. In this way only can he be made known; but words have been put to such uses since the time of Memling, that there is great difficulty in finding any which befit him.